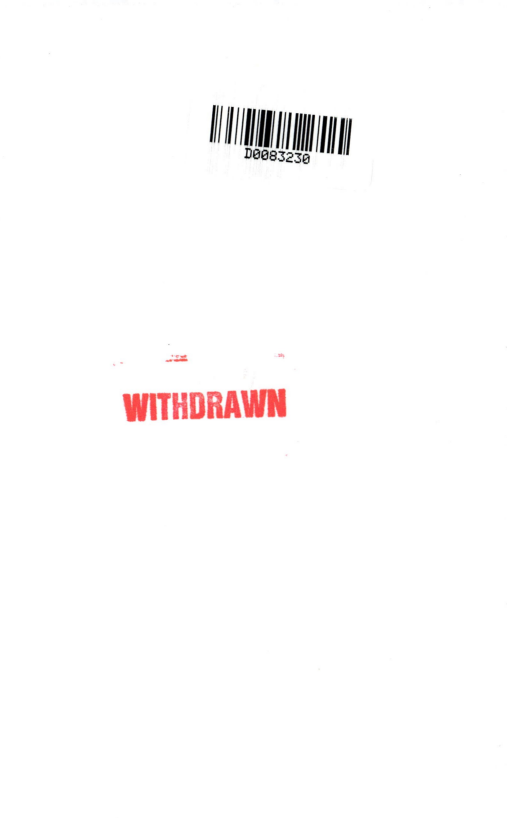

TECHNOCULTURE

The Key Concepts

ISSN 1747-6550

The series aims to cover the core disciplines and the key cross-disciplinary ideas across the Humanities and Social Sciences. Each book isolates the key concepts to map out the theoretical terrain across a specific subject or idea. Designed specifically for student readers, each book in the series includes boxed case material, summary chapter bullet points, annotated guides to further reading and questions for essays and class discussion

Film: The Key Concepts
Nitzan Ben-Shaul

Globalization: The Key Concepts
Thomas Hylland Eriksen

Food: The Key Concepts
Warren Belasco

Technoculture: The Key Concepts
Debra Benita Shaw

The Body: The Key Concepts
Lisa Blackman

TECHNOCULTURE
The Key Concepts

Debra Benita Shaw

Oxford • New York

English edition
First published in 2008 by
Berg
Editorial offices:
First Floor, Angel Court, 81 St Clements Street, Oxford OX4 1AW, UK
175 Fifth Avenue, New York, NY 10010, USA

Berg is the imprint of Oxford International Publishers Ltd.

Library of Congress Cataloging-in-Publication Data

Shaw, Debra Benita.
Technoculture / Debra Benita Shaw.—English ed.
p. cm.—(The key concepts)
Includes bibliographical references and index.
ISBN-13: 978-1-84520-297-2 (cloth)
ISBN-10: 1-84520-297-X (cloth)
ISBN-13: 978-1-84520-298-9 (pbk.)
ISBN-10: 1-84520-298-8 (pbk.)
 1. Technology—Social aspects. 2. Technological innovations—Social
aspects. 3. Science—Social aspects. 4. Popular culture. I. Title.

T14.5.S494 2008
303.48'3—dc22

2008014118

British Library Cataloguing-in-Publication Data

A catalogue record for this book is available from the British Library.

ISBN 978 1 84520 297 2 (Cloth)
 978 1 84520 298 9 (Paper)

Typeset by JS Typesetting Ltd, Porthcawl, Mid Glamorgan
Printed in the United Kingdom by Biddles Ltd, King's Lynn

www.bergpublishers.com

For Saskia and Brandon

CONTENTS

Acknowledgements   xi

1 Introduction: Technology and Social Realities   1
Machines and Modernity   6
Fordism   8
Marxism   11
Technology and Ontology   14
The Culture Industry   17
Spectacular Culture   21
Hyperreality   23
Information Technology, Networks and Globalization   24
Technocapitalism   26
Network Society   27
Global Village   31
Surveillance and Security   35
Chapter Summary   41

2 Technoscience and Power   43
Social Darwinism   44
Scientific Objectivity   46
Kuhnian Paradigms   48
Power/Knowledge   50
Truth and Embushelment   54
Chapter Summary   62

3 TechnoNature/Culture   63
Romanticism   66
Actor Network Theory   68
Haraway's Monsters   71
Chapter Summary   79

4	**TechnoBodies**	81
	Disciplined Bodies	82
	Discursive Bodies	83
	Marked Bodies	85
	Taxonomy and the Genome	87
	Cybernetics	89
	Abjection and Autopoiesis	92
	Cyborg Bodies	93
	Chapter Summary	101
5	**TechnoSpaces**	103
	The Right Stuff	104
	Outer Space and the Wilderness	105
	Simulated Space	108
	Simulacra	110
	Everyday Space	112
	Abstract Space	113
	Cyberspace	115
	Virtual War	117
	Chapter Summary	123
6	**TechnoAesthetics**	125
	Futurism	126
	Mechanical Reproduction	127
	The Aura	129
	Ideology and Aesthetics	131
	Psychotechnology	133
	Pre-Digested Culture	135
	Pop Art	136
	Industrial Music	138
	Machine Aesthetics	139
	Chapter Summary	145
7	**TechnoLinguistics**	147
	Semiotics	147
	Myth	149
	Technological Rationality	150
	Scientism	152
	Technology and Literacy	154

Incorporated Practices   156
Play Back and Spontaneity   158
Deconstruction   160
Chapter Summary   168

Conclusion   169

Glossary   173
Questions for Essays and Class Discussion   177
Notes   179
Annotated Guide for Further Reading   185
Filmography   187
References   189
Index   199

ACKNOWLEDGEMENTS

Particular thanks should go to Stephen Maddison, who took the trouble to read the whole book before I submitted the manuscript and gave me fresh insights into my own writing. Thanks also to Megan Stern who has always helped to sustain my enthusiasm for the subject and who, during long conversations involving several bottles of wine, helped to formulate the subjects for my case studies. I would also like to thank Megan for her helpful comments on an early draft of Chapter 2. Similarly, many thanks should also go to Charles Thorpe and Chris Hables Gray for their extremely encouraging and helpful comments on the manuscript. I would also like to thank my students at both the University of North London (now London Metropolitan University) and the University of East London who helped me to develop my own understanding of the subject. Particular mention should go to Andro Wieland, Andy Slaight, Annette Corbett, David Brett, Jessica White, Luisa Rovati, Matt Travers and Danny MacMahon. Finally, many thanks to Stacey Pogoda whose patience in explaining videogames and in helping me to begin to master actually playing them enabled the writing of the case study for Chapter 5.

1 INTRODUCTION: TECHNOLOGY AND SOCIAL REALITIES

In his book *Profiles of the Future*, the science fiction author Arthur C. Clarke set out three laws that, he suggested, should always be considered when we are told that something is impossible. The third of these – '[a]ny sufficiently advanced technology is indistinguishable from magic' (Clarke 1999: 2) – is often quoted but it deserves some scrutiny not least because it begs several questions. To whom, for instance, is his statement addressed? What does he mean by 'advanced'? What does he mean by 'magic'? What, even, does he mean by 'technology'? This last question has, perhaps, the most straightforward answer. When we speak about technology we are referring to the set of tools or 'techniques' that serve the requirements of any given culture. In the developed West, for instance, our working lives are constructed around the use of the internal combustion engine and data transfer devices such as the telephone and computer. We not only, in most cases, use some form of motor transport to travel to and from our places of work and some form of data transfer device to communicate with others when we arrive there, but the goods and services that many of us are engaged in producing require at least one of these methods of transportation if they are to be economically viable. Furthermore, outside of work, we tend to organize our activities similarly. In the early days of the rave scene in Europe in the 1980s, you absolutely required a telephone (preferably a mobile) and a car or van if you wanted to attend one of the illegal parties that were held at secret locations in the green belt around large cities, the details of which were available only by phoning a particular number at a particular time. So, in this regard, to speak of contemporary cultures as technocultures makes obvious sense. This bit isn't rocket science (although in some cases, actually, it is – a point to which I'll return in Chapter 5). But what of the magic?

Being a science fiction (SF) writer, Clarke was involved in the art of extrapolation. This is a term that refers to estimates about the future based on known facts and observations but it has been adopted by SF academics to describe the thought process which SF writers employ in constructing future and alternative worlds. Science fiction is never really about the future but it makes use of the future to extrapolate from the cultural conditions of the author's time and place. It is a projection of what might be, given the current state of society and, perhaps more importantly, it takes for granted that social conditions are structured by, and a fundamental structuring element in, the development of new technologies. Although all cultures are, to a certain extent, technocultures, some, arguably, are more so than others. So, what is one person's mundane, thoroughly familiar, sometimes irritating but always ubiquitous, tool for getting the job done is, from another's point of view (in another part of the world, another time, an alternative dimension), simply magic.

This is not to say that there is a hierarchy of places or times where 'progress' or 'development' marks out some cultures as more advanced or more technologically literate than others. Anyone who has seen the British Channel 4 TV programme *Time Team* will be aware of how attempts to reconstruct technologies from the distant past cause problems for contemporary engineers who no longer have access to the skills to manipulate materials that have long fallen into disuse. And, of course, the so-called 'wonders' of the ancient world like Stonehenge or the Pyramids at Giza are wonderful because the method of their construction is a mystery to us; they also are indistinguishable from magic.

In a similar sense, technology often appears to be magical in its operation and application because the development of new technologies increasingly overtakes the ability of lay persons to understand the principles of their functioning. We live daily with technologies that we take for granted but cannot repair, nor, even if we know how to replace parts, do we know the minutiae of the manufacturing process that produces those parts. Furthermore, the factory workers that put the parts together may not understand the construction of the whole or even, perhaps, how the part that they are skilled at manipulating contributes to the overall function of the machine. For that, we must rely on 'experts'; engineers, technicians, designers, programmers whose understanding of the machine on a conceptual level, as well as the relationship of parts to whole, is highly valued. The value placed on these persons reflects the importance of technology in the economic and social structure. Equally, it reflects a collective confidence in the continuing effectiveness of the production of new technologies. Technology is thus, perceived as 'magic' in yet another sense: it is expected to change our lives for the better. The question that needs to be addressed, then, is whether this is the case. Do 'labour-saving' devices really 'save' labour or do they just create different kinds of work? Do we all benefit equally from the speeding up of production and the ability to mass-produce goods and services? Do entertainment and communications technologies enrich our social lives or do they impoverish imagination and creativity? What kinds of power are mobilized by science and technology and how do they structure our politics?

The science fiction critics Brian Aldiss and David Wingrove have written about how, after the Second World War, the genre reflected a growing ambivalence about the power of technology following the events at Hiroshima and Nagasaki but the writers 'did not question the basic value of technology ... they were secure in the belief that more massive, more organised doses of technology would take care of the problem' (Aldiss and Wingrove 1988: 276) and, in Dora Russell's opinion, 'the mass of the population in America, Europe and Russia, were well satisfied with their machine god' (Russell 1983: 209). The historical and epistemological period of world history that we now refer to as modernity could, arguably, be understood as largely shaped by worship of the machine god and the conflicts of the modern era as contests for technological superiority.

Although, of course, tool use has been part of the definition of human from prehistory, the late modern period is most clearly characterized by accelerated social change driven by technological innovation. In other words, from the late eighteenth century onwards, social structures in the developed West have to be understood as organized according to the development of new technologies that changed patterns of work and social life and influenced cultural institutions and their expression in art forms like painting, architecture, dance, drama and literature. The arts that we produce not only provide us with enjoyment but also provide us with a focus for working through our responses to cultural change and can be read as representing the state of knowledge about the world in any given historical period or in any given culture. Thus certain cultural artefacts can be analysed as instrumental in both structuring and reflecting responses to the impact of technologies on social organization and everyday life.

One famous example is the French artist Marcel Duchamp's painting, *Nude Descending a Staircase, No. 2,* which caused a sensation at the Armory Show in New York in 1913. The painting is in the Cubist style but, rather than showing the same object from multiple points of view simultaneously, Duchamp's 'nude' is captured at different moments in time. The descent of the staircase is imaged as a set of overlapping repetitions, which suggest movement and speed. Duchamp later produced *Nude Descending a Staircase, No. 3* which is a copy of *No. 2* but painted on a photographic negative. While *No. 2* is rendered in warm tones and evokes, not so much the flesh tones that would be expected in the depiction of a nude but the wood in which a marionette might be crafted, *No. 3* is in shades of grey and thus makes reference to the photographic process that has originated the copy. Cinema was still very much in its infancy when Duchamp began his series (*No. 1* was a more simplified execution, sketched in oils on cardboard) but the influence of experiments with movement and photography by, for instance, Eadweard Muybridge, in the mid-nineteenth century, is undeniable. Thus a new form of art emerged, abstracted from the dynamics of the body in motion, which owed much to the technology of cinema and the way in which a series of still frames is resolved into continuous movement when they are fed through the projector. What Duchamp helps us to understand is that, as much as new technologies have an impact on everyday life, so they also, inevitably, call into question much wider questions to do with how we experience the world, the representation of these experiences and their impact on how we construct society and the environment.

The Swiss architect, Le Corbusier was also excited by the advent of cinema because he believed that it would allow us to 'enter into the truth of human consciousness' (Le Corbusier 1988: 113) by revealing the way in which psychological states are expressed at the level of the body. For Le Corbusier, psychology is important because he was concerned to 'make the true destiny of the machine age a reality'. He had no doubt that the architect, guided by both a rational understanding of the body and a clear idea of the future requirements of industry and commerce, would be instrumental in providing for an environment in which a 'new kind of consciousness' (1964 [1933]: 93) would flourish. Leaving aside for the moment the question of whether the observation of the body alone can produce a reliable psychology, we can see that what emerges from the invention of cinema is not only a new form of entertainment but a profound questioning of previous assumptions about the body and its disposition in, and occupation of, space.

I use the example of cinema here because it is another of the technologies, like cars and data transfer devices, which we now take for granted but which has had a profound influence on the contemporary world. Visual culture is currently an important field of academic study, not only because cinema and television are ubiquitous but because we recognize that any diagnosis of contemporary conditions must take into account the widespread influence of these technologies and their effects on all other aspects of culture, including the way that we experience ourselves and what this implies for the structure of societies.

We can therefore describe the study of technoculture as an enquiry into the relationship between technology and culture and the expression of that relationship in patterns of social life, economic structures, politics, art, literature and popular culture. It is also a quintessentially post-modern study in that it is a reflexive analysis from within, as it were, the belly of a beast that has grown to monstrous proportions. Postmodernism has been described in many ways and, in general, it tends to be a catch-all term used to describe the sense in which we live in a global culture, mediated by technologies of vision and computer networks, suffused by a popular culture that does not recognize previous distinctions in taste and class, such as between 'high' and 'low' culture and in which the boundaries between previously distinct categories of ideas have become fluid and unstable. There are disagreements as to when, or even if, we can reliably speak about a break between modernity and postmodernity. It is perhaps more helpful to think about postmodernity in terms of what one of the primary philosophers of postmodernity, Jean-François Lyotard (1989: xxiv) refers to as 'incredulity regarding metanarratives'. Metanarratives are discourses that legitimate what comes to be accepted as truth. For instance, since at least the mid seventeenth century, the scientific method had been lauded as the human endeavour that would deliver us into utopia. Objective knowledge about ourselves and the universe would furnish the foundation for understanding how we could provide for ourselves the best of all possible worlds. Science was understood as an inherent good that would bring nature under the control of human beings. Thus science is a metanarrative that guarantees the legitimacy of propositions and practices that come under the general rubric of 'improvement' or 'progress'.

When the director of the Manhattan Project, Robert Oppenheimer, witnessed the first nuclear test at Alamogordo, New Mexico he quoted from the Hindu sacred text, the Bhagavad-Gita, 'I have become death – the shatterer of worlds' (Thorpe, 2006: 3). Oppenheimer was treated with opprobrium for what was seen as his cowardice in the face of a technology that was heralded as the end to all wars but he was merely the first to give expression to the anxiety that would pervade the developed world when the knowledge that we could, indeed, destroy the planet had sunk in. What Oppenheimer's statement brings into focus is the realization that what might, on the one hand, deliver us from disease, hunger and toil might, on the other, plunge us into nuclear winter and eventual extinction. This ambivalence towards science and its products is what distinguishes postmodern 'incredulity' while, at the same time, we are dependent upon technology to an intensifying degree.

I am writing this book using word-processing software on a computer that also allows me access to the World Wide Web where I am able to research my subject and order books from libraries. When it is complete, I will email it to my publisher. From typescript to finished edition, it will use other data processing, as well as printing and transport technologies. Finally, it will be available for sale, not only in bookshops but through booksellers on the Web, paid for by means of electronic fund transfer systems, the same method by which I will receive my royalties. In other words, when I define myself as a writer, that definition must include my relationship with the tools that enable me to perform that function and the fact that my use of those tools is coextensive with the economic and industrial processes of postmodern technocultures. I cannot extricate myself from this set of relationships because to do so would be to deny myself the means of making a living. Neither can you. But the ambivalence with which we approach our technologies continues to define our relationships with them. The complexity of these relationships mobilizes anxieties connected to how we understand what it means to be human, how we define the limits of the social world and how we structure acceptable and unacceptable expressions of gender, race and sexuality. What this book will explore is under what terms we inhabit the technocultural universe and the ideas and methodologies that have significance for our understanding of it. It will address the kinds of questions that arise when we consider the role of technology in determining culture and the role of culture in structuring how we use, produce, define and relate to the technologies with which we effect change in the world and which, in turn, effect changes in our understanding of ourselves.

MACHINES AND MODERNITY

Charlie Chaplin's 1936 film *Modern Times* opens with a full screen shot of a clock face, which introduces a long sequence in which Chaplin's 'Little Tramp' gets into all sorts of trouble trying to hold down a job as a production line worker in a factory. The film is very funny but it is also a rather bleak analysis of the dehumanizing effects of factory work. The Tramp is subjected to a mechanical feeder, which, inevitably, slaps him in the face with a custard pie and, when he leaves the production line, his body continues to dance to the repetitive movements of the job: tightening nuts on an endless succession of metal plates. Finally, no longer able to distinguish between the processes of the job and the routine interactions of everyday life, he has a nervous breakdown. The clock is important because, as Lorenzo C. Simpson (1995: 23) points out, '[a] central goal of technology is to "stop the clock," to de-realize time … to minimize the time necessary to realize a given goal'. What he is referring to here is the shift from agrarian or rural time, dictated by the rhythms of the seasons and the day as measured by sunrise and sunset, to the segmentation and regulation of time demanded by factory work following the Industrial Revolution. Furthermore, the factory itself is a giant machine, which, to be efficient must operate like clockwork, with each component completely and continually integrated, but the Little Tramp is unable to conform and ends up out of work and homeless.

In a similar but more politically ambiguous film *Metropolis* (1927), director Fritz Lang imagines a future world where the idle rich languish in pleasure gardens high above the city while the workers and the machines, to which they must attend or die, are hidden deep underground. Two of the most enduring images from the film are the beautiful robot, Maria, symbol of the duplicity of advanced technology, and the giant clock, whose hands must be physically restrained at all times to prevent the machines from overheating and exploding, symbol of the workers' enslavement. Like Chaplin, then, Lang was critiquing technological determinism or the sense in which the requirements of machines dictate the rhythms and structure of both personal and social life. The irony, of course, is that, outside the fantasy world of the movies, at the time that these films were made, industrial capitalism had already produced a world (at least in the developed West) where the needs of the population could not be met other than by mass production. While Chaplin's tramp and the gamin (street child, played by Paulette Goddard) that he has befriended agree that they will 'get along' without conforming to the strictures of modern times, Lang's solution is to bring together the 'hand, brain and heart' of mental, physical and caring labour. However, these happy endings could not so readily be applied to the real world.

Lang's film was released just before, and Chaplin's just after, the Great Depression of the 1930s. Following the stock market crash of 1929 and the near collapse of the Austrian banking system in 1931, the world was plunged into economic chaos. In the US, '[u]nemployment climbed from under two million in 1929 to five million during the course of 1930' (Brendon, 2000: 70). The historian, Piers Brendon, writing about the conditions of the new urban poor, refers to 'nameless families squatting in doorways or bivouacking over hot-air gratings or building tar-paper shacks on waste ground or dredging through trash cans and refuse dumps for food' (Brendon 2000: 72). *Modern Times* rehearses this catastrophe in the plight of the Tramp who, determined to find work so that he and the gamin can set up home together, finds the factories closed and abandoned while the gamin's unemployed father is killed in a street riot and she and her sisters are left at the mercy of the seemingly brutal childcare authorities.

Economic historians are divided over the causes of the Depression but the start of the crash is generally understood to be 24 October 1929, referred to as 'Black Thursday', when 16 million shares of stock, purchased during the boom years of the decade, were suddenly sold by panicking investors. The boom was partly fuelled by an irrational confidence in an expanding market for the new consumer durables that became available after the end of the First World War, 'vacuum cleaners, refrigerators, washing machines, coffee percolators, phonographs, telephones and radios'. As Brendon (2000: 54) tells us, there was a 'consumer revolution', in which '[a]utomobiles, naturally, were the prime icons.' Meanwhile, companies like Seaboard Airline, 'attracted thousands of investors so intoxicated with the possibilities of aviation that they did not discover that it was actually a railroad company' (Brendon 2000: 61).

In light of this, *Metropolis* may seem to be prophetic. What Lang's workers are producing in the great caverns under the city is never specified but this only serves to make the point more poignantly. The machines must be tended so that the rich industrialist and his family can continue to enjoy the pleasures of the upper city. The towering skyscrapers, aerial walkways and flying machines, viewed in the film's opening shots, are only sustained, we discover, by forced labour and intense deprivation. The workers' dissatisfaction finds a focus in the gentle Maria, who urges them to demand better conditions for themselves but, faced with what they see as the threat of revolution, the bosses replace Maria with her robot likeness (designed by a mad scientist), who will do their bidding and sow dissent. Finally, she leads the workers to destroy their underground city. The ease with which the workers are duped by the false Maria can be read as a metaphor for the seductive power of new technologies. The robot Maria incites the workers to take action that can only end in homelessness and increased poverty. Like the investors in Seaboard Airline, they see only the surface. She is (an admittedly very beautiful) machine, dressed in the clothes of salvation.

While both *Modern Times* and *Metropolis* are indictments of the cult of the machine, it is worth remembering that, ironically, the movie industry absolutely depended on the increased spending power of the workers at the dawn of what is now referred to as consumer capitalism, as well as the changes in social life brought about by the concept of 'leisure time'. Former president of Ford Motors, Lee Iacocca, writing for the *Time 100* Web site, goes so far as to offer the opinion that 'if it hadn't been for Henry Ford's drive to create a mass market for cars, America wouldn't have a middle class today'.[1]

FORDISM

In 1905, Ford rejected the idea that the only way to succeed in the burgeoning automobile industry was to make cars for the rich. His singular idea was to produce a car that his factory workers could afford, finally realized in the now famous Model T. Ford's manufacturing method was based on the principle of interchange-ability and the introduction of the moving assembly line. Although Ford is credited with saying that his customers could buy the Model T in any colour they wanted as long as it was black, the truth was that it was actually produced in a range of colours but, in every other respect, the cars, and the parts of which they were composed, were completely interchangeable, as were most of the tasks required to assemble them and 'virtually every process involved in assembly and sub-assembly was completed on a moving line' (Batchelor 1994: 46). The price of the car came down with each rationalization and refinement of the process but the workers, understandably, hated the assembly line and labour turnover was rapid. Ford's solution, in 1913, was to double the daily rate at which they were paid and reduce the length of the working day. The result was that not only could the workers now afford to save for the day when they could own a Model T of their own but they also had the leisure in which to enjoy driving it.

However, Ford's $5 a day offer was conditional. The workers were actually paid 34 cents an hour. The additional 28.5 cents which would bring their daily wage to the $5 maximum was understood to be a share of profits, which would only be awarded to those who satisfied the requirements of the company's 'Sociological Department' that they should conform to a set of predetermined moral regulations both on and off the job. Ford disliked the idea of women working but employed them on the basis that, with good pay they could 'dress attractively and get married'. A good, moral, 'American' worker, according to Ford's Sociological Department, was married, bathed frequently, did not buy goods on credit and had a clean backyard (Batchelor 1994: 50). Thus the rationalization of the workplace, in Fordist terms, was not simply a mechanization of the production process: it also involved a rationalization of the workforce. The reward for absolute conformity, both on and off the job, was, ultimately, the chance to purchase the very item that the worker had already spent the majority of his time producing.

Essentially, Ford's achievement was to comprehensively manage both the work and leisure time of his workforce. 'Leisure time' was only won at the expense of personal privacy and was deducted from a working day determined, in the first place, by a calculation taking into account the number of machine hours required to turn a profit. Thus the significance of the clocks that feature in both *Modern Times* and *Metropolis* now comes into clearer focus, as do the herd of sheep to which Chaplin compares the factory workers in juxtaposed shots at the beginning of *Modern Times*. In a similar comparison, Lang shows legions of faceless, uniformly clothed workers, trudging in step with bowed heads. The implication is clear. The tyranny of the machines and the regulation of time that they impose deprives human beings of individuality and dignity.

Ford's system had much in common with the recommendations in Frederick W. Taylor's *Principles of Scientific Management*, first published in 1911. Taylor recommended 'the substitution of a science for the individual judgement of the workman' (Taylor 1911: 60), which, through the employment of 'elaborate motion-study and time-study' (Taylor 1911: 59) methods to simple tasks would 'in the future double the productivity of the average man engaged in industrial work' (Taylor 1911: 73). Taylor's methods found favour with, among others, Lenin, who 'expressed enthusiasm for the rational production methods and scientific job analysis incorporated in scientific management' (Boyle et al. 1984: 199). As Ray Batchelor (1994: 98) points out, '[i]t is not without irony that in post-revolutionary Russia, leading artists, architects and critics held the methods of Frederick Taylor, mass production and Henry Ford in high esteem.' The Italian Communist leader Antonio Gramsci, writing from the prison where he had been incarcerated by Mussolini in 1928, was also cautiously optimistic. He understood that the 'Americanization' of European production along Taylorist and Fordist lines would have far-reaching effects, not least that factory employees would, like the workers in *Metropolis*, who are persuaded by the sexual allure of the false Maria to destroy their own livelihood, be coerced by the lure of high wages and social competition into accepting oppressive conditions. He was also aware that the universal spread of rationalized machine production would ultimately result in unemployment and reduced wages, once factories like Ford's Highland Park no longer held a monopoly within the industry. Nevertheless, he saw possibilities in 'the need to elaborate a new type of man suited to the new type of work and productive process' (Gramsci 1971: 308), not least the fact that the work itself could be accomplished without need for the worker to engage his brain:

> The only thing that is completely mechanised is the physical gesture; the memory of the trade, reduced to simple gestures repeated at an intense rhythm, 'nestles' in the muscular and nervous centres and leaves the brain free and unencumbered for other occupations ... [N]ot only does the worker think, but the fact that he gets no immediate satisfaction from his work and realises that they are trying to reduce him to a trained gorilla, can lead him into a train of thought that is far from conformist. (Gramsci 1971: 309 and 310)

In other words, Fordism would provide the conditions under which the workers would become aware of their own alienation and exploitation. The implication is that bourgeois culture, which, as Marx and Engels pointed out in the *Communist Manifesto* was 'for the enormous majority, a mere training to act as a machine' (Marx and Engels 1988: 226) was primed to implode due to the simple fact that people are *not* machines. Like Marx, Gramsci was happy to embrace the accelerated changes brought about by industrial culture and the manifestation of these changes in the personality of the people. As he saw it, the last vestiges of aristocratic privilege in old Europe would be swept away by the spread of Americanism while the rise of the bourgeoisie and their demand for a motivated (if deskilled) workforce would provide for the conditions necessary to revolutionize the workers. As Marshall Berman explains it:

> The more furiously bourgeois society agitates its members to grow or die, the more likely they will be to outgrow it itself, the more furiously they will eventually turn on it as a drag on their growth, the more implacably they will fight it in the name of the new life it has forced them to seek. (Berman, 1983: 97)

Gramsci is understandably more circumspect than Marx in welcoming modern industrial production and the rise of the machine because he had witnessed the defeat of a workers' revolution in Italy in 1919–20. Furthermore, he had experienced the rise of fascism following the First World War, which was largely supported by the petit bourgeoisie (from whom he hoped might arise a revolutionary intelligentsia). Nevertheless, what is important here is the acknowledgement of a necessary shift in consciousness; an awareness that technology forces changes, not only in economic and social life but in the way in which we conceive our relationships to work, the products of our labour and the communities in which we live.[2]

MARXISM

Modernity, then, is distinguished by a mode of thought, an understanding of the world, in which technology becomes a problem. That is, the machines that, since the Industrial Revolution, have shaped the processes of production and imposed new divisions of labour have posed questions that have forced us to reassess the meaning of existence and experience; to examine how our knowledge of the world is shaped, not only by science, but by the uses to which we put the products of scientific understanding. This is why the work of Karl Marx is of fundamental importance to any study of modernity. 'Life', as he says, 'is not determined by consciousness, but consciousness by life' (Marx and Engels 1947: 47), meaning that the fundamental processes by which life is sustained are instrumental in determining the way that we conceptualize the world and, hence, also shape our desires and motivations. This idea is extrapolated to comic effect in *Modern Times* when Chaplin's Little Tramp leaves the production line still clutching the spanners which are the tools of his job. Apparently unable to relinquish them, he is also no longer able to distinguish between the nuts that they are designed to tighten and similar objects such as the buttons that fasten one woman's skirt and another's coat. He has begun to see all of life in terms of the process by which he earns his living. His consciousness can no longer encompass any interaction that does not involve the accomplishment of the task for which the spanners are designed. His hands have *become* the spanners to the extent that he can no longer touch anything with any sensitivity. He has become alienated from the rhythms and nuances of human interaction and thus, from himself; he has become Gramsci's 'trained gorilla'.

Although, in keeping with his hapless persona, the Tramp is arrested for being a communist agitator only because he is in the wrong place at the wrong time, Chaplin's film effectively makes the link between worker alienation and the 'train of thought that is far from conformist' by which Gramsci intends to imply the realization of inequality that will impel the proletariat to revolutionary action against the bourgeoisie. Marx is very clear that it is not the machine *itself* that dehumanizes the workforce but the way that it positions the worker within the nexus of economic and social arrangements that constitute industrial capitalism. The machine is, '[i]n short', as he says in *Capital*, 'a means for producing surplus-value' (1990 [1867]: 492). In other words, the machine is only valuable insofar as it adds value to the commodity and the transition from the 'handicraft' method of production to machine production can only produce profit if it leads to a more thorough exploitation of the workforce. In Chapter 15 (Vol. 1) of *Capital*, this is graphically illustrated by Marx's condemnation of the employment of women and children under ten in the British mining industry before it was forbidden by law. Here he makes the point that industrial machinery only became acceptable to mine owners once this source of cheap labour was no longer available to them.

> [C]apitalists considered the employment of naked women and girls, often in company with men, so far sanctioned by their moral code, and especially by their ledgers, that it was only after the passing of the Act that they had recourse to machinery. (Marx 1990 [1867]: 516)

Elsewhere, he describes the changes in the kind of labour required by machines and the way in which they provided for the employment of women and children.

> In so far as machinery dispenses with muscular power, it becomes a means of employing labourers of slight muscular strength, and those whose bodily development is incomplete, but whose limbs are all the more supple. The labour of women and children was, therefore, the first thing sought for by capitalists who used machinery. That mighty substitute for labour and labourers was forthwith changed into a means for increasing the number of wage-labourers by enrolling, under the direct sway of capital, every member of the workman's family, without distinction of age or sex ...
>
> Machinery, by throwing every member of that family on to the labour-market, spreads the value of the man's labour-power over his whole family. It thus depreciates his labour-power ... Thus we see, that machinery, while augmenting the human material that forms the principal object of capital's exploiting power, at the same time raises the degree of exploitation. (Marx 1990: 517 and 518)

However, for Marx, technology is not a neutral force that only becomes an instrument of exploitation in the hands of the ruthless capitalist. It is the needs of capital, or the market itself, which determines the rate of change, the response of different industries to how the 'motive power' of steam or electricity will be employed, the demographics of the workforce and the manufacture of machines *by* machines, in particular machines for faster communication and transportation, made necessary by more intensive production and the greater interdependence of the different branches of industry. As Marx demonstrates, these changes are also responsive to, and implicated in the development of, social institutions like the law and the family. The rate of change can only accelerate to the extent that, as Marx and Engels famously state in the *Communist Manifesto*, 'all that is solid melts into air' (Marx and Engels 1988 [1888]: 212) and this is true for all strata and institutions of modern industrial society; 'the new-fangled forces of society want only to be mastered by new-fangled men – and such are the working men. They are as much the invention of modern time as machinery itself' (Marx in Berman, 1982: 20).[3] As Berman points out, 'for all Marx's invective against the bourgeois economy, he embraces enthusiastically the personality structure that this economy has produced' (Berman 1982: 96).

I said earlier that technology was a 'problem' for modernity and the way that Marx addresses this problem is through the concept of 'alienated labour'. This concept presupposes an essential 'truth' and that is that the 'essence' of human being is in subsistence. In other words, our ontology, our 'being in the world' is inseparable from the way that we provide food, clothes and shelter for ourselves. On a very basic level, we can understand that, without these things, we would be unlikely to live very long and would certainly not be able to reproduce. Thus, for the species to survive, these things are essential. Therefore, being in the world and doing the work that ensures the continuation of that mode of being become inseparable. For Marx, '[t]he life of the species, both in men and in animals, consists physically in the fact that man (like the animal) lives on inorganic nature' (1988 [1844]: 75). Again, on a basic level, simple agriculture and the implements like hoes, rakes and spades that make it possible, provide for a direct satisfaction of our basic needs. The labour that we put into the cultivation of the soil and the harvesting of the crop is energy expended directly in the service of our own subsistence. However, with the development of complex technologies under the sway of capitalism, the energy expended by the worker results in a commodity that must be exchanged for money. The worker never receives the full value of the product (if, still on the subject of agriculture, she would if she had dug it out of the ground herself) but only a fraction of its value, in the form of wages. The remainder goes to the capitalist and/ or the shareholders. To provide for her own subsistence, she must go to the shop and buy the product that she has already laboured to produce. In terms of technology, alienated labour can thus be understood as the intervention of the machine, and the mode of production that it enables, into the relationship between the worker and the product of her labour with the result that, as Marx explains it, 'the worker is related to the *product of his labor* as to an *alien* object … The worker puts his life into the object; but now his life no longer belongs to him but to the object' (Marx 1988: 71 and 72, emphasis in translation). Furthermore, the worker herself becomes a commodity whose value is determined by the fluctuations of the market. Thus, the worker is further alienated by being in a relationship of competition, rather than cooperation, with other members of her community.

If industrial capitalism produced just enough for everyone to get by, including the capitalists, then there would be no impetus to revolution. In fact, what I have just said is patently absurd because inequality is in the nature of capitalism; it is a fundamentally unequal system. Demand must be created for new products to keep the factories in production and profit must be made to satisfy investors. According to Marx, it is under the terms of the principle of alienated labour that capitalism sows the seeds of its own demise because it is the very abundance produced by advanced industrial capitalism and its concentration in the hands of a minority that is contradicted by alienated labour. In simple terms, the fact that the people without whose labour the system could not function at all actually benefit least from it points to their eventual realization of their exploitation, along with the fact that, if the machinery of production was owned by everyone in common, then everyone would be entitled to an equal share of what is produced. Many people now, of course, would argue that Marx was incorrect in his assessment of historical conditions and point to 'human nature' as being inherently competitive[4] but this is to presuppose that we can know what human nature is, outside of its expression under prevailing conditions. What Marx teaches us is that we cannot know who we are apart from the social conditions in which we find ourselves; that the idea of the competitive individual emerges from an economic and social structure that demands that we understand ourselves in this way. A change in economic and social relations would, in this sense, lead to a change in our understanding of human being. The study of technoculture, therefore, must necessarily engage with the sense in which changes in the technologies which are an inseparable part of our social worlds, also produce changes in how we conceive of *ourselves*.

TECHNOLOGY AND ONTOLOGY

Of course, the use of tools in the pursuit of subsistence has always been part of the definition of human being and, indeed, the French philosopher Bernard Stiegler suggests that we need to examine the sense in which we accord a priority to biology over technics; that a more accurate understanding of human ontology may arise from what he calls 'a theory of technical evolution' (Stiegler 1998: 26). So what needs to be taken into account in any assessment of how we define ourselves in relation to our technologies is philosophy itself; that is, the sense in which our own reflections on the state of our knowledge must necessarily include our ontological status in connection with technology and, in particular, the advanced technologies which make modern civilization possible.

The German philosopher Martin Heidegger (1993) considered this question in his essay 'The Question Concerning Technology'. He uses the rather awkward term 'standing-reserve' to differentiate between technology as an 'object' and the 'essence' of technology; that is, he is interested in the status of technology as understood in relation to human being. Here he discusses an airliner ready for take-off:

an airliner that stands on the runway is surely an object. Certainly. We can represent the machine so. But then it conceals itself as to what and how it is. Revealed, it stands on the taxi strip only as standing-reserve, inasmuch as it is ordered to insure the possibility of transportation. For this it must be in its whole structure and in every one of its constituent parts itself on call for duty, i.e., ready for takeoff. (Heidegger 1993: 322)

This seems like stating the screamingly obvious until we take into account that what Heidegger is interested in is the sense in which technoculture can be understood in terms of a particular orientation towards instrumentality. This is what Simpson characterizes as 'the technological anticipation', which he explains as a preoccupation that 'leads to our experiencing and interrogating things and action in terms of their manifest utility or potential for use, to our experiencing them within the framework of means and ends' (Simpson, 1995: 43 and 44). 'Things and action' encompasses everything from the resources of the natural world, the ultimate 'standing-reserve' without which machines would be unimaginable but which is only imagined in relation to how it contributes to the manufacture and operation of the machine, to the activities of people who are subject to what Heidegger calls 'enframing' as much as is the machine and the resources which it commands. Enframing concerns the sense in which everything that is standing in reserve is 'revealed' in terms of a particular ordering; 'the way in which the actual reveals itself as standing-reserve' (Heidegger 1993: 329). In other words, what is standing in reserve exists in a relation of potential to other things that are standing in reserve. The parts of the aircraft are only revealed as such by their interlocking relationships, which include the fuel, the oil from which it is derived and the manner of its procurement, the materials from which the parts are made, the mining and manufacturing operations that secure them, as well as the tourist industry, among others, which, 'challenges forth' these products in its need for aircraft. The idea of 'challenging' occurs as a consequence of modern technology, which forces the natural world into patterns and speeds of production determined by industry. The danger, as Heidegger sees it, is that the whole world thus becomes enframed by the technological imperative.

The concept of enframing and its effect on how we understand ourselves is well illustrated by an episode of the acclaimed popular TV series *M*A*S*H*, first broadcast between 1972 and 1983. Major Charles Emerson Winchester III, having narrowly escaped death at the hands of a sniper, experiences an existential crisis in which he is tortured by the realization that death and, by extension, life, may have no meaning; that death may be nothing more than a cessation of life, which, by implication, must then mean that life is nothing more than a preparation for death. As a surgeon, working on the frontline of the war in Korea, it is Major Winchester's job to patch up injured soldiers, many of whom will return to fighting and the possibility that they will be killed in action. He is thus faced with a double futility in which the work to which he has dedicated his life becomes as meaningless as life itself. To think through this conundrum, Winchester instructs a mechanic to take apart a jeep, piece by piece, and lay out its constituent parts on a white sheet. Sitting in the shell of the jeep, he reflects on the fact that the jeep parts and the parts of the human body are analogous in so far as both only have meaning in terms of their potential as parts of a functioning whole but the jeep can be separated into its constituents and put back together, after which it will still function as a motor vehicle, but the same does not hold for the human body.

The question here is why Winchester should turn to a mechanical device to understand the meaning of life and death. It could be argued that he is making what philosophers call a 'category mistake',[5] in that the mode in which bodies exist is fundamentally different from the mode in which machines exist, and the comparison can thus produce nothing but despair. But, from a Heideggerian perspective, Winchester's contemplation of the jeep is entirely logical. The parts spread out on the sheet, the body shell and Winchester himself are 'standing-reserve' in the technologically enframed theatre of war. In this sense, his being in the world and the presence in the world of the soldiers that he treats only have meaning in terms of their utility and are enframed by the same technological anticipation as the parts of the jeep.

When Winchester wonders why a human body cannot be taken apart and put back together like the jeep he is falling prey to the illusion that 'everything man encounters exists only insofar as it is his construct'. He is trying to understand the body in terms of the jeep because the jeep represents the overriding logic of atomization and control promoted by the scientific method and its realization in technology. Winchester's delusion is Heidegger's 'final delusion' in which 'it seems as though man everywhere and always encounters only himself' (Heidegger 1993: 332). Winchester is trying to make sense of his own life and death in terms of a mechanical device because the mastering of the forces that have produced it, the 'challenging' which has revealed its constituents as nothing other than standing-reserve in terms of the war machine must apply equally to the way that he understands *himself*. Why else would he be using his skills to further the cause of war? The alternative, that the scientific worldview, its application to the natural world, the technology that emerges from this and its use in war is a betrayal of human being, is unimaginable. Small wonder then that Heidegger, at the end of the Second World War, described it as 'the confrontation of European humanity with global technology' (Heim, 1993: 55). In other words, following the Second World War and the first use of the atomic bomb, Europeans were confronted with their technologies in the same way that Major Winchester is confronted with the jeep and forced to ask the same uncomfortable questions.

THE CULTURE INDUSTRY

Heidegger is considered to be one of the greatest thinkers of the modern age, a fact that is difficult to reconcile with his active support for Hitler and the Nazi Party until well after the end of the war. Herbert Marcuse, a prominent member of what later became known as The Frankfurt School was one of his students up until the time he embraced Nazism in 1933 and Heidegger's influence can be discerned in Marcuse's concern with the relationship between everyday life, language and ontology. The Frankfurt School were the founders of what has become known as Critical Theory, which developed partly as a response to German fascism and partly in connection with the rise of the mass media and US-style consumer capitalism. Although fundamentally Marxist, their aim was to revise Marxism in an attempt to apply it to the economic and social developments since Marx's death.

The popularity of the Nazi Party in Germany during the 1930s is partly traceable to the fallout from the Great Depression, which resulted in unprecedented levels of unemployment. Hitler addressed this with a massive programme of public works, which merged into an equally massive programme of armaments manufacture. However, Max Horkheimer, director of the Institute for Social Research, from which the Frankfurt School emerged, from 1930 to 1958, in his essay 'The Jews and Europe' (1938) sets out an analysis that understands fascism as a logical extension of capitalism. According to his argument, the injustices of the free market, and the 'sink-or-swim' mentality which it produces, consolidates, among the bourgeoisie, an attitude of condemnation towards those who remain in poverty. A form of natural justice is evoked to establish the rectitude of the *status quo*, which provides justification for social policies that consolidate the ownership of the means of production among a power elite. Hence, '[e]xploitation no longer reproduces itself aimlessly via the market, but rather in the conscious exercise of power' (Horkheimer 1989 [1938]: 83) and '[t]he true self of the juridical owner of the means of production confronts him as the fascist commander of battalions of workers' (Horkheimer 1989 [1938]: 82). The total mobilization of a society is thus achieved and the 'battalions of workers', 'find out what they really are: soldiers' (Horkheimer 1989 [1938]: 79). What Horkheimer understood, at a time when the full horrors of Nazism had yet to be realized, was that seemingly benign manufacturing technologies can become weapons of considerable power. The infrastructure of modernity had provided a resource that the Nazis exploited in the service of war. Hitler was, as the economist John Gray writes, 'an ardent admirer of Henry Ford and American techniques of mass production, the Nazi leader saw technology as a means of enhancing human power' (Gray, 2003: 11). In fact, totalitarianism can, itself, be understood in similar terms to the management of a factory in which the lives of the population are managed in accordance with the technology of the state and human and mechanical resources become inseparable. The atrocities of the *shoah*; a technologically achieved ethnic cleansing understood as accruing from the mentality of technological anticipation, make chilling sense in terms of the logic of a power elite whose claim to dominance is founded in the mechanics and techniques of industrial capitalism.

Horkheimer also understood that it was not only the mechanical devices of capitalism that structure the fascist mentality but the techniques that drive the consumer economy:

> For decades there have been entire spheres of consumption in which only the labels change. The panoply of different qualities in which consumers revel exists only on paper ... [T]he buyer is ... paid an ideological reverence which he is not even supposed to believe entirely. He already knows enough to interpret the advertising for the great brand-name products as national slogans that one is not allowed to contradict. The discipline to which advertising appeals comes into its own in the fascist countries. In the posters the people find out what they really are: soldiers. (Horkheimer 1989 [1938]: 79)

In other words, the transition from consumer in a capitalist society to soldier in a fascist army is achieved by the same means. The technique of advertising, which constructs the self in terms of a brand image, is applied to 'remodel[ing] the populace into a combat-ready collective for civil and military purposes, so that it will function in the hands of the newly formed ruling class' (Horkheimer 1989 [1938]: 81).

Later, in *Dialectic of Enlightenment* (1944), Horkheimer and his Frankfurt School colleague, Theodor Adorno, developed a sustained critique of what they called the 'culture industry', linking the techniques of mass entertainment with the psychological effects of propaganda. Most of their argument appears to be a polemic against what, today, we often refer to as 'dumbing down' but to understand it in this way would be to miss the point. What Adorno and Horkheimer are concerned with is the tendency of mass produced culture to promote conformity and thus to prohibit the development of ideas. When they state that '[a] technological rationale is the rationale of domination itself' (Adorno & Horkheimer 1997 [1944]: 121), they are expressing a profound anxiety with regard to the pervasive influence of the media, which, itself a development of industrial technology, promotes technological production as the determining paradigm for social, as well as working life. Inherent in the culture industry is the manufacture of demand for its own products, hence the possibility of resistance is diminished if not completely eradicated. Adorno and Horkheimer's point, and it is an important one, is that what seems like benign entertainment, made possible and affordable by technology, which, itself, promises a future replete with better, cheaper, even more spectacular versions of the same, is nothing more than well disguised propaganda for continuing to feed the machine that produced it in the first place. The inequalities and injustices of industrial culture are not eradicated but displaced. On the one hand, the culture industry promotes itself as a solution to the dissatisfaction that it is largely responsible for producing. On the other, it becomes a powerful vehicle for mobilising disaffection and alienation while masking the reality of an exploitative economy.

Thus what is created is what the French sociologist Jacques Ellul refers to as a 'unifying psychism' (Ellul, 1965: 370). Writing in 1965, Ellul also made connections between the social effects of the entertainment media and what he calls 'the technical power of propaganda' (Ellul 1965: 369). By employing the word 'technical' here, Ellul connects the operation of propaganda with the concept of technique which, as he says, 'transforms everything it touches into a machine' (Ellul 1965: 4). According to Ellul, technique 'integrates the machine into society' (Ellul 1965: 5). By this he means not that the world has become mechanical in the image of the machine but that it has become increasingly rationalized in order to *accommodate* the machine. Put simply, this means that what the machine cannot use becomes worthless, and this includes the kind of people that are unable to adapt to its requirements. Although Ellul did not necessarily have in mind people with disabilities, it is worth considering, as an example, the growth of cities and the way in which they are adapted, primarily, to serve the needs of commerce and industry and *not* the needs of people who do not have the physical or mental ability to negotiate the modern workplace or the transport systems. In the name of efficiency, from which technique is largely inseparable, cities function to transport, house and entertain, only those workers who can be made the most efficient use of in the name of profit. Hence, the majority of rough sleepers in big cities are, by and large, those who have been identified as suffering from mental health problems. Therefore, when Ellul refers to the 'technical power of propaganda' he is concerned with the sense in which technique is employed to create a world in which the reality of these problems is obscured. In a technocracy:[6] 'Technique ... creates a separation between all "absolutely good" persons, who are collectively justified and who represent political, social and historic virtue, and all "absolutely evil" persons, in whom no worth or virtue is to be found' (Ellul 1965: 368).

It is not that we are easily fooled, or manipulated but that we come to experience reality as only that which can be evaluated in terms of a technical rationale, a 'common sense' sustained by the authority of pervasive media technologies. The result, according to Ellul, is 'the disappearance of reality in a world of hallucinations' (Ellul 1965: 372).

It is worth remembering that these critiques were written during and just after the Second World War and, in Ellul's case, at a time when the Cold War was at its most intense. The experience of German fascism had left onlookers in no doubt about the power of propaganda and the extent to which technocratic management was inseparable from a psychology of scapegoating. Furthermore, the ever present possibility of nuclear annihilation compounded the sense of threat from technology out of control. Ellul was voicing concerns that had significant cultural effects during the 1960s and that were at the heart of protests against the war in Vietnam and the attacks on the system of university administration in both Europe and the US. Although the hippies tend to be remembered for stunts like the attempt to levitate the Pentagon, what is often forgotten is that hippie ideology was informed by critiques such as Ellul's and, in the US, the influence of the Frankfurt School, most notably Marcuse who, in *One-Dimensional Man*, first published in 1964, coins the term 'technological rationality' (1991 [1964]: 11) to describe a system that he believed was fundamentally *ir*rational in that it operates on the basis of creating false needs: 'The people recognize themselves in their commodities; they find their soul in their automobile, hi-fi set, split-level home, kitchen equipment. The very mechanism which ties the individual to his society has changed, and social control is anchored in the new needs which it has produced' (Marcuse 1991 [1964]: 9).

For Marcuse, it is comfort, rather than deprivation, that exerts overt control in the one-dimensional society but 'the people' are nevertheless deprived, most notably of the capacity to think beyond the established paradigms: 'Its supreme promise is an ever-more-comfortable life for an ever-growing number of people who, in a strict sense, cannot imagine a qualitatively different universe of discourse and action, for the capacity to contain and manipulate subversive imagination and effort is an integral part of the given society' (Marcuse 1991 [1964]: 23).

This produces what Marcuse calls 'The Happy Consciousness – the belief that the real is rational and that the system produces the goods' (Marcuse 1991 [1964]: 84). What he means by 'the real' here is the conceptual universe produced by mass culture. In Marxist thought, the reality of worker alienation and exploitation is obscured by an ideology that disguises the interests of the ruling class as the interests of the whole society, thus producing a false reality in which the working class labours to support and maintain its own exploitation. Marx was convinced that people thus enslaved would become conscious of the irrationality of such a system and would come to understand that the power of technology could be liberated in the service of their own emancipation. What Marcuse understood was that, in postwar Western culture, because *everything* is commodified, including the kind of art and literature that challenges established ideals, there is no 'outside' in which subversive ideas can flourish. The Happy Consciousness does not describe a condition in which everyone is content and fulfilled but the sense in which people believe they *should* be happy because their desire for commodities, sold as the source of happiness, can be, at least temporarily, satisfied. Any *un*happiness is then managed by recourse to techniques like self-help groups and psychoanalysis. In short, people accept the established reality to the extent that, rather than change an irrational and exploitative system, they set about changing *themselves* to accommodate it.

Thus, despite the fact that '[t]o the extent to which the work world is conceived of as a machine and mechanized accordingly, it becomes the *potential* basis of a new freedom for man' (Marcuse 1991 [1964]: 3), its potential is obscured by 'the implanting of material and intellectual needs that perpetuate obsolete forms of the struggle for existence' (Marcuse 1991 [1964]: 4, his emphasis). In other words, under the right ideological conditions, technology would provide for our basic needs and leave us free to pursue a more creative and egalitarian existence[7] but, instead, the power of the machine is harnessed to a corrosive ideology which constructs existence as the struggle for self gratification in the form of commodities.

SPECTACULAR CULTURE

A similar argument is developed in Guy Debord's 1967 publication, *The Society of the Spectacle,* in which he states that, 'the spectacle' is 'a social relationship between people that is mediated by images' (Debord, 1995 [1967]: 12). There is some agreement in Debord's thesis with both Ellul and Marcuse but Debord's primary concern is with the increasing predominance of media technologies in the dissemination of reality. Because television, film and advertising are concerned with projecting images, the sense of sight is elevated above other senses and becomes the measure of our experiences. Driven by the logic of commodification, the world is represented to us as a series of images that we can buy into and this includes things like thoughts and feelings. Thus the capitalist economy is sustained, not only by the labour that produces the commodities themselves but by our acquiescence to the perpetuation of the spectacle. Our desire to match ourselves to the images that surround us intensifies with the development of increasingly sophisticated products that require ever greater investment of our emotional resources, as well as our money. The spectacle is thus all pervasive. In the same sense in which, for Ellul, fascist propaganda constructed the self-image of the populace as soldiers so, for Debord, the spectacle requires that we recognize ourselves as consumers. Debord compares the spectacle to the 'fallacious paradise' promoted by religious ideology, which, in promising redemption in an afterlife, allows people to invest power in an illusion and to accept suffering and cruelty in the name of what he calls 'cloud-enshrouded entities' that 'have now been brought down to earth'. 'The Spectacle', as he says, 'is hence a technological version of the exiling of human powers in a "world beyond"' (Debord 1996 [1967]: 18). In short, God has been replaced by the technologically englamoured commodity. In attempting to realize ourselves through the images associated with commodities, we are effectively separated from reality, estranged from ourselves and passively manipulated by the ideology of consumption.

Debord was a member of The Situationist International, a loose affiliation of European artists and activists who were instrumental in radicalizing the critique of technocratic capitalism. Their technique was an anarchic assault on the cultural representations of technocratic dominance, which they described as 'educative propaganda' (Knabb 1981: 8). The following is from in a self-administered questionnaire that appeared in their magazine, *Internationale Situationiste*, in 1964: 'Reality is superseding utopia. There is no longer any point in projecting an imaginary bridge between the richness of present technological capacities and the poverty of their use by the rulers of every variety. We want to put the material equipment at the disposal of everyone's creativity' (Knabb 1981: 140).

By employing the simple but effective technique of *détournement* (literally, turning around), the SI appropriated elements from familiar cultural forms like classic art and literature, films, theatre, advertisements, maps and icons of popular culture and dislocated them from their original contexts, bringing them into juxtaposition to create shocking or comic effects. Their 'anti-art' was an attack on complacency, the predominance of bourgeois sensibilities and 'contemporary artists [who] have condemned themselves to doing art as one does business' (Knabb 1981: 139). Their project was 'a conscious and collective construction of everyday life' (Knabb 1981: 310) in opposition to '[t]he world of consumption [which] is in reality the world of the mutual spectacularization of everyone, the world of everyone's separation, estrangement and nonparticipation' (Knabb 1981: 307). The SI technique of constructing 'situations' is designed to estrange us from the spectacle; to use the techniques of the spectacle against itself and promote consciousness of our own acquiescence to, and participation in, the construction of an illusive reality.

Such techniques were employed by the students who occupied the Sorbonne in Paris in May 1968. Although opinion is divided as to the extent of the SI's direct involvement in the events, they were confident that 'Situationist theory had a significant role in the origins of the generalized critique that gave rise to the first incidents of the May crisis and that developed along with that crisis.' SI influence was also apparent in the use of graffiti and slogans like 'Down with spectacle-commodity society', 'Long live communication, down with telecommunication' and 'Be realistic, demand the impossible.'[8] President Charles de Gaulle's heavy handed tactics with the students enflamed an already tense situation, while dissatisfied workers around the country demanded better conditions, leading to a general strike, which escalated to the extent that, for two weeks at least, France was poised on the brink of a workers' revolution. It was a revolution that, ultimately, failed but it is now understood to be one of the events that saw the end of the tradition of modernist thought and the beginnings of what is referred to as 'the linguistic turn' in philosophy, or, in a more general sense, postmodernism (or poststructuralism). This, essentially, is a set of methodologies concerned with deconstructing the conceptual apparatus of advanced technological cultures, rather than understanding them in terms of the progressive assumptions of classical historical materialism. In this sense, the work of the SI can be seen as foreshadowing the methods of postmodern theorists such as Jean Baudrillard who was teaching at the Sorbonne in 1968 and supported the student uprising and whose mentor, Henri Lefebvre, is often cited in SI texts. Baudrillard's ideas, in fact, have become so pervasive that they have been referenced in mass market productions, most notably in Hollywood film.

HYPERREALITY

In Andy and Larry Wachowski's 1999 film *The Matrix*, the central protagonist Neo (or Thomas Anderson, played by Keanu Reeves) is introduced to a computer-simulated environment with the words 'welcome to the desert of the real'. For initiated moviegoers this was a direct reference to Baudrillard's analysis of what he calls 'hyperreality', '*[t]he desert of the real itself*' (Baudrillard 1983: 2, his emphasis), the state of advanced consumer capitalism in which '[t]he real is produced from miniaturised units, from matrices, memory banks and command models – and with these it can be reproduced an indefinite number of times' (Baudrillard 1983: 3). The fact that a Hollywood science fiction film has paid homage to Baudrillard's ideas and the fact that he has also been published in the journal *Science Fiction Studies*, is instructive. Baudrillard brings us back to one of the propositions with which I started this chapter, which is that, as a cultural product of modernity, science fiction functions to analyse not the future but the cultural moment in which it is produced, defamiliarized by the technique of extrapolation.

Baudrillard is interested in science fiction because, in contemporary hi-tech, postmodern culture, the space between that cultural moment and the extrapolated 'other' world has collapsed. We can no longer imagine a future world in which the consequences of our present are dramatized and critiqued because the simulated reality produced by computer technologies *is* that world. In the Wachowskis' film, there *is* a world outside the matrix (the simulated world that Thomas Anderson lives in and believes is real) but it is an impoverished, cold and colourless world, only relieved by forays into the matrix to fight the machines that have enslaved humanity. Cypher, the Judas character, who betrays Neo for the taste of steak, chooses to be permanently reinserted into the matrix rather than remain in the etiolated world of the rebels because, as he says, 'ignorance is bliss'. In Baudrillard's analysis we are all Cyphers, acquiescing to a simulated reality in which we do not have to touch anything directly, or deal with the discomfort of resistance. Rob Shields, in his book *The Virtual*, gives as an example 'representations of the health of stock-markets, as expressed in, say, the charts and econometrics of a computerized news service [which] routinely stand in for the actuality of the economic life of nations half a world away' (Shields 2003: 5). These are hyperrealizations in which the 'reality' of the stock market is the movements of electronically generated graphs and charts. What we don't 'see' in these graphs is the effective exploitation of workers in countries like Indonesia and Malaysia and the way that the stock market itself is dependent on the selling of commodities that are, themselves, hyperreal. For instance, the shoes that I'm wearing today are actually copies of a sports shoe originally produced for athletes in the 1950s. You might ask why the hell I'm wearing a high performance sports shoe when I'm sitting at a desk and only my fingers are getting any exercise. The answer might be that I've paid for the *image* of the shoes, which is a technologically mediated appeal to my need to consider myself fashionable or practical or a member of a social elite. The play of images across the surface of reality that links my shoes to the electronic representations of the stock market but does not touch the deprivations of sweated labour, the damage to ecologies, consumer debt and unequal distribution of money and power on which consumer capitalism thrives and depends is what constitutes and maintains the hyperreal. Hyperreality is an intensified reification in which the excessive worlds of science fiction are our daily reality and the mode in which this excess exists is cybernetic; a function of the control, manipulation and dissemination of electronic communication which is the postmodern mode of production. We live in the matrix and it lives through us.

INFORMATION TECHNOLOGY, NETWORKS AND GLOBALIZATION

Hyperreality is a defining characteristic of what Fredric Jameson has called 'the Third Machine Age' (Jameson 1991: 36), which describes the sense in which contemporary culture reflects a shift from machines of production to machines of reproduction; that is, from manufacturing and locomotive machines to machines that reproduce sounds and visual images; from machines that were emblematic of the kinetic and motive power that they mobilized, like the turbine or railway train to machines like the computer 'whose outer shell has no emblematic or visual power' (Jameson 1991: 37). Jameson uses the eighteenth-century philosopher Edmund Burke's concept of the sublime, 'an experience bordering on terror, the fitful glimpse, in astonishment, stupor, and awe, of what was so enormous as to crush human life altogether' (Jameson 1991: 34), originally applied to the world of nature, to describe what he calls a 'postmodern or technological sublime': 'The technology of contemporary society is ... mesmerizing and fascinating not so much in its own right but because it seems to offer some privileged representational shorthand for grasping a network of power and control even more difficult for our minds and imaginations to grasp: the whole new decentered global network of the third stage of capital itself' (Jameson 1991: 37–8).

This is the kind of power that is evident in the incessant reproducibility out of which the hyperreal is constructed, from shopfronts (the global ubiquity of McDonald's, Starbucks etc.) to the ultimate medium of reproducibility: the Internet, which, itself an emblem of the third machine age, is also a third space in which the boundaries that mark out terrestrial space (countries, defence and trading zones and other lines of international demarcation) are effaced. The geography of the modern world and the politics of the nation state are thus superseded by a geography of informatics and the politics of postindustrial global capitalism.

William Gibson gives a vivid description of the geography of informatics in his novel *Neuromancer* (1983), which Jameson (1991: 38) describes as 'an exceptional literary realization within a predominantly visual or aural postmodern production':

> Program a map to display frequency of data exchange, every thousand megabytes a single pixel on a very large screen. Manhattan and Atlanta burn solid white. Then they start to pulse, the rate of traffic threatening to overload your simulation. Your map is about to go nova. Cool it down. Up your scale. Each pixel a million megabytes. At a hundred million megabytes per second, you begin to make out certain blocks in midtown Manhattan, outlines of hundred-year-old industrial parks ringing the old core of Atlanta ... (Gibson, 1983: 57)

Gibson's breathless prose captures the awe of the technological sublime while being an early example of the use of the vocabulary of electronic data processing in a literary context. His 'map' evokes intense concentrations of information exchange located in obscure but strategic regions of North American cities, which might represent nodes in the international banking system, the location of routers for the Internet or high-powered surveillance networks, or data being downloaded to 'hot sites'. According to Martin Pawley, a hot site is 'a data warehouse, an expendable and interchangeable facility':

> Virtually everything to do with its usefulness relates to the needs of information processing, for as the complexity and importance of information technology increases, so does the security problem it poses to business ... A single day of disruption across the whole United Kingdom could cost £1.4 billion. Figures of this order explain why, important as they are in computer terms, 'hot site' buildings have no status as architecture. Ideally they are run-down premises without any distinguishing features of any kind. (Pawley 1998: 178–9)

In the architecture of the modern city, buildings, like banks, department stores and company head offices were emblematic of their function and status within the system of industrial capitalism. In the 'knowledge economy' of postmodern, postindustrial capitalism, the storage and exchange of information maps a virtual city in which there is no longer any direct correspondence between the visual landmarks of power and the operations of the economy. We can bank online and receive our money from ATMs on street corners or use debit and credit cards. We still shop in stores but, increasingly, buy from sites on the World Wide Web. The administrative functions of financial and other service industries are outsourced to other parts of the world and moveable hot sites contain the wealth of multinational companies, expressed as data.

TECHNOCAPITALISM

This decentralization is characteristic of the global economy of the Third Machine Age for which Steven Best and Douglas Kellner coin the helpful term 'technocapitalism'. Technocapitalism is 'characterized by a decline of the state and enlarged power for the market, accompanied by the growing strength of transnational corporations and governmental bodies and the decreased power of the nation-state and its institutions' (Best and Kellner 2001: 212) and is 'useful to describe the synthesis of capital and technology in the present organization of society' (Best and Kellner 2001: 213). In other words, Best and Kellner's strategy in using this term is to approach the subject of globalization as a synthesis of both economic *and* technological development, rather than assuming the priority of technical processes in determining the global order or prioritizing the spread of capitalism after the fall of communism in Eastern Europe at the end of the 1980s and beginning of the 1990s.

In this synthesis, capital itself has transmogrified to the extent that it has become disconnected from specific commodities. The Henry Ford-style industrialist is long gone, replaced by chief executive officers of multinational companies that own, not factories, machines and raw materials but *brands*. In fact, although the Ford Motor Company still exists, Ford itself is one brand among many owned by the company, including Lincoln, Mercury, Mazda, Volvo, Jaguar, Land Rover and Aston Martin, as well as car rental company Hertz, car service brands and financial services. Brands are traded among companies, valorized by market share, which is largely determined by the effective manipulation of consumer taste. Thus, what is really traded is the brand *image*, itself dependent upon the effectiveness of advertising and the deployment of marketing strategies based on carefully calculated market trends and the identification and exploitation of 'niche' selling opportunities.

Hence, the ultimate commodity in this post-Fordist economic structure is *information*. The instant exchange of information made possible by the Internet promotes the development of dispersed, rather than hierarchical 'top down' management structures, instant networking between companies and their suppliers around the world, 'just in time' stock management in which stores replace their stock in response to consumer demand rather than carry a surplus, the dissemination of knowledge about purchasing habits, customer profiles and preferences and the outsourcing of customer service. Currently, Indian 'call centres', staffed by well educated middle class Indians who earn more than double the national average wage but much less than their counterparts in the West, handle the customer relations for multinational companies based in Europe and the US. These service centres train their employees to service Western clients by holding classes in, for instance, American English pronunciation and understanding Western popular culture. Employees choose Western-sounding pseudonyms and those servicing British clients learn to talk about the weather. Ironically, the English-speaking Indian middle class is itself a product of 200 years of British colonial rule.

NETWORK SOCIETY

The computer on your desk, in your backpack or pocket is not simply another mass produced, disposable product of the technical innovation that founds the economy of consumer capitalism although it is, of course, all of these things, but it is also the icon of a revolution in which it has come to stand for the momentous changes that have marked the development of what Manuel Castells (1996: 22) calls 'the Informational Society', a revolution that has been 'at least as major a historical event as was the eighteenth-century Industrial Revolution, inducing a pattern of discontinuity in the material basis of economy, society, and culture' (Castells 1996: 30). Most commentators, including Castells, cite the 1970s as the decade that saw the beginnings of this revolution although the genesis of the technologies, still designated as 'new', which mark its distinction can be traced to the mid-nineteenth century and the experiments of Charles Babbage and Ada Lovelace and their attempts to invent a 'difference engine'. What marks the 1970s is the invention of the microprocessor, the 'truly extraordinary saga' (Castells 1996: 44) of Steve Wozniak and Steve Jobs's development of the first microcomputer and the founding of Microsoft by Bill Gates and Paul Allen. Comparative developments in information routing technologies during the 1960s had already prepared the way for the instant relay of data between computers in different locations. With the advent of the personal computer, what was to become the Internet became a feasible proposition.

Anyone who lived through the first twenty to thirty years of the information revolution can testify to the extraordinary changes that accompanied the penetration of computers into all areas of social and working life. Microchip technology enabled a redefinition of the iconography of the machine, which was transformed from an imposing structure of metal and grease to an often barely visible arrangement of circuits and switches. Thus, machines often migrated from public to private spaces and from industry to the home. The personal computer has brought design, publishing, sound recording and sampling, complex accounting and, along with the camcorder, film editing within the purview of home users.

This amounts to a substantial redefinition of expertise in which many tasks previously confined to the world of work and shared among groups of workers with different forms of specialized knowledge have come within the ability of anyone with sufficient computer literacy. For instance, prior to the advent of the PC, journalists would type their stories on a typewriter and the hard copy would be passed to a typesetter who would cast the words in metal type. Originally, the metal letters were held in 'cases' (hence, upper and lower case), picked by hand and locked into a frame, ready to be transferred to the presses. Towards the end of the nineteenth century, the 'linotype' machine was introduced, which allowed the compositor to impress hot metal a line at a time. Variations on the linotype were still in use until around the mid-1960s when rudimentary computerized typesetting allowed for headlines and columns of type to be exposed onto photographic paper, bypassing the need for hot-metal compositing. From these, along with 'half tone' conversions of photographic images, 'camera-ready' finished artwork was produced by pasting the various elements into position on a board. This was then photographed and the negative used to etch the thin metal plates used in offset lithographic or 'gravure' printing or the 'blocks' used in letterpress. As late as the 1970s, hot metal was still being used for some fonts and 'blockmakers' serviced the advertising industry by setting and printing advertising copy onto specially coated paper, which would then be cut and pasted into camera-ready artwork. This would be sent back to the blockmaker who would produce blocks ready to be sent to the newspapers. Thus the production of newspapers required a conglomeration of diverse and highly valued skills and print workers' labour unions had considerable power.

In 1986–7 the Australian media magnate Rupert Murdoch, aided by new anti-union laws passed by Margaret Thatcher's government, smashed the power of the print unions in Britain when he moved production of News International titles (including *The Times*, the *Sunday Times*, the *Sun* and the *News of the World*) from Fleet Street to Wapping and introduced new printing machinery and desktop editing and compositing. When the print unions SOGAT (Society of Graphical and Allied Trades) and the NGA (National Graphical Association) came out on strike,

Murdoch simply sacked them and replaced them with members of the EETPU, the electricians, technicians and plumbers union. The new machinery did not need the skills represented by SOGAT and the NGA and not one day's newspaper production was lost during the year-long, often violent dispute. Six thousand people were involved in the strike and many of them ended up without jobs and without very much prospect of another one unless they were able to retrain. Even with retraining, many were too old to compete in the burgeoning service sector market, which demanded transferable and 'immaterial' skills. These are what Arlie Russell Hochschild has described as 'emotional labor', in which 'one's face and one's feelings take on the properties of a resource ... a resource to be used to make money' (Hochschild 1983: 55).

The Wapping dispute is certainly one of the sadder episodes in Britain's long industrial history but it also provides a very good illustration of the changes in both work and social life that heralded the dawn of the digital age. Strong labour unions like SOGAT had always stood for the power of labour in an economy characterized by vertically integrated management structures and solidarity between workers who understood that their strength was in their numbers and that union demands were made on behalf of the collective. When they were thrown back onto the labour market they met the full force of Margaret Thatcher's neoliberalist restructuring of the economy in which they forced to compete as individuals in a largely service-oriented market.

What emerges from this is a structural link between the new digital technologies and Reagan/Thatcher neoliberalism, which was, essentially, designed to free the global market from restrictions and create increased competition but which found an ally in new technologies that allowed businesses increased flexibility and the ability to streamline the workforce – essentially to dispense with centralized production and thus certain layers of middle management, as well as large numbers of manual workers. Neoliberalism promoted a return to values associated with enlightenment humanism, from which emerged the idea of the abstract individual who is understood as autonomous and whose social position is determined by a resourceful application of rationality (rather than being mandated by a higher being, as was believed prior to the seventeenth century). Thus competition is encouraged as the motor of innovation and the production of new technologies is lauded as the mark of a healthy and progressive society. What Reagan and Thatcher recognized was that trade restrictions must be removed if the kind of economy that these values promoted was to be realized.

The role of the International Monetary Fund and the World Bank in liberalizing the global economy is well documented elsewhere.[9] Essentially, they provided a conduit for international capital to exploit the productivity of developing nations and for multinational companies to export production to anywhere in the world that offered the cheapest possible labour at any given time. The instant exchange of data facilitated by global computer networks, at the same time, permitted the transfer of funds between business centres in large cities, effectively bypassing national borders. As Saskia Sassen points out, 'globalisation – as illustrated by the space economy of information industries – denationalizes national territory' (Sassen 1998: xxviii).

In September, 1999, the World Teleport Association and Telecommunications Magazine awarded Singapore the first ever Intelligent City Award in recognition of its IT2000 master plan, designed to transform the island 'into one of the key world-wide centres for business and IT'.[10] Based on the full utilization and penetration of broadband technology and wireless networks into every sphere of business, education and leisure, the plan was well underway when, in 1993, *Wired* magazine sent William Gibson to the island to 'see whether that clean dystopia represents our techno future'. Gibson, famously, referred to the 'Intelligent Island' as 'Disneyland with the death penalty'. '[C]onformity here', he writes, 'is the prime directive, and the fuzzier brands of creativity are in extremely short supply.'[11]. In a networked world, Singapore is the prime example of a twenty-first century city state, an insular and controlled environment in which the needs of technocapitalism direct the lives of the population. What this amounts to is a capitulation of culture to the processes of the information economy or to the exigencies of what Castells calls 'the network society, characterized by the pre-eminence of social morphology over social action' (Castells 1996: 469).

For Castells, networks are the fundamental organizing principle of both techno-capitalism and its social forms. As examples, Castells cites political organizations like the European Union, stock markets and their service centres around the world, banks, multinational corporations and their outsourced services, drug cartels and their associated money-laundering institutions and 'television systems, entertainment studios, computer graphics milieux, news teams, and mobile devices generating, transmitting and receiving signals, in the global network of the new media at the roots of cultural expression and public opinion in the information age' (Castells 1996: 470).

These networks interpenetrate and interact in both cooperation and competition and all submit to a logic of coordination imposed by the fluctuations of the global market, which is, itself, dependent upon speculation and future trend projections based on nothing other than the manipulations of the spectacle; the structuring of reality that, for Baudrillard, constitutes the hyperreal. Because the ideology of neoliberalism promotes choice and self-determination as the expression of our individuality, we are encouraged to communicate our identities through how we spend our money. In short, we live to shop. The majority of private sector jobs are devoted to promoting, organizing, supplying, theorizing and financing the activity of consumption. Advertising and taste manipulating TV programmes that speak to our need to identify in terms of consumption by advising us how to dress, travel, eat and decorate our houses feed the culture of consumption, which, in turn, feeds gigabytes of data representing spending patterns, consumer profiles, social class demographics, etc., as well as the revenue generated, back into the networks.

There is no time or space, as such, in the network society. The transfer of data across the globe is instantaneous so that the most valuable commodity, information itself, is always both everywhere and nowhere. Material goods travel a little more slowly but are constantly on the move and infinitely replicable so that their flow around the globe comes to resemble a constant stream rather than a fixed time/space trajectory from point of departure to point of arrival. And, as we drive around and through major cities, as a friend recently commented, 'the whole world seems to be moving at thirty miles per hour'.[12] Furthermore, the hyperreal is both constructed and experienced in the reified time of a perpetual future, in a state of yearning or existential dissatisfaction corresponding to the futurity which drives currency speculation and the stock markets.

When Castells writes '*the network is the enterprise*' (Castells 2001: 67, his emphasis), he is referring to the lateral organization of business in which different company departments, suppliers, banks, outsourced manufacturing and services, for instance, are linked together in a cooperative network for the duration of any given project; temporary affiliations facilitated by the Internet. Thus, '[b]y using the Internet as a fundamental medium of communication and information-processing, business adopts the network as its organizational form' (Castells 2001: 66). Similar forms structure the social life of the network society, maintained, as William J Mitchell points out, 'through a complex mix of local face-to-face interactions, travel, mail systems, synchronous electronic contact through telephones and video links, and asynchronous electronic contact through email and similar media'. '[I]ncreasingly', as he says, 'my sense of continuity and belonging derives from being electronically networked to the widely scattered people and places I care about' (Mitchell 2003: 17). Some of these people, he may never meet IRL (in real life) and some of the places will be fabricated by computer programs. Thus the geography of informatics also describes the dispersed and delocalized nature of communities in the network society.

GLOBAL VILLAGE

Although Marshall McLuhan's (2001 [1967]: 63) pronouncement that '[w]e now live in a global village ... a simultaneous happening' (1967: 63) has gained in significance since the advent of the network society, considered in the context of technocapitalism, the 'we' to whom he refers needs some qualification. Although capital now affects in some way, and not always beneficially, every corner of the globe, the spread of new technologies is not uniform and, even in the regions of highest access to communications and information technologies, full participation is still the preserve of an elite class. As Rob Shields points out, in 2001 '80 percent of the world's population [had] never placed a phone call' and '[m]ore people use[d] the Internet in London than in all of Africa' (Shields 2003: 87). The deregulation of world markets coupled with a bias in favour of the developed nations in world economic policies is currently fuelling an increase in global poverty, despite initiatives like the MDG (millennium development goals)[13] agreed by the world's richest nations in 1999 with the aim of halving poverty by 2015. A recent report suggests that 'despite some improvements in health and education, on current trends the target for reducing child mortality in sub-Saharan Africa will not be met for another 150 years.'[14] The campaigning organization War on Want reports that, in the same region, despite trade liberalization and the increase in FDI (foreign direct investment) trade is actually declining because '[m]ost trade is *between* developed countries and *within* TNCs [transnational corporations]'.[15] Furthermore, the transient nature of business networks has led to an increase in the casualization of labour. In Singapore, for instance, there are no homeless, no poor and no unemployed but this apparent idyll functions on the back of foreign labour migrants brought in to do menial tasks and then sent home. In March 2004, Asian Labour News reported that, in 2002, some 7,424 of these workers were forced to make salary claims against their employers who, because of cash flow problems, had simply sent them home empty handed.[16]

I would like to think that you are reading this at a future time in which these inequalities have been addressed but it may be that I have simply watched too much *Star Trek*. The rosy vision of the future presented by *Star Trek: The Next Generation* (*TNG*), first broadcast between 1987 and 1994, depends on the neoliberalist assumption that the need for money has been eradicated by human ingenuity, which has produced a world in which technological solutions fulfil the basic requirements of everyday life. Food, clothing and machine parts are produced by replicators, fuelled by infinite energy, sourced from the universe itself, and work is redefined as that which benefits the common good. The United Federation of Planets represents a cooperative drive for the accumulation of knowledge about the universe, supported by the ability to travel at 'warp' (faster than light) speed and an ethic of non-intervention in 'developing' cultures. The need for drama, of course, requires that these ethics be challenged and suitably misguided enemies are frequently vanquished (Starfleet is provided with an impressive array of weaponry) or brought to appreciate their error. Starfleet's most impressive enemy is 'The Borg', a collective 'hive mind' for whom the logic of appropriation is paramount, but what The Borg desire to appropriate is not territory but 'technological distinctiveness' (cultures deemed to be insufficiently developed are simply ignored). Thus, with every 'assimilation', they become more powerful. 'Resistance', as they say, 'is futile'.

The Federation is presented as a benign organization whose mission to explore includes the assessment of other cultures for possible inclusion and thus access to the benefits of cultural exchange. However, if space travel is, as Marina Benjamin describes it 'a metaphorical extension of the American West' (Benjamin, 2003: 46), then *Star Trek* is the American Dream achieved, an infinite and endless 'final frontier' in which expansionism is justified on the basis of technological determinism and a belief in manifest destiny – the conviction that acquisition of territory is a justified expression of the worth of a nation or civilization. As Valerie Fulton has pointed out '[t]he Federation's goals are both "to seek out new civilizations" and "to boldly go where no one has gone before" – missions that clearly contradict each other unless read through the lens of frontier ideology, which grants new civilizations existence only to the extent that the originary culture has 'found' them' (Fulton 1994: 4). If 'technological distinctiveness' is what allows the Federation to justify its attempt to colonize the universe, it is also this that makes it vulnerable to the Borg. Thus The Borg can be read as suggesting, not as at first seems obvious, a critique of international communism (although this is certainly implied) but a fear that the very efficiency of global networks may lend strength to an enemy who would appropriate the technology to challenge the ascendancy of the developed West.

The attacks on the World Trade Center and the Pentagon on 11 September 2001 signalled the beginning of these fears becoming reality. Aeroplanes are a highly symbolic technology for the information age. Representative of the triumph of twentieth-century engineering, they are, for the twenty-first century, the physical analogue of the global penetration of electronic networks and are essential to the movement of goods, people and hard copy documents around the world. They are also prodigious users of natural resources and thus a potent reminder of the dependency of technocapitalism on dwindling and contested oil reserves. In the 9/11 attacks, they became, in the hands of suicide pilots, essentially smart bombs that were turned against the very symbols of the military-industrial complex that both produces and depends upon them.

I am writing this at a time that, despite the rumours of his death, Osama bin Laden has recently proved himself very much alive by appearing on television across the world four days prior to an American election in which high voter turnout worked in favour of the incumbent, George W. Bush, rather than, as had been predicted, his challenger John Kerry. Opinion was divided as to the effect of bin Laden's re-emergence at such a sensitive time, some offering the opinion that it would work in

Bush's favour by reminding the US population that the 'war on Terror' had not yet been won. Other opinions suggested that, conversely, bin Laden's high profile made a mockery of the Bush administration's strategies in pursuing him and other high-profile terrorists and would, therefore, work against him.

Less commented upon was the fact that a man who has eluded capture for some three years and is, effectively, 'in hiding' is, in fact, as highly visible as Bush himself. Despite the fact that he is the most wanted man on the planet, bin Laden is, ironically, protected by the same networks that allow the American president global ubiquity. Both use the global reach of television to strategic affect. The US election becomes the business of everyone on the planet, not only because America's superpower status makes it relevant to everyone but because the combination of satellite and streaming video technology enables instant worldwide transmission of events. Bin Laden makes use of the same technology, courtesy of the Arab language TV station Al-Jazeera, based in Qatar, which, on this occasion, received his taped transmission via an envelope left with the security guards at their office in Pakistan. It was on air within hours, despite the American ambassador's attempts to block it. As John Gray points out 'Al Qaeda resembles less the centralised command structures of twentieth-century revolutionary parties than the cellular structures of drug cartels and the flattened networks of virtual business corporations' (Gray 2003: 76). Furthermore, he predicts that, although it is '[p]resently unchallengeable, America's military superiority will be eroded by the very processes of globalisation whose virtues the US has recently lauded' (Gray 2003: 98).

Thus, to upend my Borgian analogy, resistance, far from being futile, is actually facilitated by the structures through which American hegemony and the global 'free market' is currently maintained. The myth propagated by *Star Trek*, that cultures left to their own devices will eventually match the Federation level of technological development and will thus not only qualify for inclusion but will acquiesce to its values, is proved false by the Borg who simply steal what they require. Similarly, according to Gray (2003: 111), '[t]he Taliban were capable of using advanced technology they bought or stole; but it is unlikely that they could ever have developed it'.

Terrorism, or what Gray (2003: 73) calls 'unconventional warfare' is not new to the twenty-first century but Al Qaeda's use of the technologies and structures of contemporary commerce and media saturation means that, essentially, local acts of terror become global. Thus by a process akin to Borgian assimilation, global terrorism becomes part of the hyperreal. I can watch bin Laden deliver his message to the West on CNN and the BBC or read transcripts on a myriad of websites. On this occasion, he made no direct threats but it may be that he understands only too well that all that is necessary is that he appear on a regular basis to propagate his own myth. The filmmaker, Adam Curtis, has speculated that, although terrorism remains a threat, Al Qaeda is itself a myth constructed by the American intelligence agencies in order to identify a singular enemy when, in fact, what is identified as global terrorism is actually a loose affiliation of disparate groups, often with little or no connection to bin Laden.[17] Whether this is true or not is somewhat beside the point. As Castells (1996: 471) points out 'the new economy is organized around global networks of capital, management, and information, whose access to technological know-how is at the roots of productivity and competitiveness.' Thus, whether or not Al Qaeda has access to weapons of mass destruction and whether or not it is a global organization with the power to organize efficiently, the 'terror' that it evokes is directly related to the extent to which it is perceived as empowered by access to the same structures and expertise.

SURVEILLANCE AND SECURITY

The existence of Al Qaeda and other pernicious users of network technologies, like paedophile rings and cybercriminals, has mobilized an intensification of security surveillance worldwide. Alongside the diminished effectiveness of nation states in the control of worldwide commerce and the perception of the Internet as an effectively borderless domain, a raft of measures has been developed to intensify immigration controls, to police national borders, to collect information on supposed dissidents and to censor suspect sites on the Internet. As Sassen points out, although 'the Internet is a space of distributed power that limits the possibilities of authoritarian and monopoly control ... it is also a space for contestation and segmentation' (Sassen 1998: 191). Sassen's book was published in 1998 and her comments appear in a discussion of the rapid spread of company firewalls and local 'intranets' that were, at the time, beginning to segment the Internet into public and private domains. Since the events of 2001 and with the rise of more sophisticated infiltration techniques, like worms, viruses and 'bots' (software robots that can disable a computer system), increasingly stringent controls and surveillance strategies have been implemented, which threaten individual privacy and the previously unregulated freedoms of the World Wide Web.

In Stephen Spielberg's 2002 film *Minority Report*, Tom Cruise plays Detective John Anderton, a 'precrime' cop who works for an agency that uses human mutants with precognitive powers to identify crimes that are about to be committed. Anderton's job is to prevent the execution of the crime and arrest the potential perpetrator. But, as William J Mitchell point out, '[p]recrime does not require mutants floating in vats, as in *Minority Report* – just a database, rules and profiles, inference engines, and data mining algorithms' (Mitchell 2003: 200). These techniques are common to both commercial organizations and government security agencies. The following is from the Web site of a company called Datawatch, which sells data-mining software for commercial applications:

> When humans are trying to find causal relationships within data they will often make preconceptions about what is, and what isn't going to be there. In contrast to this, computers have the power to not bother about minimising the search to the same extent and thus find relationships which would have not been considered by a human analyst. Data mining uses this fact to produce useful inferences concerning data that human analysts would never see. In this way the data mining user doesn't exactly pose a question as much as ask the system to use a model to discover past patterns that predict future behaviour.[18]

These 'past patterns' may be purchasing decisions, registrations with sites on the World Wide Web, withdrawals from automatic teller machines, the locations of mobile phone calls made and received, data from in-car GPS devices, images from surveillance cameras, credit ratings, TV viewing habits, medical records and a host of other information gleaned from the 'digital footprints' that we leave as we access the datasphere on a daily basis. A more highly developed form of data mining is data warehousing, which performs similar operations across several, often disparate databases. According to Mitchell:

> Nationwide identity cards and numbers greatly facilitate warehousing. Such consolidation has generally been opposed by privacy advocates, and centralized, consolidated databases would provide attractive targets for break-in attempts and denial of service attacks. However, nationwide identification systems and large-scale data warehousing have had more advocates since September 2001 – particularly in the United States. (Mitchell 2003: 197)

Since 9/11, the Pentagon's Information Awareness Office has announced plans to 'build a vast warehouse of personal data about individuals and to apply data-mining and pattern recognition techniques to sniff out suspicious patterns of activity and electronically identify enemies' (Mitchell, 2003: 201). Add to this the fact that the global surveillance system Echelon, enables Comint (communications intelligence) agencies, notably the US National Security Agency and, in Britain, GCHQ in Cheltenham to monitor Internet traffic, as well as traffic passing through the INTELSAT international telephone satellites[19] and it becomes clear that Big Brother is not only watching but closely scrutinizing, sifting and matching vast amounts of the data that daily traverse the globe.

Although, to quote John Perry Barlow 'information wants to be free',[20] its freedom is being increasingly curtailed in the name of 'security', the protection of intellectual copyright and ideological concerns disguised as 'family values'. China, for instance, is alleged to have a 30,000 strong Internet police force. The 'Great Firewall of China' filters out sites deemed unsuitable for the population (this includes the BBC) and, in Shanghai, it is compulsory for Internet cafes to install video cameras and software that detect attempts to access banned sites, which are automatically reported to the authorities. 'Cyberdissidents' are regularly arrested and detained without trial.[21] However, China is not alone in attempting to police the Internet. The reason given by the Beijing authorities for the frequent inspections and closure of Internet cafes is concern about young people accessing pornographic and violent sites, and the issue of child protection is also at the heart of arguments for the regulation of Internet access in the West. As Stephen Maddison points out, 'it is clear that where advocates of privacy infringement and indiscriminate technological surveillance encounter no resistance to their programmes is in relation to the protection of children' (Maddison 2004: 54). But, as he suggests, this tends to obscure the extent to which pornography 'is integrated into the revenue streams of some of the world's most successful and recognisable corporations' (Maddison 2004: 46). Furthermore, pornography online is big business. For instance, '[i]n 2000 *Forbes* noted that shares in sex companies with internet ventures were up by up to eighty-four per cent' (Maddison 2004: 46). This produces a situation in which the demands of the free market prohibit direct intervention in the publication of pornographic material and the solution to public outrage over the ready availability of, particularly, child pornography, is seen in the same terms as 'the 'problem' of US national security and the 'problem' of copyright infringement in file-sharing networks' (Maddison 2004: 54). Thus, '[c]hild pornography is being used, along with issues of homeland security and corporate copyright protection, to extend the material field of regulations in the information society' (Maddison 2004: 56). In other words, acquiescence to increased surveillance and regulation of the Internet is secured on the basis of the anxieties mobilized by the threat of terrorism, concerns about copyright theft and child protection issues. The case for vigilance in monitoring the spread of child pornography is made on the assumption of a link between looking at sexualized images of children and active paedophilia, the so called 'stranger danger'. What this obscures is the fact that, as reported by the US Department of Health and Human Services, in 2002, 80 per cent of perpetrators of child abuse were parents.[22]

At this point, it is important to note that the employment of surveillance techniques in the context of social relations is not a postmodern invention, nor is it exclusive to capitalist societies. Fordism, for instance, can be understood as a system of industrial management that is founded in surveillance as a mechanism for the control of production. Ford's Sociological Department was not merely a whim but a calculated strategy for ensuring worker conformity that worked in concert with the controls exercised by time-management systems in the factory. Workers were encouraged to police their personal lives with the promise of higher remuneration but implied in this promise is also the threat of, on the one hand, redundancy and, on the other, social exclusion. A 'clean backyard' becomes synonymous with the higher social status that comes with higher wages so that the pressure to conform becomes self-perpetuating. At the same time, because the essence of bureaucracy is in control exercised through the collection of data and the maintenance of records, the very idea of a whole department devoted to social control is enough to ensure that its strictures are adhered to, whether or not it ever carries out an inspection. That the essential features of this system can be mapped onto the kind of controls exercised by contemporary digital surveillance makes the point that what David Lyon refers to as the 'surveillance society' (Lyon, 1994: 33) is a feature of modernity in general, rather than postmodern technoculture in particular.

This point is made forcefully by Michel Foucault in his analysis of modern disciplinary society *Discipline and Punish: The Birth of the Prison* (1991 [1975]). Foucault is interested in the shift from a 'spectacle' of punishment (public floggings, hangings etc.) which characterized the disciplinary regimes of the Middle Ages to the more dispersed and insidious forms which were developed during the eighteenth century. He offers a model for understanding how power operates in modern cultures in the form of the Panopticon, a building designed by the eighteenth-century philosopher, Jeremy Bentham. Composed of a central tower around which are arranged 'cells' which are backlit so that anyone occupying the room at the top of the tower, and looking out of the windows, can immediately see into all the cells and observe the activities of the occupants, the Panopticon facilitated total surveillance with very little cost in either money or manpower. Bentham imagined that the building could be adapted to house any body of inmates who were required to submit to a regime. Most obviously this would be convicted criminals but it also lends itself to disciplining school children, those thought to be insane, hospital patients and, presumably, university students. Foucault makes the point that the Panopticon enforces discipline, not by the constant presence of a guard or what he calls the 'director' in the tower (who can never be seen by the inmates) but by the simple fact that the inmates know that they may be observed at any moment. Because they never know whether or not they are being observed, the director be-comes hardly necessary. The surveillance becomes 'permanent in its effects, even if it is discontinuous in its action ... the inmates [are] caught up in a power situation of which they are themselves the bearers' (Foucault 1991 [1975]: 201). Thus, '[v]isibility', as he says, 'is a trap' (Foucault 1991 [1975]: 200).

Another important point to be made about the Panopticon is that it was, as Foucault points out, 'also a laboratory; it could be used as a machine to carry out experiments, to alter behaviour, to train or correct individuals' (Foucault 1991 [1975]:

203). Therefore, an important part of the administration of the Panopticon would be the keeping of files on individual inmates to record their progress towards the desired behaviour and the production of statistics from the data thus accumulated.

If this is beginning to sound familiar, it is because, as Foucault wanted us to understand, we live in a panoptic society in which the exercise of power is dispersed rather than centralized in one authority and it achieves its effectiveness through the very techniques that Bentham recommended be deployed in the Panopticon. It may be an urban myth that some of the cameras employed as speed traps on city streets and motorways are dummies but, one way or the other, it makes no difference. They work to limit the speed of drivers because, when one hoves into view, we are best advised to slow down, just in case it might be recording. Thus we police our behaviour without any direct intervention from outside forces. We internalize the discipline represented by the speed camera in the same way that we internalize the rules that limit our social interactions, our conduct as members of families, as employees, as citizens of the state and as consumers. In the absence of any direct surveillance, we survey ourselves and monitor our actions for any taint of 'abnormality', a self-discipline that is constantly reinforced by the publication of reports and statistics that identify norms and construct our responses to deviance. In Foucault's words, the system achieves 'a perpetual victory that avoids any physical confrontation and which is always decided in advance' (Foucault 1991 [1975]: 203).

In contemporary culture, new technologies enable new forms of panopticism. The speed camera, for instance, functions to symbolize a structural link between developments in photography and motor vehicles, the engineering of faster road surfaces, as well as computers and the technical application of data matching, all of which service the requirements of technocapitalism as both a consumer-led global economy and a disciplinary regime of monstrous proportions. As in my example of the Ford Motor Company's Sociological Department, the vast bureaucratic apparatus of the global network society enforces a panoptic ordering of populations, which has the effect of mobilizing demand for more of the same. We may be made to feel uneasy about the ubiquity of surveillance devices but we feel they are necessary to police those who fail to conform. At the same time, however, anxieties about our own status as citizens of the technocapitalist order (occasioned by job insecurity, consumer debt, questions about gender and sexuality and fear of terrorism) compel us to acquiesce to an intensification of panopticism.

The popularity of 'reality' TV programmes like *Survivor* and *Big Brother* testify to the increasing demand for technologies that allow us to watch others in order that we may recognize ourselves. And I use the word advisedly. To re-cognize is to know again – and again. Knowledge of the self in contemporary technocultures is the ultimate commodity. It is what we, as consumers, purchase when we indulge our need for commodities. And, with each purchase, we feed the databases that generate future demand. This is why Mark Poster refers to 'the discourse of databases' as 'the Superpanopticon', which is 'a means of controlling masses in the postmodern, postindustrial mode of information'. We subject *ourselves* to surveillance in the hope of self-confirmation; 'the population participates in its own self-constitution as subjects of the normalizing gaze of the Superpanopticon' (Poster 1990: 97). Motorists are encouraged to buy faster cars because access to advanced technology, represented as the ability to travel faster and further, is sold as confirmation of success and personal fulfilment. Thus there is a constant tension between the demands of the technocapitalist economy and the panoptic discipline that ensures its survival.

So, to return to the question that *Wired* posed for William Gibson, it may seem that, under the terms of the global Superpanopticon the 'fuzzier brands of creativity' are not only in short supply but that the forms of resistance that the phrase suggests have become meaningless; that, in fact, we have finally succumbed to totalitarianism under the terms of Herbert Marcuse's 'Happy Consciousness'. However, this would be to accept that the new technologies are monolithic; that they impose a rigidity and uniformity that does not take into account that computers, unlike industrial technologies, are highly manipulable. They lend themselves to fluidity and adaptation, rather than restriction to a single task or set of tasks and their wide dissemination and use in multiple contexts makes for unpredictability and the possibility of some surprising and subversive applications. Although, in this sense, they also elide a slippage between different materialities of power, they also offer the promise that they can be appropriated to challenge the institutions that perpetuate power hierarchies. Timothy Leary, the guru of the 1960s counter-culture, re-emerging in the 1980s after some ten years on the run from the law, wrote excitedly about the 'psybernetic' possibilities of the personal computer. Leary believed that digitalization would produce a revolution in consciousness akin to the promise of LSD and a 'cultural metamorphosis' that would 'eliminate ... dependence on the enormous bureaucracy of knowledge professionals that flourished in the industrial age' (Leary 1994: 43). Whether or not he was correct may be too early to tell but we can, at least, accept his implied suggestion that technoculture is an open field; that information itself is an always already deconstructed entity, which may finally present its own challenge to its monopolization by the neoliberal establishment.

This, then, is my premise for the remainder of this book: that the concepts that have emerged as fundamental for the study of technoculture are those that we understand as equally fundamental to the understanding of human being. Cultural responses to questions of sustenance, sex, death, aesthetics, language and space and time are and always have been rooted in informatics understood as the quality of information about the world at any given cultural moment. In this sense, an understanding of technoculture must take into account the way that knowledge about the world is produced, the uses to which it is put and the variant epistemologies that not only structure its conceptualization but which also emerge in alternative cultural forms. The following chapters will thus present case studies that draw on a wide range of cultural artefacts to demonstrate how ideas that have produced the technologies which dominate contemporary technocultures have also given rise to new forms of, often resistant, cultural expression.

CHAPTER SUMMARY

- The changes in social and cultural life brought about by machine technology are part of the definition of the historical period now known as Modernity.
- The work of Karl Marx is important for understanding the relationship between these changes and the economics of industrial capitalism.
- Our relationship with technology affects how we understand what it means to be human and how we experience our reality.
- Best and Kellner's term 'technocapitalism' describes the economics of Fredric Jameson's 'Third Machine Age' in which technologies of reproduction supersede technologies of production.
- In technocapitalism, the widespread use of information technologies enables decentralization, globalization and what Manuel Castells calls 'the Informational Society'.

2 TECHNOSCIENCE AND POWER

Science is, as Jean-François Lyotard reminds us, 'a force of production ... a moment in the circulation of capital'. What he means by this is that technology creates wealth by making production more efficient. This gives companies an edge over their competitors so that the scientific knowledge that drives the production of new technologies is valuable inasmuch as it contributes towards adding value to the product. Thus science, rather than being the pursuit of knowledge for its own sake, becomes the means by which wealth is created and, the wealthier the company, the higher its capacity for directing resources into research and development. Hence, as Lyotard (1984: 45) says, '[t]he games of scientific language become the games of the rich, in which whoever is wealthiest has the best chance of being right'. Furthermore, the 'added value' that science imparts to the product becomes part of the brand image, the 'unique selling proposition' that advertising uses to differentiate broadly similar products. Commodities are thus valorised by scientific expertise. Consequently, the slogan of the electrical goods brand Zanussi®, 'the appliance of science' now sells everything from food to face cream.

One outstanding example is the famous 'Cog' advertisement, produced by the London-based agency Wieden and Kennedy in 2003 for Honda cars, which effectively exploits the laws of physics to suggest the investment of engineering expertise in their manufacture. In what is described as 'a beautiful dance', strategically placed and, in some cases, carefully weighted car parts achieve motion and momentum by being nudged or propelled by the previous part in line. In one sequence, for instance, '[t]hree valve stems roll down a sloped bonnet. An exhaust box is pushed with just enough energy into a rear suspension link, which nudges a transmission selector arm, which releases the brake pedal loaded with a small rubber brake grommit.'[1] There is no voiceover or music attached to the sequence. It relies, instead, on the link made by the audience between expertise, efficiency and value. If the ad is successful in selling Honda cars it will not be because of any special attributes but because it suggests the application of specialized knowledge; of expertise, in the making of the ad and, by implication, also in the manufacture of the cars.

Thus, in what Neil Postman calls 'Technopoly', all experts are invested with the charisma of priestliness: 'Some of our priest-experts are called psychiatrists, some psychologists, some sociologists, some statisticians. The god they serve does not speak of righteousness or goodness or mercy or grace. Their god speaks of efficiency, precision, objectivity' (Postman 1993: 90).

Postman is concerned with the sense in which the cult of expertise now pervades institutions that were once thought inviolable. Rather than the kind of expertise that produces Honda cars, Postman has in mind what he calls '"softer" technologies such as IQ tests, SATs, standardized forms, taxonomies, and opinion polls' (Postman 1993: 90). That he finds it necessary to italicize a statement such as '*[t]here is, for example, no test that can measure a person's intelligence*' (Postman 1993: 89) is instructive. That, nevertheless, forms of IQ testing are still employed to determine 'correct' intellectual development in children and that a brief flurry of media interest was recently created by the announcement that pop star Madonna has an IQ of 140, is equally instructive. The equation is simple. Madonna is a successful businesswoman. Madonna has a high IQ. *Ergo*, people with high IQs will necessarily be successful and those lower on the scale must accept more limited prospects. This kind of equation is highly problematic if it is taken to imply that intelligence is an effect of genetic predetermination or that only certain kinds of intelligence are to be valued but this, unfortunately, *is* what is implied.

SOCIAL DARWINISM

The idea of intelligence testing was first proposed by Charles Darwin's cousin, Frances Galton, who was also responsible for inaugurating the 'science' of eugenics, which advocates selective breeding to 'improve' the human species and which provided the impetus for the atrocities of Nazi Germany. As Postman points out, what we think of as 'intelligence' is 'a word, not a thing, and a word of a very high order of abstraction' but Galton, in his day, was considered a 'major intellect' (Postman 1993: 130) and his proposition that intelligence was something that could be measured provided what appeared to be a sound scientific justification for the inequalities of the late nineteenth century capitalist order. Furthermore, at the time, his cousin's groundbreaking thesis was giving rise to what was later called social Darwinism; an idea proposed by, among others, Herbert Spencer, the British philosopher who first coined the term 'survival of the fittest', which held that natural selection could be understood to apply to social, as well as biological development.

This theory held that, under the conditions of *laissez faire* capitalism, those best 'fitted to survive' would demonstrate their natural advantage by accruing a greater share of the available resources. In other words, if successful capitalists proved themselves more adept at exploiting others this was simply because they were better adapted to the prevailing conditions, rather than because of any inherent inequalities in the system. Those that were poorly adapted would remain in poverty and would be unlikely to raise children to maturity. Thus the theory of evolution was 'proved' on a social level. Despite the fact that, as John Gray points out, 'Darwin's theory says nothing about whether the results of natural selection are good or bad. It simply describes a biological mechanism at work. So far as Darwinism is concerned, the world has no built-in tendency to improvement' (Gray 2004: 68), Social Darwinism interpreted the theory of evolution in terms of progress. Thus, not only could inequalities be justified but social policies directed towards the relief of poverty could be shown to be misguided. Similarly, Darwin himself thought that natural selection could explain the division of labour by gender. The following is from *The Descent of Man* (1871):

> The chief distinction in the intellectual powers of the two sexes is shewn by man's attaining a higher eminence, in whatever he takes up, than can woman – whether requiring deep thought, reason, or imagination, or merely the use of the senses and hands. If two lists were made of the most eminent men and women in poetry, painting, sculpture, music … history, science, and philosophy, with half-a-dozen names under each subject, the two lists would not bear comparison. We may also infer, from the law of the deviation from averages, so well illustrated by Mr Galton, in his work on Hereditary Genius, that if men are capable of a decided pre-eminence over women in many subjects, the average of mental power in man must be above that of woman. (Darwin 2004 [1871]: 629)

So much for Madonna's high IQ.

Darwin was writing at a time when the First Law of Thermodynamics was impacting on psychological theory. The idea of energy conservation, it was believed, could be applied to the human body. Physical expenditure detracted from the amount of energy available to mental activity and *vice versa*. Women's lack of mental capacity was explained as accruing from the immense physical requirements of their reproductive systems. Conversely, they were discouraged from cerebral activity because of the belief that '[e]nergy spent in cerebration was … lost to reproduction, and the intellectual maiden became a sterile matron' (Russett 1989: 118). Darwin's 'lists' would seem to prove the point but, of course, what is not taken into account is the fact that women have, historically, had primary responsibility for child care and, until the development of effective contraception, had spent a great deal of their lives either pregnant or nursing young children. Furthermore, as Linda Marie Fedigan has pointed out, 'Darwin projected onto the large screen of nature his own images of appropriate role behaviour for men and women, images which were clearly drawn from upper class Victorian culture in Britain in the 1800s' (Fedigan 1992: 105). He was therefore happy to accept his cousin's findings uncritically because they appeared to prove what he already knew. In other words, as far as Darwin was concerned, the received wisdom of his time (that women were intellectually inferior to men) had been subjected to objective scientific scrutiny and had thus been proved to be 'true'.

SCIENTIFIC OBJECTIVITY

From this it becomes evident that the truth claims of science are deeply embedded in social contexts, problematizing the commonly held view that science proceeds from an unbiased position. The motto of the Royal Society, founded in Britain in 1660 and the oldest scientific society in the world is '*Nullius in Verba*' which means 'nothing in words'. What this literally means is that the founders of this venerable institution pledged themselves to report nothing that could not be verified empirically. Speculation must be proven by experiment and the experiment must be witnessed and repeatable.

It was under the auspices of the Royal Society that Robert Boyle performed his famous air-pump experiment, which, by creating a vacuum, demonstrated that sound will not travel and fire will not burn without the presence of air. This experiment is famous for establishing the modern empirical tradition in which science becomes a public enterprise (unlike the secret and private world of the alchemists) whose knowledge claims could be tested by exhibition and demonstration. Donna J. Haraway extracts from Steven Shapin and Simon Schaffer's book *Leviathan and the Air-Pump: Hobbes, Boyle, and the Experimental Life* (Shapin and Schaffer 1985), the figure of the 'modest witness' to stand for the objective, independent observer who can confirm the veracity of the experiment and its claim to produce new knowledge. The modest witness, 'is the legitimate and authorised ventriloquist for the object world, adding nothing from his mere opinions, from his biasing embodiment' (Haraway 1997: 24). Thus the culture of science effectively promotes the scientific method as apolitical; as uninfected by emotion, belief or prejudice. The object world – that which science studies – is thus understood to become utterly transparent in the presence of the modest witness.

The epistemological conditions that produced the idea of the modest witness are inseparable from the ideology of liberal humanism, which really begins with the seventeenth-century philosopher Rene Descartes and his assertion that the essence of human being is in thinking. What is derived from the pronouncement 'I think, therefore I am' is a conception of the world as divided into two distinct but related substances, mind and body, where mind is understood as indivisible and without extension in the world and body is understood as not only capable of being divided into parts but as possessing qualities of extension like height, depth, breadth and the ability to move from place to place. Because, for Descartes, we are distinguished as human by our minds, our bodies become somewhat incidental or are part of the object world that the mind studies and seeks to understand. This clear separation between mind and body or thought and extension (*res cogitans* and *res extensa*) and the identification of the faculty of reason with human being imparts an independence to the human subject that finds its fullest expression in the claims of science to stand aloof from social relations, even when human societies are the subject of investigation.

Understandably, the knowledge claims of established science have been subjected to intense scrutiny, not least by late twentieth-century feminists, ecologists and postcolonial theorists. Ironically, however, the greatest challenge to the status of the modest witness has come from within science itself; specifically, from physics and the search for an explanation for the behaviour of subatomic particles.

The universe in which the modest witness is able to stand apart from the workings of the physical world and simply observe, for instance, that a candle flame flickers and dies when air is pumped out of the glass sphere in which it is contained, is dependent upon a rational ordering of the object world as expressed in Newtonian mechanics. The laws that Isaac Newton established express a predictable relationship between cause and effect for macroscopic events in the physical world that can be expressed as mathematical equations. These laws hold true for events anywhere in the universe which appears to operate like a giant and inexorable machine, independent of human interference but amenable to human observation.

Prior to the first formulations of quantum theory, at the beginning of the twentieth century, it was believed that the mechanical and deterministic nature of the universe would eventually yield a theory of everything, and that the increase in knowledge would lead us ever closer to perfection. However, the metaphor of the observable machine could not hold once physicists began to explore the action of particles that are too small to be seen even with the most powerful microscope. There is no doubt that they exist because experiments to measure their effects are reproducible (this is what the giant particle accelerator at CERN in Switzerland is all about)[2] but the somewhat mind-blowing discovery of quantum mechanics is that '[i]n the subatomic realm, we cannot know both the position *and* the momentum of a particle with absolute precision' (Zukav 2001 [1979]: 29). This is in direct contradiction to the laws of Newtonian mechanics, which is, fundamentally, all about making precise measurements.

We can draw up railway timetables because we can know that trains travelling at a particular speed will arrive at a given station at a particular time (except in the UK where leaves on the line or the wrong type of snow constantly confound predictions). These types of predictions are simply impossible in the subatomic realm where the scientist must decide whether to measure the momentum or position of a particle, but one cannot be inferred from the other. In other words, '[a]ccording to quantum mechanics … it is not possible, *even in principle*, to know enough about the present to make a complete prediction about the future' (Zukav, 2001 [1979]: 28, his emphasis). This means that quantum particles can only be spoken of in terms of *probabilities*. They only achieve existence in concrete terms once a physicist has decided to take a measurement. Out of all the probable states in which a particle can exist, one is actualized *only when* a human being makes the decision to observe it and decides what type of measurement to take. 'Metaphysically', as Gary Zukav points out, 'this is very close to saying that we *create* certain properties because we choose to measure those properties' (Zukav 2001 [1979]: 30). Quantum mechanics, according to Werner Heisenberg, author of the famous 'uncertainty principle' thus 'makes the sharp separation between the world and the I impossible' (Heisenberg 1997 [1958]: 128).

There are several dramatic inferences that can be drawn from quantum theory, not least the findings of the so called 'Copenhagen interpretation', which, mathematically at least, seems to prove the existence of a multidimensional universe. However, what I am concerned with here are the implications for the scientific enterprise itself, which could no longer lay claim to total objectivity once confronted with the fact that, despite Albert Einstein's protestations, God does, indeed, seem to play dice with the universe. One result is that, according to Stanley Aronowitz, 'historians, sociologists, and even a few philosophers of science have been given "permission" to interrogate science and to suggest, however meekly, that there are ideological elements of scientific theory' (Aronowitz 1988: 28–9). Aronowitz's tone is telling. In one sense it seems extraordinary to suggest that scientific practice is *not* determined by ideology, given that the technology to which it gives birth is politically enmeshed through its links with the military and commerce. On the other hand, to admit that science is ideological is to question the Enlightenment project itself and to call into doubt the distinction between 'pure' science and the cultural uses of its findings. Indeed, we may have to accept that the cognitive effects of science are structured within a nexus that includes both the worldview in which its results are interpreted and the end product or practical applicability of those results.

KUHNIAN PARADIGMS

According to Thomas Kuhn, science is produced from within and is responsive to what he calls a 'paradigm'. Scientists are trained within traditions that hold that a particular understanding of the world is true; 'science students', as he says, 'accept theories on the authority of teacher and text, not because of evidence' (Kuhn 1996: 80). At its most conservative, their project then becomes to flesh out the existing paradigm or to resolve anomalies that can be shown, under certain conditions, to confirm the paradigm. This is what Kuhn calls 'normal science' (Kuhn 1996: 24). Scientific 'revolutions' occur when the paradigm is in crisis or when too many anomalies give rise to a shift in perception. A new paradigm then emerges that satisfies the conditions for truth or reflects the state of knowledge until such time as it too becomes untenable. Kuhn has been criticized by, among others, Karl Popper for falling into relativism and thus denying that any form of objective knowledge either is or could be possible. His idea that paradigms are 'incommensurable' also seems to imply that we must accept the idea of transcendent genius (and thus also accept that intelligence is measurable) or, as Brian Easlea suggests, that scientific revolutions are 'won' by means of the same techniques as employed in revolutionary political movements (1973: 17). However, Kuhn's contribution to the study of power relations in science and technology is to offer a serious challenge to the progressive ideas of the nineteenth century and their deleterious effects in the field of social relations. He concludes:

> scientific progress is not quite what we had taken it to be ... In the sciences there need not be progress of another sort. We may, to be more precise, have to relinquish the notion, explicit or implicit, that changes of paradigm carry scientists and those who learn from them closer and closer to the truth. (Kuhn 1996: 170)

Thus, what Kuhn enables is an understanding of science as a form of knowledge that, fundamentally, is only true so long as it works under certain conditions of legitimation. Its truth is contingent and pragmatic rather than transcendental and progressive. Nevertheless, when Kuhn refers to a 'community' he is concerned with scientists and their shared methods and approaches, rather than the wider community in which the social effects of science and technology are experienced. As Ziauddin Sardar points out, Kuhn is concerned to deny that any changes within science are a result of outside influences: 'If science could reform itself, through revolutions, what need was there for outside interference with science? ... Kuhn became instrumental in marginalising all those critics of science who had argued against science's increasing involvement with the military-industrial complex' (Sardar 2000: 58).

To ignore this dimension of the production of knowledge is to, again, suggest that science stands apart from ideology or that these things are the business of the social sciences, which are in a realm apart from 'hard' sciences like physics or chemistry. As Aronowitz has demonstrated, the conditions under which both the social *and* 'natural' sciences are practised in contemporary scientific culture are not only structured towards maintaining existing paradigms but are ideologically determined through their links with the state and multinational corporations (Aronowitz 1988: 317–28). In fact, I would suggest here that we would not be wrong to think of science as *over*-determined in the sense that the divisions between scientific disciplines, the methods to be applied, the role of the scientist and, perhaps most importantly, exactly *what* is eligible as an object of knowledge appear to be presupposed.

Aronowitz gives as an example the sociological study of crime, an area of particular interest in contemporary Western culture, particularly for governments in, for instance, Britain and the US where fear of crime is mobilized to maintain the hegemony of the neoliberal establishment. Funding for crime studies is plentiful because it supports the 'tough on crime, tough on the causes of crime' rhetoric, as proclaimed by the former British Prime Minister, Tony Blair and his New Labour government. However:

> Social research devoted to discovering the causes for criminal behavior often selects the wrong object (the individual), makes the assumption that crime can be abstracted from a larger series, and that the medical model (treatment) may be applied to its cure. Thus, much of the debate in what is called in sociology "deviance" centers on options that are circumscribed by these viewpoints. Students who select "deviance" as their area of sociological study are provided with funds to complete their dissertation through their participation in projects supported by government agencies. (Aronowitz, 1988: 327)

Furthermore, the assumption that 'deviance' is a natural category presupposes that there is a corresponding normality against which it can be measured.

POWER/KNOWLEDGE

Understanding the way in which categories like 'deviant' and 'normal' are constructed is of vital importance in any study of the effects of scientific power because some of the most pernicious applications of scientific theory have emerged from studies that assumed that the elimination of a behaviour or a set of persons identified as deviant was a morally justifiable proposition. Thus, such practices as the sterilization of people believed to be 'feeble minded and insane' (as proposed by Winston Churchill when he was British Home Secretary in 1910)[3] and the lobotomization or subjection to behaviour modifying therapy of those considered to be sexually deviant (a practice only abandoned in Western Germany in 1979).[4] Furthermore, it is not only the social sciences that take such categories for granted. Molecular biology and the relatively new discipline of evolutionary psychology are also deeply immersed in paradigms which support a normative view of what constitutes 'correct' function in the human organism and are guiding influences in the funding and production of medical technologies for the rectification of functional deviance.

Because, for instance, evolutionary psychology accepts as given that *all* human behaviour is, at some level, produced out of the need for genes to replicate themselves; to provide the organism with the greatest chance of reproductive success, homosexuality has been a major cause for study because it appears to confer no reproductive advantage and yet has not died out. In 1993, Professor Dean Hamer caused a brief flurry of interest by claiming to have identified a 'gay gene' but his results were not reproducible to the standard required for scientific validity. However, this did not prevent speculation as to what evolutionary advantage might be conferred by such a predisposition and Professor Hamer himself suggested, in a documentary produced by the BBC,[5] that gay men may have simply inherited a gene that makes some women find men *extremely* attractive, thus giving them the advantage in producing offspring (thus, it seems, implying that promiscuous women will have a greater chance of passing on their genes).

More recently, in a paper for *Perspectives in Biology and Medicine*, Gregory M. Cochran, Paul W. Ewald and Kyle D. Cochran, have resurrected the argument for homosexuality as a disease by comparing it to sickle cell anaemia, a disease caused by a gene which confers immunity to malaria. 'One possible route [of infection]', they write, 'would be sexual, whereby homosexual behavior could facilitate spread because of the larger numbers of partners homosexual males may have on average, relative to heterosexual males. Alternatively, transmission could be partly or entirely by one or more nonsexual routes, and homosexual orientation be a side effect of the infection that is unrelated to transmission' (Cochran et al. 2000: 438). If it could be proved that homosexuality is a 'side effect' of immunity to a given disease, the implication is that it may be eventually eradicated and, indeed, the publication of a paper that speculates as to a potential 'cause' leaves the field dangerously open to interested parties who may pay considerable sums to further the research. Once this type of research is in the public domain, it inevitably feeds prejudice and militates against campaigns for homosexuality to be taken out of the category of deviance. While the authors state that they are aware that this 'line of logic may lead to hypotheses that we may find disturbing, distasteful, or socially disruptive' they consider, nevertheless, that 'it is better to know how nature works than to live in ignorance' (Cochran et al. 2000: 437). The reference to 'nature' points to the assumption that sexuality is biologically determined; that 'correct' function can be identified and 'incorrect' deviations be attributed to anomalous causes. What is not considered is the history of Western culture in which it is the supposed deviant sexualities that have functioned to establish the heterosexual norm in the first place. The identification of deviance enables the panoptic policing of populations and this is achieved, partly, through the dissemination of scientific 'knowledge', which sustains levels of anxiety. This, in turn, further establishes the 'truth' of this knowledge when individuals seek 'treatment' and thus give their consent to the hegemony of scientific expertise.

One of the most sustained studies of the concept of deviance and how it can be understood in connection with the history of scientific thought appears in the work of Michel Foucault. Foucault became aware that he was homosexual in the 1950s, 'the age of psychiatry and psychoanalysis'. He writes:

> Medical doctors, successors to the priests and police, now rendered sentences on the homosexual condition that were even more highly valued because they came from an apparently scientific authority and emanated a certain paternal benevolence. Each time a psychoanalyst wrote: 'I never met a happy homosexual,' I took this judgment to be a truth beyond doubt and huddled deeper into the consciousness of my woes.[6]

One way of characterizing Foucault's work would be to say that he is interested in how scientific statements are accorded the status of 'truth beyond doubt' and how these 'truths' construct cultural categories in the world beyond the laboratory or consulting room. Foucault, like Kuhn, understands the history of science in terms of change rather than progress and he calls the periods of time in which particular forms of knowledge determine what is understood as truth 'epistemes'. Foucault's epistemes are not, however, coextensive with Kuhn's paradigms because the word is used to describe a differently formulated structure of knowledge.

In his preface to *The Order of Things: An Archaeology of the Human Sciences*, he states explicitly that he is not concerned 'to describe the progress of knowledge towards an objectivity in which today's science can finally be recognized' but to understand 'its conditions of possibility' (1994 [1970]: xxii). What he means by this is that he is not interested in the continuity of knowledge or charting the breaks or revolutions that propel it in a new direction but in the social and political conditions that structure the ways in which what science says becomes acceptable as a form of truth. Foucault is primarily interested in the 'human' sciences because he is concerned to understand how it is that we became objects of our own knowledge, or, put another way, under what terms we were able to separate the category 'human' as an object of study from the human subject that does the studying. What becomes clear is that, first of all, concepts of 'normal' and 'deviant' emerge because the practice of science demands classification and calculation if it is to satisfy the empirical conditions enshrined in the idea of the modest witness. But, equally, both the scientist as human subject and the human as the object of study are, as Foucault demonstrates, products of culture. Any study of ourselves can, therefore, only produce forms of knowledge that are, at some level, culturally determined. Culture, as it were, provides 'its conditions of possibility'.

When Foucault writes about power and knowledge, he does not make the claim that scientific knowledge is all powerful or that we stupidly accept the pronouncements of scientists because they have replaced the 'priests and police' in the hierarchy of authority. What he wants us to understand is that science is what he calls a *discourse*. That is, it is a mode of *language*, a vocabulary for talking about the world which achieves validation and currency through its interaction with other powerful discourses that structure its insertion into the cultural domain. Hence, as the age of psychiatry and psychoanalysis has given way to the age of evolutionary psychology in determinations of what 'causes' homosexuality, an epistemic shift has occurred in which 'knowledge' about sexual deviancy is discussed in terms of genetic inheritance and the aetiology of infection rather than the Oedipal triangle and the incest taboo.

The discourse of deviancy, supported by pseudoscientific language, is also mobilized in the marketing of cosmetics. For instance, browsing through a current women's magazine turns up advertisements for the following: a body lotion containing something called Dermo-Nutrilium, a skin cream that lauds the rejuvenating effects of its fishy sounding Biomarine Complex and a moisturizer that promises that its Aquacellular Technology is an ingredient worth paying for. These ads, and others like them, use phrases like 'scientifically documented' and 'scientifically proven' to advance their claims and the popularity of these products is testament to the link between science and commodification. However, it is not enough to assume that the manufacturers are simply cynically exploiting the consumer by employing the acknowledged authority of scientific discourse to lend gravitas to their claims. The fact that a great many women (and, increasingly, men) are willing to pay significant sums of money for these products depends on a complex interaction of discourses concerned, significantly, with the construction of gender in contemporary Western cultures.

Standards of attractiveness for women are inextricably connected to discourses that equate youth with beauty and sexual success with confirmation of a particular, idealized feminine identity. Simply put, '[e]very woman knows that, regardless of all her other achievements, she is a failure if she is not beautiful' (Greer, 1999: 23). Thus, in keeping with the neoliberalist discourse, which marks out success and failure in terms of correct self-management and the demands of capitalist success that requires visible evidence of acquirement and consumption, 'beauty' is something to be achieved; something that, like building up a small business, requires 'work' and 'dedication'. And, in a knowledge economy that values information above all commodities, the discourse that promotes expertise equally condemns ignorance as the original sin. The informed woman is thus expected to know what is 'wrong' with her, the medicoscientific explanation for her condition and the products that will 'correct' it. To remain uninformed is to fail.

Thus the discourse that constructs scientific knowledge as truth supports and maintains the discourse of femininity, which is itself sustained by discourses in which ideas that identify health and disease also mark and condemn the female body. Equally, the discourse of feminism is implied in the scientific selling of beauty products, not only because 'feminist' has been constructed as the antithesis of desirable femininity but because, as feminists have proved Darwin to have been woefully incorrect in his analysis of female intelligence, the use of scientific language in media explicitly aimed at women suggests a postfeminist acknowledgement of their intellectual status.

Of course, the bottom line, in the case of so called 'skin-care' products is that they, quite simply, do not work in the way that they claim. In March 2007, the BBC broadcast a special report on beauty products in which a dermatologist tested several anti-ageing creams and came to the conclusion that only one, Boots' Protect and Perfect, *might* work. Following the broadcast, women lined up outside branches of the pharmacy chain, which sold out of the product and had to restrict purchases to one per customer. The South Florida *Sun-Sentinel* reported that the chain had to increase production from 20,000 bottles per week to 20,000 bottles per day.[7] Like the massive sales of Viagra and other 'performance-enhancing' drugs, which achieve valorization through discourses that medicalize male sexuality,[8] so, in the case of anti-ageing creams, what is, in effect, a culturally produced anxiety connected to the discursive production of gender norms becomes, under the terms of the discourse of scientific expertise, a 'condition' to be 'cured' by investment in technology in the form of drugs and cosmetics.

TRUTH AND EMBUSHELMENT

Thus, despite the fact that, as Lyotard has determined, '[t]he grand narrative has lost its credibility' (Lyotard 1984: 37), the scientific narrative retains its power as a major force in the discursive construction of postmodern consumer identities. Fredric Jameson, in his foreword to *The Postmodern Condition* refers to the 'persistence of buried master-narratives' and posits 'not the disappearance of the great master-narratives, but their passage underground as it were, their continuing but now *un-conscious* effectivity as a way of "thinking about" and acting in our current situation' (Lyotard 1984: xii, his emphasis). In the case of science, its claims to the production of truth may be questioned and its embeddedness in a particular Western cultural context may be understood but it nevertheless emerges as a structural determinant in a myriad of cultural productions from advertising to environmental awareness campaigns, not only as legitimation for powerful systems of belief but equally, in the form of technological icons, which work to shore up the fading hegemony of the nation state.

Rob Wilson (1994: 219) has shown persuasively how the 'Patriot missile speech' given by President George Bush Snr. to the workers at the Raytheon Corporation at the beginning of the first Gulf War made use of 'technophilic euphoria' (Wilson 1994: 217) to galvanize belief in American techno-military supremacy despite the fact that '[t]hese smart weapons, as *Business Week* soon pointed out, have foreign [Japanese] brains' (Wilson 1994: 222). 'Patriot works' Bush Snr. told the workers, 'because of patriots like you … [W]hat has taken place here is the triumph of American technology … keeping this country strong, firing the engines of economic growth' (Wilson 1994: 220).

As David Nye has demonstrated, the technological sublime has, since the early nineteenth century, been associated in American minds with Manifest Destiny, the ideology that justified US expansion, originally into what is now the Western States and, ultimately, beyond North America. 'By the 1830s', he writes, 'sublime technological objects were assumed to be active forces working for democracy … The citizen who contemplated such public improvements … saw himself as part of the moral vanguard, leading the world toward universal democracy' (Nye 1994: 33 and 36) and '[m]any asserted that industrial development was not merely compatible with democracy but a direct outgrowth of it' (Nye 1994: 38). Thus, the sublime experience inspired by the natural landscape of the US, which had been appropriated 'as a natural symbol of the nation' (Nye 1994: 37) was transferred to the symbols of ingenuity and expertise, which were not only transforming the landscape and thus demonstrating the power of science over nature but were assuring American dominance over the 'old world'. As Nye points out, 'sublimity is not inherent but a social construction' (Nye 1994: 27) and a considerable factor in popular scientific discourse to which it lends moral and hegemonic authority. '[D]emocratic virtue', as Nye explains it, 'could be invigorated by the powerful experience of sublimity' (Nye 1994: 36), a fact that the Patriot Missile Speech seems to confirm.[9]

As Ziauddin Sardar points out, '[s]cience is simply not what realists and idealists claim it to be. Its ideological and value-laden character has been exposed beyond doubt' (Sardar 2000: 63). Nevertheless, he suggests that a 'doctrine of 'double truth'' or what Steve Fuller calls 'embushelment' operates in which 'significant cultural artefacts are doubly encoded, with one message intended to appease the masses by reinforcing their prejudices and the other meant only for elite inquirers who are mentally prepared to assimilate a strongly counter-intuitive truth.'

He goes so far as to charge that Kuhn himself expressed embushelment in his conclusion 'that in a fickle, bipolar world, the autonomy of science had to be defended and protected from marauding outsiders such as Marxists and New Agers' (Sardar 2000: 60). However, he believes we are now entering a 'post-normal' (Sardar 2000: 61) episteme, which 'requires the gap between scientific expertise and public concerns to be bridged'. Post-normal science 'becomes a dialogue among all the stakeholders in a problem, from scientists themselves to social scientists, journalists, activists and housewives' (Sardar 2000: 64).

But for the project of postnormal science to be realized there needs to be a substantial re-evaluation of the terms under which science enters the public domain, not only in the way that scientific knowledge is disseminated but in the way that it is applied. As I have demonstrated, whatever the intentions of scientists themselves, the knowledge that they produce is ideologically structured from the first appeal for funding, which must be couched in terms attractive to potential investors, to the

Case Study: Biotechnology and Frankenstein Foods

In 1994, Calgene Inc. won approval from the US Food and Drugs Administration to market the Flavr Savr tomato, the first genetically modified fruit. Since then, the term 'Frankenstein Foods' has been coined to describe these and other biotechnologically produced hybrids of everyday foodstuffs, which are engineered to retard decay, enhance appearance and produce varieties resistant to infection. The opposition to GM Foods is thus expressed in terms of anxieties about the misuse of scientific power and the misapplication of technology as symbolized by the character in Mary Shelley's novel, first published nearly two centuries ago.

Shelley's monster, initially, is far from the marauding demon that is portrayed in most of the Hollywood films adapted from the novel. Actually, he is rather sweet. He evidences an endearing, childlike curiosity about the world and tries desperately to be accepted but everyone he meets reacts with horror because he is so obviously *wrong*. At the end of the novel you are left with the impression that Victor Frankenstein's mistake was not in the creation of an artificial form of life but in not taking account of the prejudices of nineteenth-century

European culture. On the other hand the monster is a full-grown human with the moral imperatives of a child and thus his wrongness and the violence to which he eventually succumbs can be directly attributed to his being manufactured in a laboratory rather than born and nurtured to adulthood by acculturated parents.

This ambivalence, which makes Shelley's novel a far more complex document than any of the succeeding films, lends a somewhat poignant accuracy to the Frankenstein epithet when applied to biotechnologically produced foods. There is evidence to suggest that some of the arguments against their production are based in prejudice born of mistrust. Arguments against transgenics benefit from comparison with transuranics, the science that produced not only the atom bomb but environmental nuclear disasters such as the accidents at Chernobyl in Russia in 1986 and the Three Mile Island power plant in Pennsylvania in 1979. Indeed, '[i]mmediately after the [Second World] [W]ar, the Atomic Energy Commission's programme on radiation genetics paid for much American biological research' (Turney 1998: 122). Furthermore, as Jon Turney points way that it is employed in the production of technologies, which must appeal to consumers already convinced that they have a need for them. As Foucault's work has shown, the development and application of science cannot be separated from social history or from the ideas that structure attitudes and beliefs, which, themselves, are inseparable from the economic structures that determine social life and in which science is deeply embedded. But the power of science is also expressed in the very real effects that technologies produce. The affective charge of the technological sublime is, in large part, due to the realization that increased knowledge of the workings of the universe can produce changes in our life worlds that are little short of miraculous. Thus where embushelment has its most pernicious effects is when people must make decisions to accept technologies which effectively give us power over life and death.

---

out, 'anxieties about the most apocalyptic of physical technologies often focused on possible biological effects.'

'The discussion of the potential consequences of nuclear fallout promoted public awareness of a number of the biological facts of life, as they were then understood. There arose a greater interest in genes and mutations, and a renewed interest in the centrality of genes in determining characteristics' (Turney 1998: 127).

Thus it is possible to argue, as Turney does, that part of the discursive construction of transgenic technologies is the vocabulary of biological mutation inherited from earlier debates about nuclear power. Of equal importance is the still historically close experience of Nazism and its particular interpretation of the science of eugenics. The production of transgenic foods raises the spectre of human genetic manipulation and all that it implies for the elimination of racial characteristics deemed 'undesirable' in an increasingly racist and intolerant world.

Already, concerns have been expressed regarding the potential for those with access to the resources to spearhead the movement into genetic enhancement of offspring to thus set the standard for 'humanness'. This would necessarily create considerable disadvantage in the poorer nations of the world and create divisions between those who embrace the new technologies and those who have a religious or ethical objection to them (Frankel and Chapman 2000: 41). Indeed, the surviving member of the duo of scientists credited with the discovery of the structure of DNA, James Watson, has already suggested that genetic engineering should be used to 'raise intelligence'.[10] Aside from the ethical issues raised by the notion of selective 'improvement' and the assumption that intelligence can, in fact, be measured, Watson is also assuming that the Human Genome Project will eventually reveal a combination of genes 'for' intelligence. Currently there is no evidence for a simple one-to-one correspondence between particular genes and corresponding traits, making the possibility of such a scenario highly unlikely. Therefore, in the developed countries, opposition to GM foods on the grounds that they may have unforeseen consequences for human health, in the absence of any defining evidence, needs to be understood in the context of the power relations through which science becomes both a political tool and a commodity.

This is not to say, of course, that the fears are unfounded or that opposition to GM technologies is misguided. An independent review of over 600 scientific papers conducted in the UK in 2003 concluded that that the risk to human health from GMOs was very low.[11] Nevertheless, the creation of what Harvard biologist, Mark L. Winston calls '[a] new type of biologist ... an entrepreneurial scientist working for a multinational company with access to staggering amounts of funding and resources' (Winston 2002: 42–3) raises, again, the spectre of Victor Frankenstein and the pursuit of knowledge unregulated by recourse to ethics or democratic consultation. The 'town-and-gown' partnerships, which have led to senior biotechnologists moving out of the university and into the employ of multinational companies and the patenting of genes under intellectual copyright laws have, unsurprisingly, led to the accusation that the companies (and, by implication, the scientists) are putting profit before people and the environment. Winston spoke to a biologist working for Aventis, one of the massive conglomerates involved in the development and marketing of GM crops, who told him: 'I have opinions which may not be those of the company, and I am reluctant to speak them. I'm an industry person now, like it or not, and I either say nothing or say what the company likes' (Winston 2002: 55).

At the time of writing, Aventis is one of only six global companies that control 'almost 100 per cent of the transgenic seeds market' (Ali Brac de la Perrière and Seuret 2000: 11). By the time you read this, it is quite possible that acquisitions and mergers will have led to that number being reduced. What emerges from this is the potential for a few corporations to acquire a global monopoly on production, with farmers worldwide becoming consumers, rather than owners, of the seeds that ensure their livelihood. Although it is theoretically possible for farmers to refuse to purchase the seeds

that these companies produce, the reality is that they may simply have no choice.

In Canada, for instance, most canola farmers 'view the environmental and food safety risks of GM crops as small to nonexistent, and see diversification of GM products as the only viable way to increase farm income and profits ... In the year 2000 over 80 percent of growers planted one of the genetically modified, herbicide-tolerant canola varieties on 55 percent of Canada's canola acreage' (Winston 2002: 149 and 135). But what of the 20 per cent who do not conform? Winston reports the case of Perry Schmeiser who was sued by Monsanto, the *bête noir* of the anti-GMO movement, because he harvested seeds that, he claimed, had been inadvertently fertilized by wind-blown pollen from neighbouring GM fields, which he saved to plant the following year, thus violating patents which protect the herbicide-resistant genes in Mansanto's Roundup Ready canola. Schmeiser counter-sued for defamation of character but lost. 'The court's ruling stated that it was irrelevant whether Roundup Ready canola originally was planted or blew into Schmeiser's fields. Either way, he knowingly replanted and grew Monsanto's seeds in subsequent years without its permission' (Winston 2002: 140). 'Permission' in this case, would mean that Schmeiser would have had to buy the seeds from Monsanto in the first place and then sign a TUA (technical use agreement), barring him from saving harvested seeds to plant in the following year, a practice that has been a mainstay of farming for centuries. Monsanto customers must buy a new batch of seeds from the company year by year, thus ensuring Monsanto's profits.

Schmeiser's case highlights the precarious position of small farmers who hold out against the biotechnology revolution. There is little room for ethical objections or demands to remain independent when traditionally farmed fields can so easily be contaminated or, more to the point, when neighbouring farms that have converted to GM crops are showing increased profits and expanding. Winston found that a majority of the

Canadian farmers were happy to accept TUAs because 'it is more economical to buy seed from specialty companies that excel at selecting and producing certified seed. Buying selected seed has many advantages, not the least of which is the increased production of [higher yielding] hybrid varieties' (Winston 2002: 144).

However, there are dangers from GMOs that may yet threaten the livelihood of the Canadian farmers, not least the possibility that the weeds that herbicide-resistant strains initially allow to be easily disposed of, without danger to the crop or overuse of herbicides and pesticides, may cross breed and become infected with the resistant gene. Currently there is some evidence that, if this happens, the gene will die out in one or two generations but this does not mean that farmers are safe from herbicide-resistant weeds. As with the yet-to-be-proved health dangers from the presence of GMOs in foods, the fallout from biotechnology in the field may simply not yet be apparent.

Furthermore, whatever the consequences for farmers in the developed north of the planet, the presence of GMOs in wild plant varieties may have catastrophic effects on biodiversity. In the less-developed south, where GM crops have been offered as the answer to hunger and malnutrition, the threat to biodiversity, and the consequent effects for farmers, is more pronounced due to the fact that transgenics would replace more traditional farming methods in which a greater variety of species are cultivated. One immediate effect of monoculture farming is the possibility for plant diseases, which would normally be contained by encountering a naturally resistant species, to spread over a wide area. This was one of the effects of the so called 'Green Revolution', a pre-GM initiative to relieve world hunger by supplying farmers in developing nations with HYV (high-yield varieties) of wheat and rice.

[T]he scientific research behind the Green Revolution was not structured to meet local needs. The international research institutes for the different crop types did not decentralize their work into various countries or local communities, where research could better take local needs and ecologies into account. Furthermore, the new varieties of seeds emerged from laboratory research, not from local communities, where there were hundreds of varieties of non-standard seeds that often matched the local ecology in ways that had never been studied. (Hess 1995: 236)

High-yield varieties require large amounts of water as well as quantities of pesticide and herbicide that, of course, have to be purchased from the seed producing companies. In the state of Andhra Pradesh in India, farmers who had bought seeds and pesticides on credit at high rates of interest, only to find that they had to buy more pesticides when the pests became immune, 'committed suicide by swallowing their own pesticides' when the crop failed (Notes from Nowhere 2003: 162).

Winston believes that 'GM crops do have a role to play in third world farming but their overuse would lead to some of the same problems that beset the Green Revolution' (Winston 2002: 250). But biotechnology also brings its own, unique problems, one of which is the fact that 'transgenesis offers buyers the possibility of diversifying their supply sources and therefore strengthening their negotiating power' (Ali Brac de la Perrière and Seuret 2000: 16). Genetic manipulation of plants means that, theoretically, any plant can be engineered to produce any product. If farmers in the developed north can adapt their fields to produce crops that express a characteristic previously only available from regions in the developing world, the price will be driven down and farmers in poorer regions would not survive the competition. For instance, Robert Ali Brac de la Perrière and Franck Seuret report that Filipino farmers are under threat from genetically modified rape which can be grown in the US to produce lauric acid, a raw material used by the cosmetic and soap industries: '[t]raditionally this acid is extracted from palm and coconut oils, 80 per cent of which are produced in Indonesia and the Philippines' (Ali Brac de la Perrière and Seuret 2000: 19).

A further effect of the patenting of genetic material, which allows the multinationals to impose TUAs and which led to Perry Schmeiser's defeat, is that the diversity produced by decades and, in some cases, centuries of selective breeding to adapt plant varieties to local ecologies is not protected under international laws, which favour the major seed producers. The TRIPS (Trade Related Aspects of Intellectual Property Rights) agreement adopted by the World Trade Organisation (WTO) and the somewhat more flexible but still essentially biased Union for the Protection of New Varieties of Plants (UPOV) are both in contradiction with the spirit of the Convention on Biological Diversity (CBD). 'Whereas TRIPS and UPOV aim at imposing exclusive private intellectual property rights on biodiversity, the CBD, adopted in 1992 by 170 countries at the Earth Summit in Rio (Brazil), recognises the collective rights of communities to this very resource' (Ali Brac de la Perrière and Seuret, 2000: 90).

However, as Winston points out, '[i]n spite of the lofty and carefully negotiated rhetoric in the Draft Convention on Biodiversity, the key clause remains Article 4.1, added largely to get the United States to sign: "The Guidelines are voluntary"' (Winston 2002: 188). What this essentially means is that farmers cannot be said to 'own' the rights to crops developed by generations of their ancestors, which can thus be 'coopted for genetic modification without payment' (Winston, 2002: 186).

Despite Monsanto's commitment to '[b]uilding strong relationships through: customer involvement, consultation with stakeholders, collaboration and partnering [and] listening to diverse views',[12] there seems to be little evidence for the practice of 'postnormal' science in the development of GMOs. 'GMOs prevail', according to Ali Brac de la Perrière and Seuret, 'even before civil society

has had an opportunity to raise its voice' (2000: 76). Rather, the case seems to be that organized opposition emerges in response to field trials and experimental plantings that are initiated by the companies without consultation. For instance, the burning of GM planted fields by activists which began in India in 1998 was a response to farmer Basanna Hunsole's discovery that 'the 'experimental' seeds Monsanto had given him to plant were 'genetically modified ... When Hunsole discovered this, he helped KRRS (Karnataka State Farmers' Association) activists rip up the crop – the first trial of GM cotton in India – then they threw the plants into a pile and made a bonfire' (News from Nowhere, 2003: 152).

Similar protests accompanied the introduction of the infamous 'Terminator Technology ... a kind of biological lock' (Ali Brac de la Perrière and Seuret: 2000: 24), which obviates the requirement for TUAs by forcing crops to produce sterile seeds in the next generation. The withdrawal of Terminator by Monsanto, who had purchased its originator, the Delta and Pine Seed Company, in order to secure the patent was a victory for the antibiotechnology movement but other companies have not provided the same assurances. Terminator, in fact, is aptly named. Not only does the technology assure the termination of seed saving practices, thus protecting the interests of the multinational seed producers, it equally threatens to obliterate small farmers who, under conditions where they are struggling to survive, are tempted to sell their fields to the more prosperous farming organizations. The result is that they often then join the ranks of the urban poor, competing for scarce jobs in the cities.

Ironically, the idea of Terminator Technology evokes another fictional heir to Frankenstein's monster, as played by Arnold Schwartzenegger in *The Terminator* (1984), *Terminator Two: Judgement Day* (1991) and *Terminator Three: The Rise of the Machines* (2002). The Terminator is a biotechnologically engineered cyborg, sent back in time by a multinational corporation to kill the mother of a rebel, John Connor, who leads a successful resistance against them in the future, before he can be born. However, the Terminator not only fails to kill Sarah Connor but, because John survives to adulthood, he is able to acquire and reprogram another Terminator, which he sends back to protect his younger self.

Thus modified, Schwartzenneger's Terminator stands as a symbol for the kind of resistance suggested by Donna J. Haraway's cyborg myth, which appropriates the concept of the human/machine hybrid as a means to challenge the conceptual boundaries that distinguish Western thought. Cyborgs, for Haraway, allow us to think the previously unthinkable. Rather than being horrified by Frankenstein's monster, she suggests that we need to challenge the preconceptions that determine how 'life' is understood; the 'origin stories' that legitimate particular bodies and practices, while marginalizing and demonizing others. She wants us to understand that categories are culturally produced and that other, more imaginative configurations are not only possible but are essential to the way that we live in Jameson's Third Machine Age, in which we are always already cyborg, 'theorized and fabricated hybrids of machine and organism' (Haraway 1991: 150).

We can be nothing other than cyborg when we use advanced technology to understand the composition of cells, to sequence the human genome or to splice tomato genes with a gene from a bacteria to slow down the rate at which the fruit decays. Once these hybrids have entered the world, we are all forever changed in the sense that our way of understanding the world must now contain the concepts that they evoke: hybridity, changeability, mutability, along with different scales of time and space to accommodate fruits that decay 'more slowly' and seeds without a successor generation. The concept of 'seed' here is irrevocably changed, as are our ideas of what constitutes reproduction. Terminator seeds replicate or reduplicate rather than reproduce, confounding concepts of 'inheritance' and 'lineage'

and connecting, in cyborg fashion, with Baudrillard's simulacra, the entities that inhabit the hyperreal (see last chapter); copies without originals and thus with a life of their own. Where Baudrillard is pessimistic about the future for a world of inauthenticity, Haraway, a feminist and an activist, is suspicious of authenticity in the first place. Cyborgs are 'somehow "trans" to what once counted as normal and natural' (Haraway 1995: xv), they are 'beings in whose presence the categories themselves break down' (Myerson 2000: 21). Cyborgs confound the normal/deviant dichotomy required by 'normal' science and are thus uniquely placed to disrupt its paradigmatic essentialism. Equally, they 'refuse both technological determinism, whether of a cultural-industrial or biological-genetic sort, and back-to-nature mysticism' (Haraway 1995: xvii). They remind us, in other words, that myth making is what culture does and that the myth of a pre-lapsarian world is as redundant, and as damaging, as the determinist myth that accompanies the experience of the technological sublime. Haraway writes:

> taking responsibility for the social relations of science and technology means refusing an anti-science metaphysics, a demonology of technology, and so means embracing the skilful task of re-constructing the boundaries of daily life, in partial connection with others, in communication with all of our parts. It is not just that science and technology are possible means of great human satisfaction, as well as a matrix of complex dominations. Cyborg imagery can suggest a way out of the maze of dualisms in which we have explained our bodies and our tools to ourselves. (Haraway 1991: 181)

Perhaps then, doing post-normal science thus requires the kind of activism implicit in John Connor's appropriation of Terminator Technology in the *Terminator* series. As Forest Pyle has pointed out, '[w]hat *The Terminator* defines as fundamentally human is the routing of technological mastery into a rebellious subjectivity' (Pyle 2000: 128). This is what Haraway means when she demands of feminists that we 'seize ... the tools to mark the world that marked [us] as other' (Haraway 1991: 175).

Contemporary activism, as evidenced by India's KRRS and similar organizations, is thus an informed cyborg position in which farmers challenge the cult of expertise by asserting the value of local knowledge while being open to the integration of new technologies. The KRRS, for instance, have used solar power to construct an electric fence around their Global Centre for Sustainable Development in the South of Karnataka. Their criteria for rejection or acceptance of new technologies is based on 'whether the technology can be directly operated and managed by the people who use it, whether it is labour-intensive or capital-intensive, and other political criteria'.[13] They do not assert the value of 'pure' farming over the new gene-spliced hybrids but remind us that they had always been in the business of gene manipulation but in a local context attuned to a specific ecology. This is postnormal science at the grassroots level where contests over what counts as a viable technique for future agriculture confound both the process of embushelment and the cult of expertise.

CHAPTER SUMMARY

- Scientific expertise is fetishized in contemporary consumer culture.
- Nineteenth-century social Darwinism used the idea of natural selection to legitimate the *laissez faire* economy.
- The work of Thomas Kuhn and Michel Foucault helps us to interrogate the truth claims of science.
- 'Embushelment' describes the disjuncture between expert knowledge and the way in which it is received in social contexts.

3 TECHNONATURE/CULTURE

In traditional Western scientific thought, 'nature' is understood to be the raw resource that is studied by science and is worked upon and transformed by technology. In modern societies, nature is thus opposed to culture and represented as that which civilization has permitted an escape from while, conversely, being that which we are urged to escape *to* in our search for a means to transcend the impositions of civilized life. Identified variously with the countryside, animals, agriculture, landscape and female reproductivity, 'nature' has become a category into which is crammed all the displaced anxieties of modern life. In postmodern cultures, these anxieties re-emerge in debates about the effects of environmental change and the correct management of human health, which is frequently represented as being under siege by medical science. Nature is invoked to do battle against medical intervention in childbirth and 'natural' remedies are offered for everything from the common cold to impotence. Medical doctor Ben Goldacre's highly amusing 'Bad Science' column in the British daily newspaper the *Guardian* offers weekly excoriations of the claims made for these products, which are often based on misleading interpretations of published research.

In the current climate, nature sells, promoted by discourses that structure civic responsibility in terms of correct management of the body. Current 'health advice', which advocates walking (10,000 steps per day), restrictions on fat intake, five portions of fruit and vegetables per day and limiting stimulants like nicotine, alcohol and coffee is the contemporary equivalent of the Victorian obsession with 'fresh' air and concerns about working-class health in newly industrialized cities. As Donald S. Moore, Anand Pandian and Jake Kosek point out, the discourse of contemporary environmentalism also evokes '[m]emories of Eden ... that catastrophic fall from original natural leisure into the degraded toil of a working world' (Moore et al. 2003: 7). Anxieties about work and the technologies from which it is inseparable are expressed as concerns about damage to 'nature' and, by implication, the 'human nature' with which it is associated. These same concerns were expressed in European colonial discourses, which, in determining a hierarchy of races, situated colonized peoples in a reified idea of nature. The 'Noble Savage' ideal romanticized races thought to have retained an association with nature that the supposed 'civilized' races had lost. They could then be represented as custodians of a prehistorical environment, awaiting appropriation by European settlers who would then, themselves, be reacquainted with the invigoration of the natural world.

Nature as antidote to the privations of labour also enabled states to relinquish responsibility for workers' ill health. In South Africa, miners infected with tuberculosis were 'dumped by state administrators and mining companies into the welcoming pastoral care of rural environs. These rural landscapes and communities – spatially and racially removed from white privilege – were celebrated by officials for their allegedly natural capacities to nurture the afflicted bodies of miners, thus obviating the need for state assistance' (Moore et al. 2003: 22).

Similarly, the female body has functioned to contain anxieties connected to industrialization and worker alienation by being represented as 'closer' to nature than the male and thus an object to be revered and protected while being simultaneously associated with primitivism and thus in need of containment. Thus 'nature' is a highly charged symbol in the construction of the oppositional categories, masculine/feminine, primitive/civilized, proletariat/bourgeoisie, town/country, which perpetuate distinctions of race, class and gender.

'Nature' is also what Shelley's Victor Frankenstein is determined to 'penetrate into ... and show how she works in her hiding places' (1912 [1818]: 40), echoing 'Isaac Barrow, [Isaac] Newton's teacher [who] declared that the aim of [science] was to 'search Nature out of her Concealments, and unfold her dark Mysteries' (Easlea 1981: 83). Thus, what Brian Easlea calls 'the scientific quest as a masculine penetration into a female nature' has cast the body of nature as 'a woman passively awaiting the display of male virility and the subsequent birth of a race of machines' (Easlea 1981: 86); a technological offspring imaged as equally virile. Consequently, the practice of science has, traditionally been jealously guarded by a masculine power elite and technology has often been somewhat ludicrously gendered. Carol Cohn's analysis of the 'technostrategic' (Cohn 1987: 690) discourse of defence intellectuals working on US nuclear policy in the 1980s refers to 'vertical erector launches, thrust-to-weight ratios, soft lay downs [and] deep penetration' (Cohn 1987: 693). In similar terms, the science fiction writer James Tiptree Jr's description of a rocket ship as 'a planet-testicle pushing a monster penis towards the stars' (Tiptree 1978: 65), is a succinct comment on the gender bias implicit in space technology made doubly ironic by the fact that Tiptree was actually the psychologist and CIA operative Alice Sheldon, writing under a male pseudonym.[1]

Unsurprisingly, feminist historians of science have been concerned to address the gender imbalance in scientific practice and the development of technologies and the result has been a new understanding of the role of women in the genesis of important scientific ideas and technological breakthroughs and similar work has been done by anthropologists concerned to establish the technological credentials of cultures previously condemned as 'pre-civilized'. Arguably, the fight of Indian farmers for recognition of their traditional agricultural techniques in opposition to GMOs (see case study, Chapter 2) can be cast as a similar demand. Nevertheless, the idea of nature as an oppositional force that 'fights back' and constantly threatens to overwhelm our technological defences is implicit in debates about global warming, the destruction of the rainforests, the threat to the ozone layer from the burning of fossil fuels and the use of aerosol chemicals, concerns about the depletion of traditional food sources, ecological imbalance caused by over farming and species extinction caused by the erosion of natural habitats.

For example, in Roland Emmerich's 2004 disaster movie *The Day After Tomorrow*, the northern hemisphere experiences a sudden and violent return to the Ice Age when melting polar ice causes the north Atlantic current to desalinize (needless to say, an unlikely scenario). Mass evacuations to the southern hemisphere are organized but Mexico refuses to admit the refugees until the American President agrees to write-off all Latin American debt. The film ends with the President thanking the 'Third World' for its hospitality. Aside from the somewhat ludicrous suggestion that the impoverished nations of the southern hemisphere will readily agree to accommodate a further drain on their resources from the region that has, historically, subjected them to privation, the clear implication is that human magnanimity and empathy will win out over the forces of unforgiving nature. The film suggests that nature's revenge for the excesses of the developed north is to ensure its ultimate dependency on the less developed and therefore more 'natural' south; to force a return to the 'state of nature' (Rousseau 1952 [1754]: 333), in which, according to Jean-Jacques Rousseau the 'inequality of mankind is hardly felt, and ... its influence is next to nothing' (Rousseau 1952 [1754]: 347). For Rousseau, the 'state of society' (Rousseau 1952 [1754]: 336) necessarily produces inequality because it presupposes private property and its attendant class based division of labour. While Rousseau ends his dissertation by recognizing that a return to 'primitive' conditions is neither possible nor desirable, his argument leaves the overwhelming impression that industrialization spells the degeneration of the species. 'The more our capital cities strike the vulgar eye with admiration' he writes, 'the greater reason is there to lament the sight of the abandoned countryside, the large tracts of land that lie uncultivated, the roads crowded with unfortunate citizens turned beggars or highwaymen' (Rousseau 1952 [1754]: 365–6).

ROMANTICISM

Rousseau is recognized as a precursor of Romanticism, a political and cultural movement that spread throughout Europe and the US during the late eighteenth and early nineteenth centuries and which has had a profound effect on ideas about the relationship between the individual and society and attitudes towards nature. It was, according to Alfred North Whitehead, 'a protest on behalf of the organic view of nature' (Whitehead in Marx 1964: 19). Most clearly expressed in the art, literature and poetry of the period, Romanticism emphasized emotion over reason and sentimentalized the spontaneous art of the common people and the grandeur of the landscape. Ruined buildings were elevated to iconic status as representative of the power of nature to reclaim the land from civilization. However, according to Paul A. Cantor, the Romantics did not simply oppose technology to a classical conception of nature but were concerned that our alienation from nature would blind us to its true potential. This was not the fault of science and technology *per se* but a failure of the imagination as applied to the possibilities that it offered for transcendence. Romanticism gave philosophical and poetical expression to the sublime; the sense that '[t]he mind is always in some sense larger than the object of contemplation – even if that object is effectively infinite' (Turney 2004: 93). Critics of this position, such as Theodor Adorno could see that what it implied was simply a capitulation to Heidegger's 'final delusion' (see Chapter 1). '[W]ith this concept', he writes, 'nothing in the world is worthy of attention except that for which the autonomous subject has itself to thank' (Adorno 2000: 81). Thus, according to Cantor, 'the nature of [William] Blake and the other Romantics, is a thoroughly *humanized* nature, a nature filtered through, represented in, and in the deepest sense produced by a human consciousness' (Cantor 1993: 117).

It is this Romantic sense of the sublime which, according to Leo Marx, sustained the 'pastoral ideal' of nineteenth-century America. '[I]t seemed', he writes, 'that mankind actually might realize what had been thought a poetic fantasy. Soon the dream of a retreat to an oasis of harmony and joy was removed from its traditional literary context. It was embodied in various utopian schemes for making America the site of a new beginning for Western society' (Marx 1964: 3). Central to this new beginning was the bucolic ideal of what Marx calls the 'middle landscape' (Marx 1964: 71), located in a middle ground somewhere '"between," yet in a transcendent relation to, the opposing forces of civilization and nature' (Marx 1964: 23). This 'middle landscape' is what supports the myth of the American technological sublime (see last chapter). It is not the machines in isolation that promote awe but their function as an emblem of progress in the context of the abundance which the American landscape seems to promise.

Many American writers, contemplating industrialization, could not conceive of it bringing the dirt, disease and danger of the European factories to the New World. According to Marx, the 'popular American attitude toward mechanization' was that '[l]ike a divining rod, the machine [would] unearth the hidden graces of landscape. There [were] to be no satanic mills in America' (Marx 1964: 234–5). Thinkers like Thomas Jefferson and Ralph Waldo Emerson were confident 'that under native conditions science and technology [could] be made to serve a rural ideal'. Emerson, in particular, regarded 'the virgin landscape as a source of spiritual therapy, a divine hieroglyph awaiting translation by Americans into aims worthy of their vast new powers' (Marx 1964: 236).

It is for good reason that Marx calls his book *The Machine in the Garden*. The ideology of the garden evokes both a pastoral idyll and the sense in which cultivation tames and manipulates nature and the machine is an essential artefact for achieving the dream of the middle landscape. What is perpetuated is the sense of technology as both transforming and sustaining. The labour of the people, aided by the machine, would reveal and make usable the unlimited resources that the myth implied were contained in the beauty and the wildness of the landscape. Thus, for Americans to contemplate a limit both to the machine and the resources that it hungrily uses is essentially to admit an end to the American dream. If nature is used up and exhausted, the promise of the middle landscape is unrealizable. The alternative, as proposed by *The Day After Tomorrow*, is nature as an agent of, ultimately, beneficial change. Not only does the new Ice Age affecting the northern hemisphere heal the fiscal and political rifts that divide it from the south but, once the storm has cleared and the temperature stabilized, the Earth is healed of the ravages of pollution and global warming. 'Look at that', says a Russian cosmonaut on board the International Space Station, with wonder in his voice, 'have you ever seen the air so clear?' We are not so much punished for our excesses as excoriated to begin anew by a redemptive and forgiving nature.

The Day After Tomorrow perpetuates several myths associated with the cultural construction of nature, not least that it is what Kate Soper (1995: 30) calls a 'redemptive resource', an idea that hails from the legacy of Romanticism and that, as she points out, was an idea that was also 'crucial to the construction of Nazi ideology' (Soper 1995: 32). Indeed, in *The Day After Tomorrow*, there is an uncomfortable reference to this idea in the way that the rapidly freezing environment claims the lives of those that take it upon themselves to ignore the advice of the hero scientist (paleo-climatologist Jack Hall, played by Dennis Quaid), while those who heed his advice to remain under cover until the worst of the storm has passed (including his son, Sam, played by Jake Gyllenhaal) are spared. Those that are saved give due deference to the power of nature *and* to the greater wisdom of science, as did National

Socialism, which drew on 'Romantic conceptions of "nature" as wholesome salvation from cultural decadence and racial degeneration' (Soper 1995: 32) while espousing the power of science and technology 'to transform the human condition, without regard to the moralities of the past' (Gray 2004: 175). However, it is important to recognize that this apparent contradiction is not exclusive to Nazi ideology but is deeply embedded in Enlightenment thinking and the political situations to which it gave rise. Put simply, in the Cartesian elevation of human consciousness over the world of matter, 'nature' becomes the Object over which the human Subject presides. At the same time, it is cast as a worthy adversary, deserving of respect. Francis Bacon, father of the scientific method, as Raphael Sassower points out, referred to nature in terms of 'conquest … exploitation, and abuse. But Bacon also understood that nature, in order to be controlled, must be obeyed' (Sassower 1997: 29).

Films like *The Day After Tomorrow* use the legacy of these ideas to its fullest potential in the current climate of environmentalism and eco-awareness. The film mobilizes aspects of the sublime to promote awe as nature ravages the Northern Hemisphere and reduces the city of New York to a frozen wasteland. The Statue of Liberty emerges, draped in frozen garments, from a pristine ice field that, hours before, had been a teeming metropolis. But this is, ultimately, a benevolent nature, attuned to human concerns. It thus stands as a good example of Kate Soper's argument that nature is 'thought through a process of anthropomorphism, in which we project on to that which we are not those very qualities and attitudes we deem exclusive to humanity.' And, as I have pointed out, this process has produced a thoroughly feminized nature, 'equally lover, mother and virago: a source of sensual delight, a nurturing bosom, a site of treacherous and vindictive forces bent on retribution for her human violation' (Soper, 1995: 71). Thus gendered, nature is to culture what women are to men, the 'other' whose qualities and attributes are understood in opposition but which, paradoxically, are essential to maintaining our self-definitions. These oppositional but wholly dependent categories are deeply political constructs, which affect our moral judgements and underpin many of the laws that shape our cultures.

ACTOR NETWORK THEORY

'Nature', then, is not simply that which is external to us but which we share through the needs and demands of our bodies but is a complex mix of real phenomena, conventional tropes and political fictions. It is, simultaneously, 'what science studies' and what scientists conjure into existence; what is deemed elusive and beyond our ability to comprehend and what we nevertheless 'know' about through science teaching and observation. For the French sociologist, Bruno Latour, 'nature' was what was brought into existence along with the birth of 'modern man'. It might have always been 'there' but we brought it into the here and now as a category only when we recreated ourselves in opposition to 'things, or objects, or beasts' (Latour 1993: 13). Properties are then lent to 'nature' in contradistinction to 'society', for example that it is eternal and unchanging while society is shaped and reshaped by the circumstances of history or that there are 'Laws of Nature' which exist before science but which it is able to prove by experiment while the laws of society are created by people.

Of course, there *are* laws of nature or, at least, certain facts that are indisputable such as, for instance, that gravity exists and that the Earth moves around the Sun but even these are not 'pure' knowledge in the sense that they are unaffected by human concerns. Our knowledge about gravity and the movement of the planets is inseparable from the way that it is employed in social contexts. Hence, Latour can claim that '[p]olitical ecology claims to speak about nature, but it actually speaks of countless imbroglios that always presuppose human participation' (Latour 2004: 20). In questioning what it means to 'speak about nature', Latour demonstrates how the term refers to what amounts to an ontological absurdity. 'Nature', in the singular, is abstracted from the social and historical context from which it has received its definition and, in this reified state, stands in for the complexity of concerns for which political ecology claims to speak. Thus, environmental and ecological issues are referred to in terms of what Latour calls 'modern, smooth, risk-free stratified objects in successive gradations from the cosmos to microbes by way of Mother Earth' (Latour 2004: 26). In other words, the closing off of nature in a separate domain from culture or society, the separation into human subject and natural object, the idea of nature as prior to culture – all these are assumed in any speech about 'nature'.

Latour is recognized as one of the leading exponents of Actor Network Theory (ANT), which was largely a response to the problems posed by the so called 'science wars' of the 1990s. When social scientists and cultural theorists turned their attention to deconstructing the politics of science (see Chapter 1), some scientists reacted angrily to the suggestion that the results of scientific experiment are discursively constructed. That is, that they are received, and understood, in a social context, mediated by language and given meaning through their insertion into the cultural domain where they become not so much established facts as mutable ideas.[2] Latour demonstrates that this division between facts and ideas, or between essentialism and social constructionism, is not a division at all. In fact, both positions depend upon maintaining certain modernist myths such as what Latour calls 'the aberrant opposition between mute nature and speaking facts' (Latour 2004: 68). In Western modernist thought 'it is not men who make Nature; Nature has always existed and has always already been there; we are only discovering its secrets' (Latour 1993: 30). The intermediaries that 'speak' for mute nature are scientists but the work that they do to give it a voice and the processes which secure the results are obscured so that what scientists say emerges as what Latour calls '*indisputable speech*' (1993: 68, his emphasis). Or, as Donna Haraway puts it, '"Science says" is represented as a univocal language' (Haraway 1991: 204). This univocal language presents what it says *as if* facts were 'speaking for themselves' and then, in Latour's words, '"All you have to do is shut up!"' (Latour 2004: 68).

In what Latour calls 'mononaturalism', 'nature' is overdetermined and singular and is opposed to multiculturalism, which allows for a plurality of social constructions but demands that we acknowledge an underlying reality on which all cultures are built. What emerges from this is that the 'green' movements and their demands to 'save the planet', 'protect the environment' and 'show respect for the natural world' are founded on the assumption that 'nature' is a universally understood concept. But, as Latour says, '[n]on-Western cultures *have never been interested* in nature; they have never adopted it as a category; they have never found a use for it' (Latour 2004: 43, his emphasis). It is Western modernism that has insisted on separating out nature as a universal category; on there being 'one nature' and 'multiple cultures' (Latour 2004: 184). It then arrogates to itself the authority to proclaim what should be included in each category. Thus, 'Nature', as he says, 'is an unmarked category', much as was 'man' before the advent of the feminist movements questioned the assumption of Western masculinity as that from which all other genders and sexualities were differentiated. 'Culture' is the marked category; the deviant 'Other' which, like 'woman' is subject to qualification. Thus Latour can claim that: '*the very notion of culture is an artefact created by bracketing Nature off*. Cultures – different or universal – do not exist, any more than Nature does. There are only natures-cultures, and these offer the only possible basis for comparison' (Latour 1993: 104, his emphasis).

While I would hesitate to agree with Latour when he asserts that '[n]o Westerner today would take the word "man" to be unmarked', the analogy, nevertheless, is telling. Feminisms have at least done the job of challenging the linguistic norms that designated 'man' as 'the totality of thinking beings' while separating out 'woman' as 'apart from thinking beings' (Latour 1993: 49) and it is a similar challenge that Latour sets out for political ecology. In the same way that the deconstruction of the man/woman dichotomy brought to light the fact that the former category 'man' had only, in reality, a very small and select membership so the job of a truly *political* ecology would be to deconstruct the nature/society and object/subject dichotomies in order to question the terms under which membership is admitted. Objects and subjects, being already opposed in advance, '*can never associate with one another*'

(Latour 1993: 76, his emphasis). The designation, 'humans and nonhumans' on the other hand, allows for the kind of complex association that Latour names 'the collective' (Latour 1993: 7). In other words, objects could only ever be abject; belonging to the category of what is expelled in order for subjects to establish themselves. Nonhumans trouble subjectivity in the sense that they too can become what Latour terms 'social actors' (Latour 1993: 76) or 'actants' (Latour 1993: 75).

HARAWAY'S MONSTERS

It is important to note that there is nothing mysterious about actants. They may have been 'socialized by the complex equipment of laboratories' (Latour 2004: 77) but they are not exclusive products of science. This is a point made forcefully by Donna Haraway in her essay 'The Promises of Monsters: A Regenerative Politics for Inappropriate/d Others' (1992b). Haraway likes the idea of monsters because they are both what we live with everyday and a concept that we need to explore in order not to succumb to apocalyptic paranoia in our search for a solution to environmental crises. What do we mean, for instance, when we talk about entities like bacteria, viruses, genes, molecules, protons and quarks? In common representation, these entities are complete unto themselves; they are understood as having boundaries; as belonging to nature; as being the stuff of which the world (and our bodies) is made. However, this is to give undue determinacy to the logic of 'discovery', which implies that these entities had simply been waiting for us to recognize them in all their ontological distinction; that they, in effect, had voices that could clamour for our attention. But if you think of them as ontologically indistinct monsters; as stories told about the world from a particular perspective; as contingent fictions built up from the confluence of many diverse interests, at a particular point in time and serving a particular purpose then their ontological status becomes less clear.

The first entry for monster in dictionary.com defines it as 'An imaginary or legendary creature, such as a centaur or Harpy, that combines parts from various animal or human forms.' The entities that emerge from laboratories are definitely imaginary and undeniably combinations of different parts. We cannot *see* a virus without the aid of an electron microscope and, even if we can 'see' it, we need to ask ourselves how we know *what* we are seeing. Even with the evidence before our eyes, we 'imagine' the virus, and our imagination is fed by metaphors of war and battle propagated by popular science texts (we, conventionally, 'fight' viruses), the elation of the technological and natural sublime (particularly if we are seeing it on Discovery channel and the accompanying music is suitably dramatic) and the slight frisson of fear that accompanies the realization that we harbour such things inside ourselves. These responses, in turn, are connected to our own socialization within modernist cultures, the history of Enlightenment science and its investment in the idea of 'progress', the Christian salvation story, capitalist economics and the investment strategies of corporations involved in medical research. All these things (and many more) make up the monster that is our virus. The thing 'in itself' is unknowable in any clear and transparent sense but it is this very hydra-headed, connective and contingent monstrosity that can form a model for Latour's 'collective' informed by what Haraway calls 'articulatory practices', in which '[b]oundaries take provisional, neverfinished shape' (Haraway 1992b: 313). As she says, 'In obsolete English, to articulate meant to make terms of agreement. Perhaps we should live in such an "obsolete," amodern world again. To articulate is to signify. It is to put things together, scary things, risky things, contingent things. I want to live in an articulate world' (Haraway 1992b: 324).

If we can imagine our virus as never finished; as a node in a series of networks where its significance is strategic and where it is defined neither as a natural artefact nor a socially produced entity but a product of a nature-culture, then we can go some way towards appreciating the way in which it emerges as an actant in the kinds of life-changing dramas associated with, for example, HIV/AIDS and SARS. The kinds of articulatory practices that have already gone some way to establishing these entities as 'facts' in the public domain as practised by, for instance, networked TV news and newspapers, Hollywood, scientific research departments, scientific journals, drug companies, representatives of state religions, governments, hospitals, manufacturers of condoms, dental dams, breathing masks and the machines that aid the scientists in their work (to name but a few) can be enlisted by activists attuned to the propagation of monsters.

Haraway gives as an example the AIDS Coalition to Unleash Power (ACTUP) which, as she says, 'is a collective built from many articulations among unlike kinds of actors' (Haraway 1992b: 323). These 'unlike' actors [actants] include such diverse groups as 'biomedical machines, government bureaucracies, gay and lesbian worlds ... IV drug-users, pharmaceutical companies, publishers, virus components ... and more ...'

Case Study: Sex, Reproduction and Cloning

It is important to state at the outset that whether or not human cloning is, or will be, actually possible is not at issue here. The cloning of animals has already been realized and the knowledge exists that could, theoretically, lead to human cloning in the future. Indeed, it may be the case that some of my future readers will owe their origins to SCNT (somatic cell nuclear transfer) or a similar procedure and would

The actors, however, are not all equal. ACT UP has an animating center-PWAs [people with AIDS], who are to the damage wrought by AIDS and the work for restored health around the world as the indigenous peoples of the Amazon are to forest destruction and environmentalism. These are the actors with whom others must articulate. That structure of action is a fundamental consequence of learning to visualize the heterogeneous, artifactual body that is our "social nature," instead of narrowing our vision that "saving nature" and repelling alien invaders from an unspoiled organic eden called the autonomous self. (Haraway 1992b: 324)

Thus, Haraway reminds us that we, ourselves are always already monstrous and that a necessary part of learning to negotiate for more egalitarian social worlds is to recognize that the boundaries we draw around 'human nature' are a product of the same modernist practices that 'bracketed Nature off'.

Nature, then, has become an increasingly disputed category as we have challenged the univocality of science and problematized the distinctions that separated nature from culture. Thinking in terms of Latour's concept of 'natures-cultures' forces us to recognize that nature and history are inseparable. 'Natures' is pluralized because it is a concept that is deeply affected by cultural change and by its insertion into the very multiple and differing contexts which give rise to 'matters of concern' (Latour 2004: 51) in political and social life. In the current concern with the consequences of environmental change, what counts as nature is being constantly tested. Environmental 'awareness' is, fundamentally, a recognition of what ANT proposes: that is, that we are not the only actors that have agency in the world. Of course, the fact remains that it is difficult to see how actants with which it is impossible to have a dialogue (plants, animals, rocks etc.) can be allowed to 'speak' but this is to reckon without the communities who live in everyday negotiation with such actants and who give voice to these articulations in their cultural practices. Therefore, we must learn the process of articulation if we are to negotiate for a responsible science, rather than reject what we have only understood through the mythology of a 'bracketed off' nature.

---

consider any discussion that threw doubt on the efficacy of the science to be redundant and any debate about the ethics of producing human beings in this way to be personally insulting. Nevertheless, in the current state of knowledge, the clone is an important actant; perhaps an 'animating centre' that provides the impetus for the network and draws the collective together. The ontology of clones, then, is, at the present time, a function of the debate itself. As I write there are no (to my knowledge) functioning human clones but they, nevertheless, crowd our imaginations, clamour for space in the popular press and provide idiomatic ammunition for derogating those whose individuality is supposedly in doubt. What is highly ironic, of course, is that, in the current political milieu of possessive individualism, such insults merely expose the anxieties that shape attitudes towards cloning in the first place. The former British Prime Minister, Margaret Thatcher, famously declared that 'There is no such thing as society. There are individual men and women and there are families.' If we agree with Mrs Thatcher, then anything other than sexual reproduction is anathema. Her statement entails the assumption that democracy is a function of a social order, which emerges out of heterosexual affiliation in alliance with capitalist economics. There are no 'collectives' in Mrs Thatcher's world but neither are there divergent sexualities and definitely no clones. This is the world that we have, by and large, inherited, here at the start of the twenty-first century but the problem is that there *are* clones and they are set to trouble taken-for-granted terms such as 'individual' and 'family'.

'[P]robably the most famous sheep in history', Dolly, was born in 1997 at the Roslin Insitute in Scotland. 'Right from the start' as Federico Neresini reports, 'the discussion created by Dolly's appearance revolved around the issue of human cloning' (Neresini 2000: 359). This led to the creation, in August 2001, of the President's Council on Bioethics by the American President George W. Bush, 'to address the ethical and policy ramifications of biomedical intervention' (see foreword by Kass in President's Council on Bioethics 2002: xv), which, in 2002, published a report entitled *Human Cloning and Human Dignity* (hereafter HCAHD). The Chairman of the Committee, Leon Kass' foreword to the report contains the following statement:

[T]he burgeoning technological power to intervene in the human body and mind, justly celebrated for its contributions to human welfare, is also available for uses that could slide us down the dehumanising path toward ... the abolition of man. Thus, just as we must do battle with anti-modern fanaticism and barbaric disregard for human life, so we must avoid runaway technology, 'scientism,' and the utopian project to remake humankind in our own image. Safeguarding the human future rests on our ability to steer a prudent middle course, avoiding the inhuman Osama Bin Ladens on the one side and the post-human Brave New Worlders on the other. (Kass in President's Council on Bioethics 2002: xvi)

The actants in Kass' collective are a shady bunch: terrorists, barbarians, utopians, identikit clones, anti-moderns, as well as (presumably) unscrupulous scientists, 'runaway' technology and 'man'. So, in the same way that 'Dolly became an excellent argument to strengthen the opposition to IVF and abortion' (Neresini 2000: 369),[3] so Kass enlists the clone in the fight against terrorism, on the one side, and the preservation of the white, Western 'autonomous self' on the other.

Kass's statement thus joins the voices that have established cloning as scientific 'fact' while, at the same time, determining how that fact is to be understood. In what follows, I will sketch Neresini's analysis of the network of actants that determined Dolly's emergence into public consciousness in order to see how Kass' additions to the collective conjure the clone into existence. What sort of monster has our clone become?

Neresini studied the coverage of Dolly's birth in the Italian press during February and March 1997. What he discovered was that the progression of the debate enlisted an increasing list of actants from beyond the scientific community, including politicians, the Catholic Church, IVF and abortion practitioners, 'public opinion' (which entered the network through opinion polls conducted in Italy and the US) and, by extension, embryos, monozygotic twins (those produced by a split zygote rather than the fertilization of two separate eggs, thus making them, effectively, clones), childless couples and, inevitably, the family. In the case of the Catholic Church:

> the debate on cloning represents not only an opportunity for the Church to expound her point of view, but also to reopen the debates surrounding abortion, contraception, and the social definition of "family." This is a clear example of translation: the Catholic Church uses the debate on cloning to pursue goals that are unimaginable by the scientists who worked on the Dolly experiment, who are mainly interested in confirming cloning as a scientific fact. Even the Catholic Church is interested in establishing mammal cloning from somatic cells as a scientific fact, but not for enhancing her own scientific reputation nor for protecting the freedom of science, but for furthering her condemnation of abortion using scientific arguments, for reaffirming a specific model of family (one defined by Catholic morality as "natural"), and for reclaiming the Church's authority to define what is meant by "human being." (Neresini 2000: 376)

In Actor Network Theory, as Latour explains it, translation is 'the interpretation given by the fact-builders of their interests and that of the people they enrol' (Latour 1987: 108). As Neresini explains it 'the differences in the term's translation lead to its establishment as a fact; the term, in all its translations, can rely on a network of stronger and more heterogeneous allies' (Latour 1987: 362). With the enrolment of the Catholic Church the fact of cloning is not only strengthened but is given credence in terms of its insertion into debates that predate Dolly's birth and which are outside the purview of the scientists who performed the experiment; they only cloned a sheep. Once the fact escapes the laboratory (and this happens the moment that a peer reviewed paper has been published), its significance becomes a function of the articulations which the reports in the media enable and the other actants who join the collective, often by default. While the Catholic Church understands the possibility of human cloning to be an ally in its drive to add moral substance to a particular view of how human reproduction should proceed, its pronouncements enrol, as actants, gay, lesbian, bisexual and transgendered persons, lone parents and people with physical and mental disabilities, who have a stake in challenging the 'natural' family, as well as pro and anti-abortion activists and feminists. What is particularly interesting here is that a 'fact' which is not yet established as 'natural' (cloning) comes up against one that has been well established historically (the family) but is under siege because other facts that are beginning to gain allies (such as that sexuality and gender are not necessarily biological givens) are militating against it. Therefore, before proceeding to analyse the translation represented by Leon Kass' pronouncements, it is worth pausing to study the terms under which the family enters the debate.

In her book *Primate Visions: Gender, Race, and Nature in the World of Modern Science*, Donna Haraway (1992a) tells the history of Carl Akeley's Hall of African Mammals at the American Museum of Natural History. Akeley was a pioneering explorer, taxidermist, sculptor and photographer who was concerned to preserve for posterity the flora and fauna of Africa, which, at the start of the twentieth century, was already disappearing. The African Hall contains twenty-eight dioramas containing carefully preserved and mounted specimens that evoke the habitats in which Akeley encountered the animals. 'Most groups', as Haraway reports, 'are made up of only a few animals, usually a large and vigilant male, a female or two and one baby' (Haraway 1992a: 30). In the centre of the Hall, a group of four elephants stands 'like a high altar in the nave of a great cathedral' (Haraway 1992a: 29). The photograph that forms the template for this group shows, 'unmistakeably ... a perfect family' (Haraway 1992a: 41).

Haraway's qualification here is telling. Akeley, as she points out, was concerned that the captured specimens should conform to a particular notion of perfection. Thus, '[a]n animal with asymmetrical tusks was rejected' (Haraway 1992a: 40–1). The hunt was to be accomplished as 'a meeting of equals'. Any animal displaying 'cowardice' was also rejected and there was a 'hierarchy of game according to species ... The gorilla was the supreme achievement, almost a definition of perfection' (Haraway 1992a: 41). Hence, the 'perfect family' is, in the same terms, both composed of 'perfect' specimens, as determined by certain visible, physical criteria and the achievement of capturing, by means of Akeley's specially adapted camera, a group most nearly resembling the ideal human family, as understood in white, Anglo-American ideology. An elephant family, as is now well known, actually consists of only females, led by a matriarch. The males visit for mating and immediately return to the bachelor herd. Akeley's diorama thus functions to establish a sociobiological verification of the white, bourgeois, nuclear family, rather than the truth about the way that elephants live in Africa. Or, as Haraway explains it, for Akeley, '[n]ature's biographical unit, the reproductive group had the moral and epistemological status of truth-tellers' (Haraway 1992a: 41). The elephants are enrolled as actants in the establishment of a particular form of family as a scientific fact.

This then, is nature as 'tool for the reproduction of man' (Haraway 1992: 296); for the naturalization and legitimation of a social order which privileges monogamous heterosexual mating and a particular, gendered division of labour. Akeley's dioramas, with their insistence on 'perfection' also reinforce the sense in which the idea of the family is inseparable from concerns about who should be accorded the privilege of reproduction. The discourses which structure these concerns echo nineteenth-century anxieties about the

containment of sexuality and, particularly from the European perspective, the control of colonized others.

Michel Foucault has written extensively about the connection between sexology and bourgeois hegemony and argues persuasively for an understanding of Victorian sexual anxiety and the development of what he calls 'bio-power' (Foucault 1978: 140) as coextensive with the rise of racism in its modern form. The development of branches of knowledge concerned exclusively with the control and regulation of the body, particularly in its reproductive capacities, he understands as receiving justification from 'the mythical concern with protecting the purity of the blood and ensuring the triumph of the race' (Foucault 1978: 149). This mythologizing of racial dominance as something fragile and in need of protection is directly related to fears that the 'noble savage', the romanticized association of so called pre-civilized cultures with the wildness of nature, will exact a just revenge, either by taking up arms against a colonizer weakened by sexual excess or by infiltrating the gene pool through impregnating women whose sexuality has been insufficiently contained.

Furthermore, as Judith Butler points out, these same anxieties are at the root of oppositions to gay marriage in contemporary culture. The claim that marriage is, primarily, a filial concern and that 'parents' must, by definition, be one from each biological sex, resurrects structuralist notions of the perpetuation of the 'clan' through the exchange of women. At the same time, the incest taboo and the structuring of the psyche through the Oedipal transition are evoked as mechanisms for the transmission of a cultural form deemed to be universal. Thus, '[t]he woman from elsewhere makes sure that the men from here will reproduce their own kind. She secures the reproduction of a cultural identity in this way' (Butler 2002: 32):

> Marriage must take place outside the clan. There must be exogamy. But there must also be a limit to exogamy; that is, marriage must

be outside the clan but not outside a certain racial self-understanding or racial commonality. So the incest taboo mandates exogamy, but the taboo against miscegenation limits the exogamy that the incest taboo mandates. Cornered, then, between a compulsory heterosexuality and a prohibited miscegenation, something called culture, saturated with the anxiety and identity of European whiteness, reproduces itself in and as universality itself. (Butler 2002: 33)

Anxiety about miscegenation also reasserts itself in 'fear[s] that lesbians and gay men will start to fabricate human beings, exaggerating the biotechnology of reproduction' and that these '"unnatural" practices will eventuate in a wholesale social engineering of the human' (Butler 2002: 36).

Here, then, are Kass's 'inhuman Osama bin Ladens' and 'posthuman Brave New Worlders'. Like the Catholic Church, President Bush's Council on Bioethics is interested in establishing cloning as a scientific fact but in the interests not only of 'reaffirming a specific model of family' but of setting up the family as that which is most at threat from 'terrorism' and its supposed project 'to remake humankind in [its] own image'. Bin Laden joins the collective as a cipher for fears about racial identity and the preservation of the white, bourgeois family and Aldous Huxley's technocratic, dystopian society of mass produced worker clones is enrolled as a surrogate for the risk posed by the exaggeration of the biotechnology of reproduction by 'imperfect' families: lesbians and gay men, single and aged parents, 'criminals' and others deemed unfit in the discourse of familial and bodily 'health'. As Roddey Reid reminds us '[i]n familial discourse the production of "family" as desirable norm has always required freaks and outcasts that name the norm indirectly by virtue of their departure from it' (Reid 1995: 191). In the biopolitics of the besieged twenty-first century family the clone is always already

a 'freak' and 'outcast' by virtue of the fact that, as in Huxley's novel, it demands that we examine the necessity of Oedipal psychic structuring. In this sense, it is also always already posthuman in that, far from 'threatening' the family, it has no need for it in the first place. It describes a world where, in fact, Kass's careful bracketing of the human by 'inhuman' and 'posthuman' makes no sense.

Brave New World (1932) is not so much a critique of the possible misuse of biotechnology as a satire on the political consequences of the separation of sexuality and reproduction and the decline of romantic love, a legacy of the 'new domesticity' of the late eighteenth century, 'based on heterosexual monogamy, love matches, and sentimental intimacy focused on children' (Reid 1995: 187). As Reid points out, '[t]hen as now, therein lay the sense of what it meant to be "human," and it was the domestic family and its sentimental narratives that grounded and lent meaning to all other social arrangements' (Reid 1995: 186). Freudian psychoanalysis ensured the legitimacy of these arrangements by confirming them within a narrative of human origins backed by the authority of scientific reasoning. The clone fits only awkwardly into the Oedipal narrative, if at all. Thus, it already inhabits a post-familial world and can only ever be abject 'other' in the discourse of the human family. Hence, Kass's team find it necessary to point out that '[t]he problems of being and rearing an adolescent could become complicated should the teenage clone of the mother "reappear" as the double of the woman the father once fell in love with' (President's Council on Bioethics 2002: 125), a statement that delicately avoids mention of, but nevertheless raises the spectre of, not only incest but child abuse; a powerful enough argument against cloning in an era in which unfitness to parent is often conceived of in terms of abuse and inappropriate relationships. We are reminded that at the heart of family rhetoric is the incest taboo and the subsequent Freudian connotations attached to its perceived fragility.

This is a subject addressed in Michael Winterbottom's film *Code 46* (2003), set in the near future, where the prevalence of cloning and *in vitro* fertilization means that laws have been instituted to prevent the possibility of incest between unsuspecting near relatives. Tim Robbins plays William, a detective who investigates identity fraud who falls in love with a woman called Maria (Samantha Morton) who is a suspect in one of his cases. The film dramatizes the close links between sex, reproduction and social order.

Maria is a clone of William's dead mother and the Code 46 of the title is the law that applies when she is discovered to be pregnant with his child. One of the film's conceits is that designer viruses can be manufactured to induce emotional responses and, in William's case, to enhance his empathic responses to enable him to 'read' emotions. Maria's child is aborted, her memory is selectively wiped to expunge her relationship with William and she is infected with a virus that triggers a 'flight or fight' response if he attempts to touch her. William hunts her down and takes her to the *afeura*, the outside, where they have been led to believe they will be safe but, while they are able to overcome Maria's defensive response to William's touch, what they cannot overcome is that the virus also encodes a compulsion to confess. William, a valued member of the privileged classes, has his memory wiped and goes back to his old life but Maria has effectively condemned herself and is banished permanently to the *afuera*. As the trailer for the film tells us 'society is divided. Your life is determined. Including who you can love.' What seems to be implied is that technological intervention in 'natural' processes can only lead to totalitarianism; that Mrs Thatcher was correct to imply a direct relationship between sexual reproduction and democracy.

However, the film can also be read as suggesting that clones themselves have become scapegoats for a social order that is maintained through the management of sexuality and reproduction. In other words, one not unlike our own at the present time. For instance, the film makes much of William's 'happy' family life with his wife and child, contrasted with Maria's lonely existence in a small apartment in Shanghai. In breaching Code 46, William and Maria have effectively committed the same 'crime' but it is Maria who is banished while William, made compliant by medical intervention, returns to his family. The bourgeois family is thus protected from incursion. Maria stands for the threat of incest, which must be banished by social taboo so that the making of families can proceed by exogamy and the exchange of women. As a clone, she is thus doubly conceived of as a 'crime against nature', she both tempts incest and is a reminder that clones trouble the lines of heredity that determine bourgeois inheritance and generational privilege. Equally, as a woman, she is the temptress who is blamed for leading men astray. While, within the narrative, these representations provide justification for her banishment, the film elicits sympathy on her behalf, which leads to an ambiguous response. While on the one hand, suspicion about the potential for biotechnology to usher in a totalitarian order is confirmed, on the other, we are lead to the conclusion that it is not the presence of clones themselves that permits oppression but a social order that, in attempting to secure the nuclear family as a site of privilege by retaining 'heterosexual monogamy, love matches and sentimental intimacy focused on children' has need to implement controls that lead to increased surveillance and social exclusion. We are forced to consider the possibility that the exaggeration of biotechnological reproduction may usher in a post-Freudian, posthuman world where categories like 'nature' and 'culture' are neither exclusive nor mutually defining and where the concept of 'family' must necessarily be contested.

CHAPTER SUMMARY

■ 'Nature' is constructed as a category in opposition to 'culture'.
■ Romanticism emphasized the sublimity of the natural landscape and the redemptive properties of nature.
■ These ideas underpin contemporary debates about the role of science in environmental politics.
■ Bruno Latour and Donna Haraway suggest that we think in terms of 'natures-cultures' in order to deconstruct the way that nature is determined under the terms of contemporary ideologies.

4 TECHNOBODIES

The Australian performance artist, Stelarc, has announced that 'the body is obsolete'. Committed to a postevolutionary, extraterrestrial future, Stelarc's work deorganizes the body by drawing attention to the way that technology extends, amplifies, invades and shapes contemporary bodies. He invites us to consider the absurdity of the 'natural' body and to contemplate the idea of human evolution as aided and determined by technology. 'We have always' he says, 'been prosthetic bodies'.[1] In other words, technology should not be considered an adjunct to the body or in opposition to it but as a determinant of its ontology. Machines, for Stelarc, 'R' us.

Stelarc is not alone in believing that we need to dispense with the idea of the human body as an inviolable structure, contained by the skin, which produces but is never itself produced by, the technologies that it needs to continue its existence. The philosopher Bernard Stiegler has argued that we are in error if we believe that the tools that we use are something that 'we' invent, where the 'we' presupposes a human essence which remains, in some sense, separate from technology. '[T]he human', he says, 'invents himself in the technical by inventing the tool – by becoming exteriorised techno-logically' (Stiegler 1998: 141). In other words, the concept of 'human' is unthinkable without technology but we act as if it is.

Stiegler's argument is complex but it can be illustrated quite simply by thinking about successive understandings of the body in Western culture, beginning with, for instance, William Harvey's discovery of the circulatory system in the early seventeenth century. Prior to Harvey, the findings of Galen, a Greek physician and philosopher who lived in the second century AD were the accepted wisdom. Galen knew that the heart had a role in the distribution of blood but thought that it sucked it from the veins. He also thought that the liver made a different type of blood, which was absorbed or consumed by the organs. Harvey's innovation was to demonstrate that blood actually circulated around the body and was pumped by the heart. Thus, Harvey was not only responsible for introducing the concept of the circulatory system but also for an idea of the constitution of the body that survives to this day.

Having a 'bloodstream' is part of our understanding of what makes us human and it is our understanding of how it works that produces medical technologies, both machine and pharmocological, which enable us to affect the body in many ways, from making the circulation of the blood visible to moving various drugs and other agents around the body. On the one hand, we could say that our idea of the body (as containing a circulatory system) is *produced* by technology in the simple sense that Harvey had necessarily to use tools to examine the workings of the heart. But, in a more complex sense, we could also say that technology continually *produces* the body both because, once the idea of the circulatory system is established, increasingly complex and sophisticated technologies allow us to examine it in more detail and because other (chiefly medical) technologies are introduced into the body on the basis of the new understandings that these produce. These, in turn, help to maintain our idea of what a fully functional body *is*.

DISCIPLINED BODIES

Michel Foucault was particularly interested in the body as an object of knowledge and in his book, *Discipline and Punish: The Birth of the Prison* (1977) he discusses what he calls the 'docile' body, the exemplary form of which is the soldier. The body of the soldier is 'manipulated, shaped, trained' so that it 'obeys, responds, becomes skilful and increases its forces' (Foucault 1991 [1977]: 136). A well disciplined army, in fact, can be compared to a well oiled machine. All the parts function smoothly and in tandem but this is only achieved because the individual parts have been tailored to fit an exact function. The raw material of the human body is, in a sense, crafted according to the dictates of certain requirements of the state (for protection, security and so forth), which exercises power through control of the soldier's body. Control may take the form of exercises, punishments and regimes but the soldier is also controlled by the technologies of war of which the army, in its totality, is one, but also the guns, vehicles and other machines which serve its purposes.

There are distinct comparisons between the way that the soldier's body is rendered docile and the way that power disciplined workers under the regimes of industrial capitalism. According to Marx, '[m]achinery is put to a wrong use, with the object of transforming the workman, from his very childhood, into a part of a specialized machine' (Marx 1990 [1867]: 547). According to Jonathan Benthall, 'when Marx writes of *labour, exploitation* and so forth, he is not using abstract theoretical terms; we are constantly reminded of the sweating, suffering body of the labourer' (Benthall 1976: 142). Thus, despite the fact that Foucault disagreed with Marx about the way that power operates to determine our work and social lives, they fundamentally agree that power has marked effects at the level of the body. How we *use* our bodies and how we understand what it means to *be* embodied is a function of power relations that operate to distinguish a hierarchy of bodies in terms of function and appearance. In Marxist terms, the worker's body is a commodity to be bought and whose value is determined by the fluctuations of the market. As such, it is subject to a disciplinary regime that determines its effectiveness as an adjunct to machinery but which extends way beyond training for the job or learning the ritualized movements of factory production (something of which Charlie Chaplin's Little Tramp is incapable, see Chapter 1).

The fundamental basis of the capitalist system is a belief in the priority of the self-determining individual. According to the doctrine of liberal humanism, the 'self' is fundamentally rational, free (see Chapter 1) and thus capable of making informed choices. The system of liberal democracy is, in fact, based on this idea. The ideology of liberal humanism determines what we mean when we speak about 'human nature', which is understood as fundamentally competitive, inquisitive and acquisitive. According to this ideology the worker is free to sell his or her labour to the highest bidder but what is also implied, of course, is that, under conditions where there is a surplus of labour, the capitalist, or owner of the means of production, is free to pick and choose from what is on offer. Workers must therefore be prepared to tailor themselves to the fluctuating requirements of the labour market. Thus, although the concept of the liberal humanist individual prioritizes the faculty of reason as the determinant of what makes us human and relegates the body to a subsidiary function, it is the body that bears the marks of status and social class. In terms of industrial capitalism, the capabilities of the manual, or blue collar worker are distinguished by physicality; by a body that bears the marks of responsiveness to the industrial machine.

DISCURSIVE BODIES

The continuing importance of the worker's body as an icon of industrial culture, at least up until the late twentieth century, is emphasized by Fred Pfeil's analysis of Bruce Springsteen as a 'swaggering, solidly muscled working-class rocker' and his monotonous 'stamping out of the lyrics, a "singing" that functions … as a metonymy for the monotonous oppression of male working-class life' (Pfeil 1995: 84). As Pfeil points out, '[a]t a moment in the Reagan eighties characterized by the decline of traditional manufacturing sectors and the loss of those jobs' (Pfeil 1995: 85), in Springsteen's performances, 'a certain kind of white working-class masculinity associated with Fordist regimes of mass production and capital accumulation is being rendered artifactual. Bruce's worker's body circa 1984–86 pins down and neutralizes all the other meanings in his music by becoming, finally, an object of nostalgia' (Pfeil 1995: 88).

Thus Springsteen's body, its shape, the clothes that he wears and the way that he moves activate a form of consciousness that refers to industrial technology for confirmation of a particular masculine identity in a time of insecurity and flux.[2]

Springsteen's body can help us to understand how power works to determine what Foucault called 'subject positions' and how these are structured by technocapitalist institutions. Although Foucault acknowledges that Marxism is concerned with the body of the worker, he nevertheless disagrees with the Marxist notion of 'ideology' or, at least, with the way in which it tends to privilege consciousness as the site of control. Nor does he agree that power is necessarily repressive. '[O]ne must set aside', he says, 'the widely held thesis that power, in our bourgeois, capitalist societies has denied the reality of the body in favour of the soul, consciousness, ideality. In fact nothing is more material, physical, corporal than the exercise of power' (Foucault 1980: 57–8). Power, for Foucault, is productive (see Chapter 1) and it produces forms of knowledge that provide us with understandings of embodiment, which, in turn, have real, physical effects.

The function of discourse is to make distinctions between what we understand to be 'normal' or 'deviant'. When we condemn someone's behaviour or bodily comportment as 'abnormal', we are perpetuating the discursive construction of certain bodies in terms of knowledge that often originates in scientific analysis but gains currency through its wider dissemination by institutions of the state (such as the law, education or the Church) as well as the media and simple word of mouth. Foucault is particularly concerned with discourses that structure ideas about the sexualized body and he disagrees with, for instance, Herbert Marcuse, for whom power is repressive in that it appears to prohibit the free expression of sexuality. In fact, the production of subject positions is at its most intense in struggles to define 'proper' expressions of sexual desire. Thus, 'homosexual' is a subject position that only emerges in the late nineteenth century (Foucault 1978 : 43) along with 'the hysterical woman, the masturbating child, the Malthusian couple . . .' (Foucault 1978: 105). In a historical and cultural milieu in which the European colonial powers are concerned with the preservation of racial purity and the maintenance of a healthy middle class, the discourse of sexuality produces forms of knowledge that allay fears about miscegenation, infertility and the sexuality of children. In more recent times, we might consider the production of the subject position PWA (Person With AIDS) that emerges from the confluence of discourses about the immune system, sexuality, race and gender as well as financial and legal discourses concerned with entitlement to treatments and the funding of drugs research and, perhaps crucially for my argument, discussions of ethical responsibility that are, themselves, based on contemporary forms of knowledge which consider 'fitness' (which we might consider to be one's personal responsibility) over 'health' (the responsibility of the social body and the state). In Foucault's terms the PWA is a 'marked' body. That is, it corresponds with a discursively produced truth that it represents, confirms and perpetuates.

MARKED BODIES

In light of this, we could say that Bruce Springsteen's body, which is 'fit' in terms both of appearance and conformity and corresponds to the requirements of a particular type of labour, is equally marked. Or rather, that it straddles the divide between the 'norm' that is invisible and assumed and thus unmarked and those bodies that, by their very visibility, work to confirm it; the old, the infirm, women, people of colour and, perhaps crucially, those who live with a physical disability. Springsteen's 'fitness' is of a type that, in the period that Pfeil refers to, was increasingly achieved in a gym, rather than as a result of heavy labour. He thus signifies the passage from the body of the industrial worker, marked by social class, to the body of the late capitalist consumer who, whatever his occupation, is required to purchase his fitness in accordance with new discourses of sexuality and health. This is what Foucault refers to as 'control by stimulation'. 'Get undressed – but be slim, good-looking, tanned!' (Foucault 1980: 57). Nostalgia for the worker's body is exploited in the service of eroticized consumption.

Another way of understanding this is in terms of Anne Balsamo's assertion that we are 'incurably informed' (1996: 134), a phrase that she borrows from Pat Cadigan's cyberpunk novel, *Synners* (1991). *Synners*, in common with all cyberpunk fiction, is concerned with the effects of technological liminality; more precisely, the ontological insecurity that attends the interface between the human body and the datasphere or realm of information that William Gibson famously named 'cyberspace' (Gibson 1986: 67 – see Chapter 5, this volume). The four central characters in the novel represent four conceptual understandings of the body in a space in which information defines social and corporeal relationships that Balsamo names 'the marked body, the disappearing body, the laboring body and the repressed body' (Balsamo 1996: 140) and which she reads as aspects of gendered corporeality in postindustrial culture.

Cadigan's 'disappearing' and 'repressed' bodies are Visual Mark and Gabe Ludovic who, in common with other cyberpunk 'heroes' are emaciated, demasculinized males who represent the extreme of a subject position that, in contemporary culture, might be labelled 'geek' or 'technophile'. Geeks are marked by unfitness. The stereotype lives on take away pizza and canned drinks and, with few exceptions, is portrayed as an inexperienced heterosexual male with little to recommend him to women. The geek, however, can emerge as a hero in the domain of cyberspace where 'virtual' bodies can be constructed (and changed at will) and gender boundaries can be explored, as well as opportunities for 'safe (fluidless) sex' (Balsamo, 1996: 146). In *Synners*, Visual Mark achieves the geek dream of dumping the 'meat' body for permanent existence in what Gibson calls the 'bodiless exultation of cyberspace' (Gibson 1986: 12) while Gabe escapes the demands of embodied reality in his increasing infatuation with inhabiting an avatar 'headhunter' in a virtual reality game. Mark and Gabe represent the reconfiguration of the masculine body under post-industrial conditions in which, unlike Springsteen, it no longer 'works' as an instrument and sign of gendered labour division.

Nevertheless, in common with Springsteen, they are ciphers for the body as formed, discursively, in connection with technology. In the novel, Gabe Ludovic works as a 'simulation producer' (Cadigan 1991: 434), making virtual reality ads for commodities while Visual Mark is a 'synner', a human synthesizer with the ability to merge sound and visuals into a form of rock video in which consumers can 'finally *be* the music' (Cadigan 1991: 83). In the late capitalist circuit of production both are hot property, their value determined by their ability to manipulate, synthesize and produce information. In this context, their retreat from the flesh marks the dissolution of the body in an incurably informed world in which the 'meat' is constantly manipulated and thoroughly mediated.

For instance, Gabe is employed in making commercials for 'Gilding Body-shields' whose function is never specified but is implied in the strapline '*Gilding Bodyshields Can Save Your Life*' (Cadigan 1991: 43). Thus the function of the body-shield, within the novel, is to stand in for the way in which the market produces anxieties about the body at the same time as it offers solutions to those anxieties in the form of commodities. Hence, to be 'incurably informed' is to understand ourselves in terms of the constantly disseminated information about health and fit-ness and the desirability of the 'perfect' body for which there is, in fact, no 'cure' other than more of the same. We are, in effect, constantly 'plugged in' to the tech-nology through which this information is disseminated while we employ increasingly elaborate technological solutions to keep ahead of the game. Women, for instance, are constantly reminded that our body hair is unacceptable but there is a simple technological solution to our 'problem' in the nearest supermarket. On the one hand, the body 'disappears' as a cogent materiality and becomes another 'screen' for the projection of the shifting images of late capitalism while, on the other, the repression of desire is manipulated into new forms and satisfaction is constantly deferred in the service of consumerism.

However, for Balsamo, *Synners* articulates a structure of oppositions in which the 'marked' and 'laboring' bodies of the female characters reassert 'the critical importance of the materiality of bodies in any analysis of the information age' (Balsamo 1996: 144). Gina, the only black character in the novel, is marked by racial difference and Sam, Gabe's daughter, is a talented hacker who pierces her own skin to become a 'potato' (Cadigan 1991: 413) and provide 'a power source that can't be compromised' (Cadigan 1991: 392) when a living virus invades the datasphere and threatens the electricity supply. Gina and Sam remind us that female bodies have always been marked by difference and that difference is enshrined in the division of labour in which women labour both to produce and reproduce. Gina's racial difference equally marks the distinction that divides off the white, male body, which is unmarked because it is the 'norm' from which all other bodies deviate. Indeed, it is the body of the white, middle-class male that 'disappears' in the liberal humanist elevation of mental labour over physical or reproductive labour. As Allucquere Rosanne Stone has pointed out, 'Forgetting about the body is an old Cartesian trick, one that has unpleasant consequences for those bodies whose speech is silenced by the act of our forgetting; that is to say, those upon whose labor the act of forgetting the body is founded – usually women and minorities' (Stone 1991: 113).

If we are not to forget about the body, then the task for science and technology studies is to determine how new understandings of corporeality can be articulated, under the terms of technologically mediated cultures, which do not simply conform to accepted hierarchies.

TAXONOMY AND THE GENOME

I began this chapter by suggesting, along with Stelarc and Bernard Stiegler, that 'bodies are obsolete'. This claim can now be clarified as depending upon a recognition that the modern idea of the human body is utterly dependent on accepted differentiations, not least that between humans and machines but also humans and animals. These differentiations, in turn, support and make sense of racial, gender and class divisions. The body has become obsolete because, under the conditions provided by postindustrial, silicon-chip technologies, these divisions are increasingly difficult to maintain.

Consider, for instance, the sequencing of the human genome, a task akin to 'taking 10 copies of the complete Oxford English Dictionary, all 12 volumes, ripping each page into 300,000 minute pieces, placing all of the pieces in to a large barrel, thoroughly mixing them and then trying to put all the pieces back together again'.[3] The technique for mapping the human genome was known in the 1970s but the project did not become feasible until the late 1980s when supercomputers became available that were capable of processing and storing vast quantities of data. Researchers originally estimated that, based on relative complexity, the map of the human genome would contain around 100,000 genes but, when the project was completed, in April 2003, estimates were revised downward to between 20,000 and 25,000. Comparative genomics, which looks for genetic similarities across species has revealed that humans and fruit flies share a core set of genes and similar comparisons can be made between the human genome and that of *Canis familiaris*, the domestic dog.

Findings like these force us to think seriously about the way in which we have historically determined the meaning of 'human'. Taxonomy, a system developed by Carolus Linneaeus in 1735 and still in use today, groups species according to structural similarity and common ancestry. We are classified under the genus *homo* (human) within the order of primates which is a Latin word meaning, essentially, 'first', and belonging to the family *Hominidae* (bipedal). *Homo Sapiens* distinguishes us further as possessing language and the ability to make and use complex tools. But what happens when those tools force us to re-examine our self-classification?

The computers that made possible the Human Genome Project have thrown into doubt the distinctions that kept us apart from other species and have, at the same time, contributed to new ontological discourses in which we comprehend our bodies in terms of the binaries of computer code. We may have 'made' these machines but now, in a very real sense, they make us. Where once we understood ourselves in terms of anatomy and visible differences, so now we refer to those differences made visible by the 'computer-generated topological maps used by the Human Genome Project' (Hayles 1999: 13). Where once the description of the circulatory system forced us to recognize ourselves in terms of its role in structuring our anatomy, so now we describe ourselves in the language of genetics and recognize ourselves as coded in-formational entities. We have, of course, not dispensed with the idea of the circula-tory system as part of our corporeal structure but the blood that it carries is, like other bodily organs, understood in terms of cells containing chromosomes on which genes are located which are, themselves, composed of DNA (deoxyribonucleic acid). DNA stores genetic information which determines the specialism of the cell in the form of linked chains of four nitrogen 'bases' called adenine (A), thymine (T), guanine (G) and cytosine (C). The distribution of these bases on the DNA molecule (the famous twisted ladder described by James Watson and Francis Crick) is represented by combinations of the four letters A, T, G and C. Different combinations 'code' for different attributes. Understanding the way that the bases combine is what has led to scientists' ability to transfer genes between species and the development of recombinant DNA technology (genetic engineering – see Chapter 2).

The implications of this for the way that we understand the body is explored in the work of 'transgenic' artist Eduardo Kac whose most controversial project was 'GFP Bunny'. GFP stands for 'green fluorescent protein', an attribute of jellyfish, which glow in the dark, the gene for which was added to the DNA of a rabbit, named Alba by Kac's family, who was born in a laboratory in France in February, 2000. As Kac tells us on his Web site, the project was designed to be 'a complex social event that starts with the creation of a chimerical animal that does not exist in nature'.[4] As part of the ongoing project, Kac's aim was to take Alba home and socialize her as a family pet. Ultimately, the lab refused to let Kac take Alba home, claiming that '[s]uch an action ... would be a scientific and ethical impropriety' (Lynch 2003: 76). However, the very existence of Alba as a transgenic animal, the product of computerized gene sequencing, born in a laboratory and commissioned by an artist serves, in itself, to raise questions about the arbitrariness of the divisions we have made between art and science and between different species of animal (and, therefore, by implication between us and other species). Furthermore, we are brought to question the distinctions between 'self' and 'other', between 'natural' and 'unnatural' (see Chapter 3) and, perhaps most fundamentally, between information and materiality.

CYBERNETICS

As N. Katherine Hayles writes, '[i]t is not for nothing that "Beam me up, Scotty," has become a cultural icon for the global informational society' (Hayles 1999: 2). As long ago as 1950, Norbert Wiener, the 'father' of cybernetics, offered the observation that '[w]e are not stuff that abides, but patterns that perpetuate themselves' and speculated as to 'what would happen if we were to transmit the whole pattern of the human body' (Wiener 1950: 96) in the same way that radios transmit patterns of sound and televisions transmit patterns of light. Because DNA is constantly perpetuating the 'pattern' of a human being and DNA can be understood as coded information that can be transmitted in the same way as email is transmitted across the world, teleportation becomes, at least, theoretically possible.

Cybernetics is, fundamentally, concerned with control and communication and the relationship between a mechanism and its environment. Wiener was primarily interested in the dynamics of the human nervous system and the method of communication between the exterior senses and the muscles. By observing people who suffered from varying forms of ataxia – a breakdown in this communication resulting in a loss of control over the simple actions necessary to respond to stimulus from their immediate environment – he was able to conclude:

> The central nervous system no longer appears as a self-contained organ, receiving inputs from the senses and discharging into the muscles. On the contrary, some of its most characteristic activities are explicable only as circular processes, emerging from the nervous system into the muscles, and re-entering the nervous system through the sense organs. (Wiener 1948: 8)

Wiener realized that in order for these 'characteristic activities' to be duplicated by machinery, a similar system of mechanical feedback would be required whereby 'messages' could be transmitted to influence a series of actions, the outcome of which would in turn generate further messages. For example, the action of picking up a pencil, for a machine, would require a simulation of at least two senses (sight and touch), along with an information processing mechanism that would 'know' at any given moment, from initiation to completion of the action, what had so far been accomplished by the moving parts. It would then have the capacity to relay this information back to the 'senses', which would in turn pass back information from the environment.

Contemporary robots are cybernetic systems but so are large organizations, which depend upon nested series of feedback and feedforward loops, involving both people and machines and, in the case of, for instance, multinational companies, over vast distances. My computer and I also constitute a cybernetic system. In such a simple operation as word processing, our bodies are adapted to transmit language as patterns of key strokes that are interpreted by levels of computer software and returned to me as words on the screen which I edit in a continual loop of information between the machine and myself. This book is an informatted artefact in the sense that it conveys (hopefully) information that you will find useful but, at the same time, it exists as a pattern of zeros and ones at the most basic level of machine code that can be transmitted electronically and appear as words on my editor's screen. But it is not just my thoughts transcribed into words that my editor will read but the patterns of my fingers as they move across the keyboard in the same way that it is not just words on the screen that you are reading when you receive e-mail but a series of electronic pulses which would be meaningless without the hardware to receive them and the software to translate them. In other words, the mode of transmission and the content of the message are interdependent and mutually determining.

When Hayles (1999: 2) writes about 'how information lost its body', she traces the history of cybernetics to the point where researchers were forced to recognize that we do not merely observe cybernetic systems but that 'feedback can also loop *through* the observers, drawing them in to become part of the system being observed' (Hayles 1999: 9). In my word-processing/email example above, the system consisting of myself, my computer, my editor and his computer will be 'observed' by my readers who become part of the system by taking on board the fact that, they too, are structured by being part of one or several cybernetic systems and this changed perspective both confirms and effects the output from *my* system. Hayles also gives as an analogy Bruno Latour's idea that 'scientific experiments are shown to produce the nature whose existence they predicate as their condition of possibility' (Hayles 1999 – see Chapter 3, this volume). This 'reflexive turn' (Hayles 1999: 10) in cybernetics can also be seen to parallel the implications of quantum mechanics for how we understand the world (see Chapter 1, this volume). The final move, made by Humberto Maturana and Francisco Varela in 1980, was to expand the reflexive turn 'into a fully articulated epistemology that sees the world as a set of informationally closed systems.' 'Organisms respond to their environment in ways determined by their internal self-organisation. Their one and only goal is continually to produce and reproduce the organization that defines them as systems. Hence, they not only are self-organizing but also are autopoietic, or self-making' (Hayles, 1999: 10).

If we remember here that 'systems' are not discrete but are in reflexive relationships with their environment, then the implication is that, as Wendy Wheeler puts it, 'the world is not simply out there as 'information' to be processed by our senses; our human nervous/endocrine/immune system ... actively contributes to the world it thus calls forth' (Wheeler 2006: 108). We are not 'minds' that observe and process an informational world that includes our own bodies but complex systems that reproduce themselves in connection with their environment. Machines are not simply prostheses that we 'add on' to our minds or bodies in order to facilitate and extend our capabilities but part of the environment out of which we produce ourselves.

Thinking of minds and bodies in this way enables us to conceive of ourselves in terms that evade the opposing responses of technophobia and technophilia in which we either see technology as a threat to the coherence of the body or celebrate it as allowing us to escape from the 'meat'. Both responses presuppose the liberal humanist body and both are invested in maintaining the divisions between body and mind, inside and outside and nature and culture, with all that these divisions imply for dividing a 'good' body from a 'bad' or imperfect body. In the case of technophobia the 'bad' body would be conceived of as 'unnatural' or inappropriately modified whereas technophilia creates a hierarchy of bodies under the sign of evolution or progress with Balsamo's disappearing body at the top and marked and labouring bodies at the bottom.

The new descriptions of bodily reality that emerge from considerations of our embededness in cybernetic systems trouble the ties that bind us to specific subjectivities. If these ideas have been prompted by the realization of our necessary relationship with machines, we can also imagine them as the unarticulated 'other' of the system of representations in which we have struggled to pin down and normalize what it means to have or be a body. In other words, concepts like autopoiesis allow us to question the way in which our ideas of what a correctly functioning body looks like or behaves are dependent upon ideologically structured power relations.

ABJECTION AND AUTOPOIESIS

For instance, although, in every day life, we may not consciously refer to Freudian psychoanalysis when we talk about bodies, nevertheless, in contemporary Western cultures, the language in which we discuss our feelings, sensations and desires are deeply mired in Freudian concepts. Although Freud is generally thought to have been interested primarily in the mind, his particular contribution to our understanding of the development of the personality was to demonstrate how the desires of the body are controlled and directed in civilized society. His discussions of infant sexuality, although shocking at the time, demonstrated the link between our pleasure seeking drives and the way in which those drives are manipulated so that we learn to defer their satisfaction so that we may gain from entering into productive relationships with others. Of course, the organ of ultimate control is the brain, generally associated with the mind, which is privileged as the site of personality. We do not talk about 'a healthy mind in a healthy body' for nothing and we consider mental health to be demonstrated by correct control of bodily functions and appropriate bodily responses. We have thus developed a hierarchy of organs where those concerned with the disposal of bodily wastes and sexual functioning are relegated to the status of unmentionables. We not only find the natural functions of our body distasteful but go to great lengths to deny that these functions exist while, as Foucault has pointed out, continually drawing attention to them in the very language that seeks to deny them.

The ideal body is a continent body and we react with disgust to the incontinence of the body, which, as Julia Kristeva has pointed out, reminds us of death and the dissolution of the body when it returns to dust. 'It is', as she says, 'death infecting life. ... something rejected from which one does not part' (Kristeva 1982: 4). In a sense, then, we could say that we hate our own bodies, which seem to betray us at every turn and we can understand the history of Western civilization as a series of attempts to escape from the body or at least to bring it under control to the extent that it serves us efficiently in our quest for rational solutions to the human condition. As long ago as 1944 Adorno and Horkheimer wrote that '[t]he feats of civilization are the product of sublimation, that acquired love-cum-hatred for the body and earth from which the rulers have separated all men. Medicine uses the mental reaction to the physical incarnation of man for productive purposes, while technology uses the reaction to the reification of nature as a whole' (Adorno and Horkheimer 1997 [1944]: 234).

The body, as thus understood in terms of its connection to the earth and nature as, in Heidegger's terms, 'standing-reserve' (see Chapter 1) becomes merely instrumental and, in effect, dead, lifeless and awaiting animation by the right mind, technique or political regime. But, if the body is understood as in autopoietic relationship to its environment then it becomes both less and more than mere matter or, as Steve Grand suggests:

> The matter is *not* the organism ... Atoms are form. They are self-organising, self-maintaining systems in flux. People are self-organising, self-maintaining systems in flux too ... Think of atoms as mere markers, pegging out ever-changing relationships. It is these relationships that make us. They extend into the body and outward into society. What counts is the rules that govern the changing relationships, not the stuff of which we are made. (Kember, 2003: 200)

CYBORG BODIES

One way of thinking this through in connection with how we might conceive of embodiment is in terms of Gilles Deleuze and Felix Guattari's Body without Organs (BwO). The BwO is an anti-Oedipal body in that it refuses the conformity to structures of desire demanded by the Freudian schema predicated on bodily organization. They refer to the ideal body, which corresponds to a suitably organized mind, as 'molar'. This is the body under the conditions of social order where it is 'overcoded' (Deleuze and Guattari 1987: 46) in terms of gender, species, class, race, sexuality and so forth. In other words, molarity describes the disciplined body, which conforms to ideas derived from Cartesian dualism (the separation of mind from body) Linnean taxonomy and social Darwinism, as well as Freudian psychoanalysis. This is the type of body required by liberal humanism because it lends itself to classification. The ideas that we have about our own bodies are limited and organized by the kinds of expertise which sustain the technocapitalist order. The joke that introduces William Gibson's *Neuromancer*, 'It's not like I'm using ... It's like my body's developed this massive drug deficiency' (Gibson 1986: 9) tropes on the way that 'using' refers to a practice condemned because it is understood as choosing to 'pollute' the body whereas 'deficiency' is understood as a lack which it is our business (or the business of the medical establishment) to put right. While they are opposed concepts, they are also (like all opposed concepts) inseparable because both refer to the way in which the molar body is maintained, both in discourse and in practice.

The Body without Organs, on the other hand, is 'the unformed, unorganized, nonstratified, or destratified body' (Deleuze & Guattari 1987: 49). The BwO forces us to question why we accept limits to how we understand our bodies, particularly when the kinds of science that produced the molar body in the first place have not been supplanted, but have certainly been challenged, by the worldviews of cybernetics and its associated disciplines and concepts like autopoiesis.

Deleuze and Guattari think of the body as creating 'assemblages' (Deleuze and Guattari 1987: 4), which is a term that evokes the way that it responds to the ever-changing physical stimuli of the environment in which it exists, the way in which it exchanges its substance with its environment (eating, defecating, sweating, having sex, ingesting bacteria, blood transfusions, being bitten by insects and so forth), as well as the way that, for instance, the immune system adjusts to antigens or the way that the body adjusts to tolerate certain substances. We can also think of assemblages in terms of the kinds of articulations suggested by actor network theory (see last chapter), in which a variety of actants have to be taken into account in understanding how the body is socially produced. Some of these actants will inevitably be what the discourse of the molar body elides, or the kinds of things that figure in Kristeva's formulation of the abject.

The concept of abjection, in fact, can help us to understand what Deleuze and Guattari mean when they speak about 'becomings' (Deleuze and Guattari 1987: 11). Abjection is a mode of desire in which we are attracted to, and fascinated by, the things that we exclude in order to establish the continent body. 'Becoming' describes this desire as an active principle, 'as a desire to escape bodily limitations' (Massumi, 1993: 94). It is a way of recognizing the autopoietic nature of bodies as a mode of existence in the world while, at the same time, understanding that the identities that we cling to with such tenacity are provisional and that in 'becoming-other' (Deleuze & Guattari 1987: 320–2) we produce ourselves, not by imitating or adopting other identities but in exploring the process of desiring them. In recognizing that they are

Case Study: Dead Bodies and Lively Machines

In Pedro Almodovar's 2002 film *Talk To Her*, a man called Benigro (Javier Cámara) is in love with a girl who is in a persistent vegetative state. Trained as a nurse, he caters to her every need, washing and massaging her body, cutting her hair and talking to her constantly while imagining her responses to his stories. Eventually, he is arrested for raping and impregnating her and, while in prison, he takes an overdose of drugs in the hope that he too will fall into a coma and join her in her state of undeath. Ironically, he misjudges the part of our self-description, we also recognize the way that our bodies are in fluid interaction with them. These bodily assemblages, like Donna Haraway's cyborg (see Chapter 2), are 'needy for connection' (Haraway, 1991: 151). Like the BwO, the cyborg is 'a condensed image of both imagination and material reality' (Haraway 1991: 150). Configured as cyborgs, we are no longer other to the machines that increasingly determine our self-understandings. As Haraway says, these machines have 'made thoroughly ambiguous the difference between natural and artificial, mind and body, self-developing and externally designed, and many other distinctions that used to apply to organisms and machines' (Haraway 1991: 151).

What Deleuze and Guattari and Haraway enable us to realize is that the tyranny of the machine (or technophobia) can only be experienced by bodies that conceive of themselves as separate, distinct and subject to significations which determine them. These culturally conditioned (mis)perceptions of ourselves are threatened by, for instance, the idea of what Slavoj Žižek refers to as the 'uncanny experience of the human mind directly integrated into a machine'. This, he says

> is not the vision of a future or of something new but the insight into something that is always-already going on, which was here from the very beginning since it is co-substantial with the symbolic order.[5] What changes is that, confronted with the direct materialization of the machine, its direct integration into the neuronal network, one can no longer sustain the illusion of the autonomy of personhood. (Žižek 2004: 18)

In other words, we are fighting a losing battle in our attempts to sustain the illusion of an essential body that exists prior to its insertion into social categories. The cyberpunk characters that take for granted the direct integration of the machine into the neuronal network are not a nightmare vision of the future but a representation of ourselves, right *now*. We may not yet be able to access computer networks through direct interface with our nervous systems but the difference is marginal. We have been cyborged by our own machines.

---

dose and dies while the girl revives during the birth of his dead child.

Although the film raises uncomfortable issues to do with the connection between male fantasies of feminine passivity, rape and death, it is, ultimately, a twenty-first century love story enacted under the sign of medical technology. A great deal of the action takes place in a specially equipped clinic where Benigro meets Marco (Dario Grandinetti), whose girlfriend Lydia (Rosario Flores) has been gored by a bull and is also in a coma, and instructs him in how to care for her. While Benigro is the hero who, at least in his fantasies, is sacrificed on the altar of love, Marco is the hapless lover who, equally devoted, is supplanted by his rival. Absent for most of the film, Lydia's previous lover emerges near the end to declare that they had reconciled just before her untimely accident.

The important point here is that these romantic fantasies are enacted over the bodies of women suspended in a state somewhere between life and death so that the film effectively makes a link between modern medical technologies and the technology of cinema itself, both of which have the power to foster fantasies of a romantic undeath which denies the decay of the body and preserves the illusion that death need not be final. What is significant about *Talk to Her* is that it questions our investment in these fantasies by demonstrating how they encode the desire for happy endings. Both Benigro and Marco are thwarted in their attempts to act out the resolution of a typical Hollywood love story where the man gets to marry the girl once he has proved his dedication through romantic gestures and attention to her concerns. The fact that the two women are in comas and sustained by machines, enables these fantasies, so that the film makes the link between technological undeath and the fantasy of human perfectibility – the ultimate happy ending.

While cinema has always had the power to preserve dead stars in the larger than life format of the big screen, more recently the technology has evolved to the point where the barrier between live and dead 'performances' has become very flimsy indeed. The following is from a review of *Sinatra at the Palladium* on Theatre.com:

Fifty-six years after Sinatra made his European debut at the London Palladium--and nearly eight years since his death--Ol' Blue Eyes has returned to the same theatre and thrillingly lives again. He proves that, whether dead or alive, his legacy will endure forever; and this frequently phenomenal show comes close to transporting us right back into the heart and art of the man.

Another Web site gives thanks to 'advances in digital technology and film donated by the Sinatra family' enabling Frank to 'once again do what he does best – entertain'.[6] While it may be argued that Frank himself can, in fact, do nothing of the sort, the star of these shows is not Sinatra but the technology that allows us the illusion that he 'lives again'. In effect, they enact the ultimate promise of the technological sublime; that the machine is, indeed, our salvation.

Hence, the hope invested in cryonic suspension and other forms of 'undeath' that depend, ultimately, upon taking for granted that 'Moore's Law',[7] the observation that computing power doubles every two years, will continue to hold (and, of course, that no untimely cataclysm will wipe out the human race altogether). Nick Bostrom, Professor of Philosophy at Oxford University and dedicated transhumanist refers to what he calls 'the singularity' (Bostrom 2005: 2). This is the prediction that there will come a point where the development of artificial intelligence, the perfection of the technique of uploading the human brain into a supercomputer and the perfection of nanotechnology will, singly or in tandem, push the human race into a new mode of existence in which current social structures, laws and moral values will no longer be relevant. The task of philosophy, for Bostrom and his associates in the World Transhumanist Association, is to prepare for likelihood of this event and to 'create forums where people can rationally debate what needs to be done, and a social order where responsible decisions can be implemented' (Bostrom 2005: 15).

According to Bostrom, the term 'transhumanism' was first introduced by the distinguished biologist and brother of Aldous, Julian Huxley in his book *Religion Without Revelation* (1927). He refers to transhumanism as a 'belief', having to do with 'man remaining man, but transcending himself, by realizing new possibilities of and for his human nature' (Bostrom, 2005: 5). For contemporary transhumanists, transcendence tends to be understood in terms of preserving individuality while either arresting the decay of the body or doing away with it altogether. In any case, the prime concern seems to be with eluding, evading or displacing the inevitability of death while preserving the idea of individuality.

As James J. Hughes says in his introduction to a speculative paper on 'The Future of Death':

[t]echnology is problematizing death ... Until the advent of the respirator, the cessation of spontaneous breathing immediately led to the cessation of circulation and unrecoverable brain damage. Since the 1960s we have continually expanded the gray areas between life and death, stabilizing one process after another in the previously inexorable path from life to dust. (Hughes 2001: 3)

Ultimately, Hughes predicts, '[t]he ability to repair brain damage, and even brain death, will spur a re-definition of the end of life' (2001: 5). The problem is that this redefinition will have to be adjusted continually in order to account for subsequent advances in medical technologies. Already, laws that determine brain death vary from country to country and across the US, and the right to determine one's time of death in the event of serious illness is a subject of critical debate. Consequently, the end of life is increasingly understood in terms of the disconnection of the body from a machine. Medication once only legally employed as an antidote to death is now often employed in assisted suicide.

Of course, techniques for prolonging life and maintaining the body in a state of undeath are only available to people in the developed West and, even then, often only to those with sufficient medical insurance. Death is therefore an aspect of consumption, as evidenced, in particular, by the debates around cryonic suspension; the technique of freezing the body at the point of death with the hope of reanimation into a future world with more advanced technologies for curing disease. Currently, the Alcor Life Extension Foundation requires members to pay an annual fee of $398 and to take out life insurance to fund suspension to the value of $150,000 for whole body suspension and $80,000 for neurosuspension (head only). Non-members requiring emergency suspension are charged $25,000. Alcor's claim that '[f]or a young person, the lifetime cost of cryonics is no greater than that of smoking, cable TV, regular eating out, or even a daily cup of coffee'[8] confirms the fact that life extension is now part of the panoply of consumer 'choices', which are marketed on the basis of neoliberal anxieties about the body. For those interpellated by the discourse of health and efficiency, in which the maintenance of the body is the mark of civic responsibility, to die is, in effect, to fail. In a culture in which ageing is anathema and nonconformist bodies are required to submit to the rigours of diet and exercise in order not to be marked as subversive and unruly it is no surprise that the ability to purchase a form of undeath attains status in the power hierarchy as a mark of fiscal and cultural success. Suspension is, in fact, legitimated by the technocapitalist world order on several counts. Firstly, as a speculative investment attuned to the gambling ethic inherent in stock speculation and the futures market. Secondly, as an indication of confidence in, and thus legitimation of, the ascendancy of scientific and technical expertise. And, thirdly, as a demonstration of belief in the continued ontological security and integrity of the individual human being.

Equally, it can be understood as legitimated by the consumerist ethic that has increasingly replaced the older, paternalistic model of medicine in which the hegemony of medical expertise ensured that doctors always 'knew best'. As Megan Stern writes

In recent years ... patients have become consumers of health care with contractual relationships to service providers. In the new order consumers' rights over their bodies and the bodies of their relatives are paramount. Furthermore, as state paternalism has diminished, health-care systems place increasing responsibility on individuals for maintaining their own health. Health, in other words, is less a matter of social welfare and more a matter of individual choice, self-awareness and responsibility. (Stern 2003b: 4)

What this means is that choices are governed, not only by cost effectiveness and prestige but by how they confirm ideals of self identity. Consequently, in order for cryonics to be marketed as a viable investment, consumers must be convinced that the technique can not only arrest death but can ensure that, upon revival, the integrity of the individual will not be compromised.

For instance, Max More, cofounder and Chairman of the Extropy Institute, understands 'dead' as a contingent term, opposed to the finality of 'death', which he uses to distinguish a state of the body that is irreversible under any circumstances. 'Dead' refers to the condition of a body under existing medico-technological conditions where it would necessarily progress to 'death' without intervention because the technology is not available to arrest the process. More (1995: 34, his emphasis) proposes a 'third term ... *deanimate*' to refer to 'patients' whose progress from dead to death has been arrested by cryonic suspension or another form of suspended animation. These patients are not 'alive' because they cannot (yet) be restored to full function but neither are they 'dead' because, despite the failure of neocortical function, disintegration has not yet occurred. As far as Alcor is concerned, a preserved brain is like a computer that is disconnected from the electricity supply or, perhaps a better analogy, a computer that has ceased to function but about which someone must make the decision whether to call in a technical expert and get it working again or destroy it and get a new one. Cryonic suspension is a bit like waiting for the right technical expert to come along. More makes it very clear that

Alcor understands a 'person' as inhering in what he calls 'identity-critical information'. 'Persons', he asserts, 'can continue to exist despite being neocortically dead.' In what he calls 'Informational Continuity', '[p]hysical structure may be destroyed, but all the information necessary potentially to allow reconstruction of the brain (or other consciousness-support structure) and thus restoration of its function persists' (More 1994: 31). 'We might say', he concludes, 'that we are software and not hardware; the psychological relations that are me are currently instantiated in *this* neocortex, but I am not *essentially* this neocortex nor even (more controversially) any neocortex' (More 1995: 34).

More thus effectively produces an understanding of human being in which the mind is understood, not only by analogy with computers but as translateable into a form that is meaningful in terms of information processing. The brain, for More, can be replaced with an 'other consciousness-support structure' because the structure of the brain is, itself, translateable into information. This view accords with the informational paradigm produced by ventures like the Human Genome Project as well as suggesting that a coherent and localizable 'self' can be abstracted from the structure of the brain and retained in the form of code.

But cryonic preservation does not guarantee against injury to the supposed organ of consciousness. James Hughes, in fact, goes so far as to consider the possibility that 'reanimated' people may have to be accorded the status of 'a successor or relative of the deceased, but not the same person' (Hughes 2001: 16) in cases where severe brain injury means 'we will be faced with the meaning of putting back together a living person who has lost all identity-critical information' (Hughes 2001). He predicts that '[t]echnology will eventually develop the capacity to translate human thought into alternative media ... Full nano-replication of the mental process opens the possibility of identity cloning, distributing one's identity over multiple platforms, sharing of mental components with others, and the merging of several individuals into one identity' (Hughes 2001: 17).

Contemplating damage to the brain during the retrieval of identity-critical information, More suggests uploading into 'an appropriately-configured parallel-processing computer constructed according to the information gained from the destructive scanning of [a] brain' (More 1994: 35). We are left to wonder why anyone should bother, considering that such a powerful computer may, conceivably, pass the Turing Test[9] with or without the upload of a human brain and thus be self-aware and, presumably, subject to full rights under the law and a 'person' in its own right. Similarly, if a consciousness is revived and can only legally be considered to be a near relative of the dead person, why would anyone invest in their own continuity rather than in the futures of their children or other near kin?

But continuity, of course, is the point. The concept of 'identity-critical information' not only abstracts the mind from the body but does so in a way that makes the 'trans' human intelligible in terms of religious notions of transcendence in which the body returns to dust while the mind or soul continues into eternity. It also accords with various versions of the afterlife in which the individual is 'saved' but, in this case, salvation is the reward for wise investment rather than an exemplary moral life. Despite Hughes' claim that 'once some individuals begin to abandon individuality for new forms of collective identity then the edifice of Western ethical thought since the Enlightenment will be in crisis', he is making his claim within the context of transhumanism which he understands as a drive 'to complete the project of the Enlightenment, the shift to a consciousness-based standard of law and ethics' (Hughes 2001: 19). In other words, he agrees with Max More in privileging consciousness as the determinant of humanity. This is a position supported by Nick Bostrom's 'Transhumanist Declaration', which advocates the moral right of 'those who so wish to use technology to extend their mental and physical ... capacities and to improve their control over their own lives.' 'We seek', it states, 'personal growth beyond our current biological limitations'. This quest for

personal transcendence through technology can be read through a social Darwinist ethic that understands the purpose of human reason to be the direction of our own evolution.

Nineteenth-century social Darwinism interpreted evolutionary theory as a justification for *laissez faire* ideals. Accordingly, 'the surivival of the fittest' was interpreted as a legitimation of the emerging capitalist economy, with natural selection supposedly favouring the 'captains of industry'. In this interpretation, power would naturally accrue to monied families who instructed their children correctly in the management and maintenance of wealth, progress being commensurate with economic prudence and privileging those who engaged all their energies in the competitive process. In the words of William Graham Sumner, a leading proponent of this system of thought, 'millionaires are a product of natural selection, acting on the whole body of men to pick out those who can meet the requirements of certain work to be done' (Hofstadter 1959: 58). This idea was supported by the assumption that natural selection naturally tends towards progress, despite the fact that, as Peter Bowler reminds us 'in a truly Darwinian universe there [is] no guarantee of progress' (Bowler 1984: 209). Nevertheless, the operation of progress was claimed to be apparent in the distinction between the less technologically advanced and socially sophisticated races and the so called 'civilized' and 'superior' white, industrialized races. Bowler reports that it was 'even suggested that women represented a stage of growth lower than that of men' (Bowler 1984: 286).

The transhumanist concept of 'personal growth' can thus be read as encoding similar assumptions about progress and entitlement. 'Cryonauts' are self-selecting individuals who understand the body as a 'limitation' that can be overcome by superior purchasing power; they are Balsamo's 'disappearing bodies' who claim their right to what they conceive of as immortality at the expense of, not only those labouring bodies who are involved in the maintenance and production of the equipment but also, by implication, those who, by choice or circumstance, remain fettered to the flesh. Ultimately, they presuppose the primacy of the mind with all that that implies, not only for the status of women and minorities but also in terms of technocratic assumptions in which faith is invested in science as the guarantor of the future.

Transhumanists are, in fact, committed to a future in which technological transcendence will ultimately produce a new human species. According to Nick Bostrom (2005: 202) 'Ultimately, it is possible that [technological] enhancements may make us, or our descendants, "posthuman", beings who may have indefinite health-spans, much greater intellectual faculties than any current human being — and perhaps entirely new sensibilities or modalities.'

Bostrom takes several things for granted here. Notwithstanding the assumption that science will provide for a future of such possibilities there is also the much more problematic assumption that 'human' is a condition or state of being that is universally understood and recognizable such that the state of being 'posthuman' will be equally distinguishable.

We already have longer life spans than our predecessors and conceive of ourselves as having greater intellectual faculties but this judgement needs to be understood in the context of the progressive ethic that pervades contemporary Western culture. Bostrom inherits from Enlightenment humanism a linear and progressive concept of evolution measured in terms of consciousness and control; what Donna J. Haraway calls 'C³I, command-control-communication-intelligence' (Haraway 1991: 150), a formula that determines the tactics of twenty-first century military planners as well as neatly encapsulating the dream of perfect control of the unruly human organism through rational future planning that cryonics seems to promise.

But, as I have demonstrated, 'human' has only ever been a retrospective category, marked out through signification and determined on the basis of difference. In other words, we only know that we are human because we keep close at hand significant others that

we have labelled 'other than' human; animals, machines and the inorganic, as well as, historically, slaves, women and, perhaps most significantly for my current discussion, the corpse.

In Julia Kristeva's theory of abjection, the coherence of the modern subject is produced by the continued expulsion from consciousness of those things that cause revulsion. This includes the waste products of the body, culturally proscribed foodstuffs, sexual behaviours that have been deemed 'perverse' and, almost universally, dead bodies. We constantly reconfirm what is 'I' by bringing close to us and then rejecting all that has been deemed 'Not-I'. Our love of horror films is testament to our fascination with the abject and our need for reconfirmation by confining it to, in the case of cinema, a technologically produced fantasy or virtual world controlled by culturally sanctioned rituals.

Discussing Gunther von Hagen's 'Body Worlds' exhibition of 'plastinated' dissected corpses, first staged in 1996, Megan Stern points out that 'Real, decaying corpses are messy and smelly, qualities which play a crucial role in rendering the corpse taboo, the destabilizing abject that must be made safe through rituals of purification and detachment. Plastination arguably constitutes just such a ritual, so that instead of shocking visitors by confronting them with abject corpses, "Body Worlds" renders these corpses safe, unthreatening' (Stern 2003b: 3).

Equally, cryonic preservation freezes (in this case, literally) the body at the moment before death and before the putrefaction, which must ultimately follow, renders the corpse unrecognizable, abject and reminiscent of the instability of bodily boundaries. It is not so much perhaps the hope of revival that appeals to cryonauts but the same impulse that motivates visitors to Von Hagen's exhibition to donate their own bodies for future plastination. As Stern tells us, '[i]n the comments of many donors, the avoidance of physical decay is prominent among the reasons given for registering as a donor. "Body Worlds" is, quite literally, a consumer heaven' (Stern 2003b: 3).

It should perhaps, then, come as no surprise that the spectacle of plastination and the technique of cryo-preservation are offered for consumption at a time when the types of technological interventions that make both procedures possible threaten the stability of the human subject. As Rosi Braidotti suggests, '[t]he same post-industrial culture that is undergoing such transformations of the practices, the social status and the representation of subjectivity is also simultaneously in the grip of a techno-teratological imaginary. That is to say it simultaneously fears and desires the machine-like self/other' (Braidotti 2002: 233).

But it is also possible to argue that the techno-teratological imaginary has always played a part in the way that we define ourselves. In the early nineteenth century, Dr Frankenstein's lumbering monster was testament to the fear produced by the possibilities of technological intervention in 'natural' processes but, unlike his more recent cinematic reincarnations, Mary Shelley's original creation was, in many ways, simply misunderstood. It is only when he is continually rejected because of his deformed appearance that he becomes the murderous archetype for which he is mythologized.

It is possible that we have similarly misrecognized ourselves in the drive to substantiate a version of the human that accords with the ideals of abstract individualism; ideals only ever attainable within the purview of a minority of mostly white, middle-class heterosexual males. Donna Haraway's cyborg and Deleuze and Guattari's BwO are techno-teratological constructions that, while arising from within postindustrial culture, nevertheless are only fully intelligible within the terms that Bernard Stiegler proposes; that is, that we are always already posthuman – in Haraway's words, 'theorized and fabricated hybrids of machine and organism' (Haraway 1991: 150). In light of this it is worth considering that the more urgent task would be to develop a politics of the body that attends to the fluid and changeable aspects of the embodied subjects that we already are, rather than deferring responsibility to future generations while attempting to shore up the fiction of a ghostly consciousness awaiting transplant into a more efficient machine. While technocapitalism requires the fantasy of cheating death by the application of technological expertise it equally requires that the life that is preserved conforms to pre-established ideas about what counts as a viable individual. Ironically, that same expertise is forcing us to confront the fact that the terms under which we distinguish ourselves as such are challenged by the machines that it is engaged in producing.

CHAPTER SUMMARY

- In contemporary culture, bodies are 'disciplined' in accordance with ideas of appropriate health and fitness as well as gender, race and sexuality.
- Information technologies, applied to understanding, visualizing and manipulating the human body have problematized the distinction between 'us', other species and machines.
- The theory of cybernetics positions the body as both produced *by* and the producer *of* the environment in which it exists.
- Donna Haraway's cyborg and Deleuze and Guattari's BwO (Body without Organs) are theoretical constructs which enable us to think through the politics of contemporary bodies.

5 TECHNOSPACES

This chapter is really a continuation of the last, in that what is constantly implied in any discussion of the body is its configuration in terms of the space that it inhabits, traverses or occupies. Deleuze and Guattari's BwO, for instance, is a body conceived in terms of its deterritorializations and reterritorializations. While the molar body, the organism, colonizes and fixes space, the BwO is committed to destructuring the territory of fixed organic hierarchies. In other words, we cannot think through the implications of specific forms of embodiment without paying attention to the territoriality that is the condition of their existence.

In simple terms we need to ask questions like: what is the significance of the location of bodies in space? What are the implications of our habituation to specific spaces and places? What role does the technological imaginary play in our under-standing of how space is defined and, perhaps most significantly for the concerns of this book, how do successive new technologies construct and reconstruct our notions of space? How do we conceive of spatiality in terms of technology and how do notions of how space is thus understood effect our social relationships?

In Ridley Scott's celebrated film *Blade Runner* (1982/92), floating satellites advertising life in the 'off world' colonies describe a new frontier, already partially conquered by 'genetically engineered replicants developed specially for your needs'. What becomes clear is that the promise of a 'new life' for the inhabitants of Earth conceals a bloody colonization battle while, increasingly, the home world is becoming a ghetto for the poor, the medically unfit and employees of the Tyrell Corporation, which dominates the industry that produces the replicants. Similarly, in Gibson's *Neuromancer* (1983), the Villa Straylight, home of the decadent and corrupt Tessier-Ashpool dynasty is constructed as part of an orbiting space station, dedicated to consumerism and gambling. Thus, the cyberpunk imaginary, indebted to the spatial organization of hierarchy in Lang's *Metropolis* (see Chapter 1, this volume), extrapolates a future in which privilege buys the right to emigrate to outer space while the dregs of humanity are left clinging to the surface of a dying Earth.

THE RIGHT STUFF

To date, no one has been to the moon since 1972 but, on 14 January 2004, the American President, George W. Bush, announced his intention to call upon Congress to 'to increase NASA's budget by roughly a billion dollars, spread out over the next five years', to enable, not only a return to the Moon but 'to take the next steps of space exploration: human missions to Mars and to worlds beyond'.[1] Evoking the spirit of Lewis and Clark,[2] the President told his audience, '[w]e have undertaken space travel because the desire to explore and understand is part of our character … Mankind is drawn to the heavens for the same reason we were once drawn into unknown lands and across the open sea. We choose to explore space because doing so improves our lives, and lifts our national spirit.'

Space travel is thus associated, in American consciousness, with the territorial expansion of the US in the early nineteenth century; the so-called 'Age of Manifest Destiny' when the belief that American ideals of social democracy, liberty and progress should be spread to benefit the world drove the quest to annexe and explore the remaining continent and, by implication, beyond. The idea of travel into outer space consequently encodes a confirmation of the value of liberal humanist ideals and the myth of progress as exemplified by the awe inspiring technology of space flight, despite the fact that, following the Colombia disaster in February 2003,[3] voices were raised in opposition to the continuation of manned space exploration.

The *Telegraph* suggested that human space exploration is 'little more than a dangerous form of entertainment, with almost no scientific or economic benefit'[4] and an April edition of *Pravda*, contemplating the possibility of manned flight to Mars, concluded that 'it is much more reasonable to pursue [the] scientific goals of space exploration with the help of unmanned spacecraft; this became clear back in the 1970s'.[5] However, in the same month, Chris Flynn, MD, a NASA flight surgeon and chief of psychiatry at the Johnson Space Center in Houston, in an interview with Michael Jonathan Grinfeld for *Psychiatric Times*, offered the opinion that '[e]liminating manned space flight would mean the disappearance of heroic icons who symbolize the best human traits'.[6]

There is, of course, a high level of assumption in this statement, which turns on the belief that 'the best human traits' are universally understood and recognized. But, over and above this, what Flynn is expressing is a continued faith in the myth of the 'right stuff' (Wolfe 2005 [1979]), an idea that Tom Wolfe discovered in the culture of NASA and which he discusses in his book of the same name which describes the way in which astronauts were selected for the *Mercury* programme. As the blurb on the back cover of the 2005 Vintage edition puts it, the right stuff is 'the quality beyond bravery, beyond courage'. The astronaut is cast as the quintessential modern human.

Those proven as having the right stuff could be shown to be not only resourceful and brave but able to push technology beyond its known limits. They demonstrated implicit faith in science and technology to the extent that they were willing to risk their lives, over and over again and thus were thought to be worthy pioneers of what many believed to be the next stage of human evolution. Like the cryonauts, waiting in suspended animation for human ingenuity to improve their chances of claiming the future (see case study, Chapter 4), so astronauts are invested with the hope of salvation through technology. No matter that astronauts are, in most cases, no more than what Dale Carter (1988: 161) refers to as 'pre-packed human cannonballs'. It is the human presence in outer space that is important if it is to function as 'the final frontier'.

OUTER SPACE AND THE WILDERNESS

The impetus to carry human beings beyond the confines of Earth emerged out of the ideological struggles of the Cold War in which the US and the USSR competed for the strategic achievement of being the first to land a human being on the Moon. Neil Armstrong's 'one small step for man' was significant in terms of Cold War politics, not only because the US won the 'race' but because it demonstrated the triumph of liberal democracy over totalitarian socialism in terms of technological achievement. Although the USSR had been the first to launch a satellite into orbit (*Sputnik*, 1957) and sent a dog (Laika) into space in the same year, the significance of *Apollo 11* (1969) is that it effectively extended the territory over which humanity could, theoretically, claim dominion.

The concept of the 'right stuff' is thus deeply imbued with a sense of entitlement. In their association with the early pioneers of the American West, astronauts signify as exemplars of the progressive spirit, which, in its association with the concept of manifest destiny, marks outer space as a territory that those exhibiting 'the best human traits' can claim for themselves. They encode the promise of the 'new life' in the 'off world colonies' that makes sense of the burning, polluted and rain drenched future city of Los Angeles in *Blade Runner*. Recalling the spirit of social Darwinism (see Chapter 2) there is a strong suggestion that those who conform to the ideals of neoliberal entrepreneurialism will earn the chance to leave the depleted Earth behind and take up residence in a new tax haven beyond the stars. As David J. Gunkel points out, '[t]he new world is always posited as a world of riches waiting to be exploited. The frontiers of the American West and Alaska were organized and articulated around the concept of gold and the gold rush. Justifications for the American space program, which set out to explore the "final frontier," were often couched in the discourse of wealth' (Gunkel 2001: 38).

Thus outer space is produced, in the popular imagination, as a territory on which the inequalities of wealth and social class can be reproduced, re-enacted and justified.[7]

Equally, like the promise of the wilderness that constructed previously unexplored territory as a space in which the hero would discover *himself*, so outer space promises an escape from the restraints of civilization and the world of everyday life. '"[T]he American myth"', writes Frederic I. Carpenter, 'has sometimes imagined an innocent Adam before the fall, and sometimes a fallen Adam seeking to regain a wise innocence (or "simplicity") in a new, industrial America' (Carpenter 1959: 602). Needless to say, the American Adam, in all his ambiguity, has no need of Eve, or must consciously reject her, and the wilderness thus promises escape from the domesticating power of women as an essential condition of innocence regained. The wilderness embodies 'the essential quality of America'. It offers itself to the individual 'as the medium on which he may inscribe, unhindered, his own destiny and his own nature', free from 'the encroaching, constricting, destroying society' (Baym 1986: 72). 'Most Americans', writes Carpenter, 'have idealized the wild as an antidote to excessive civilization, as a figurative mountain-top from which man can gain perspective on civilized society, and perhaps as a point of leverage from which he can hope to move it' (Carpenter 1959: 605). It is thus possible to read outer space in terms of a similar idealization; a new territory in which the 'right stuff' can prove their worth and, looking down on the Earth, can proclaim its beauty and confirm its potential. As Marina Benjamin writes

> [f]rom *Apollo 8* onwards, it became increasingly clear that what most preoccupied astronauts was not the Moon, but the Earth … For the first time mankind was able to stand outside of itself and turn a cold eye on its innermost contradictions. As purveyors of the new knowledge, the astronauts were aggrandised by the act of travelling upwards, their thoughts at once elevated and rarefied. They'd become privy to the vantage point of God. (Benjamin 2003: 57)

Like the unsettled wilderness, outer space offers the assurance 'that individuals come before society, that they exist in some meaningful sense prior to, and apart from, societies in which they happen to find themselves' (Baym, 1986: 71). The astronaut is the indicative confirmation of abstract individuation, what Donna Haraway (1991: 151) has referred to as 'an ultimate self untied at last from all dependency, a man in space.'

The significance of both the wilderness and outer space is that they are conceived of as *empty* and thus ripe for colonization and outer space has the further advantage of not, as yet, producing any prior inhabitants, other than in our imaginations. The many species of aliens that crowd fictional extraterrestrial space are projections of otherness that serve to reflect our culturally determined self-descriptions. *Star*

Trek's 'prime directive', for instance, which forbids contact with alien civilizations considered 'primitive' because they have not yet attained 'warp' capability (the ability to travel faster than light), entails the assumption that cultural development is linear, progressive and technologically determined. With typical *Trek* paternalism, General Order number 1, 'the most prominent guiding principle of the United Federation of Planets', 'forbids any effort to improve or change in any way the natural course of such a society, even if that change is well-intentioned and kept totally secret … Starfleet allows scientific missions to investigate and move amongst pre-warp civilizations as long as no advanced technology is left behind, and there is no interference with events or no revelation of their identity.'[8] The assumption here is that technological and moral development are concomitant; that, in effect, the 'primitive' species are not ethically capable of making 'correct' decisions regarding the use of advanced technology, particularly, it is implied, weapons and space craft; that their ideology has not yet progressed to a full understanding of their place in the wider cosmos.

This is revealing in light of the space race, which was primarily a race to prove technological superiority but what was also implied, when *Apollo 11* planted the American flag on the moon, was the triumph of liberal democracy and its attendant ideological structuring of nation and personhood, as well as military supremacy. It proved, in effect, the moral and ethical superiority of the winning side; the side with the wealth and expertise sufficient to the task. Hence, George Bush's reference to 'national spirit' in his reinauguration of the space programme at a time when the initial fervour of support for the war in Iraq was beginning to give way to cynicism and dismay. Thus, outer space is constructed as a field on which culturally produced notions of supremacy can be enacted and confirmed. But, as Megan Stern has pointed out 'the only object man is finally capable of encountering in the technologically enframed universe is himself' (Stern 2000: 207). In other words, in the absence of any real aliens, the drive to conquer space is simply an expensive re-enactment of the scientific enterprise itself; the pursuit of truth and self-confirmation through domination of nature. Linking the spectacle of the rocket launch to David Nye's analysis of the 'American technological sublime', Stern suggests that '[t]he technological sublime creates a transition between the subject as embodied, North American individual to the subject as abstract, and of course, scientific.' 'Gazing down on a planet which appears untouched by human culture, the astronaut-subject sees the unseeable; the pre-historic, pre-human earth. He is timeless, bodiless, primordial; containing time and space within his all-encompassing gaze' (Stern 2000: 205).

This is what Donna Haraway (1991: 189) calls 'the god-trick of seeing everything from nowhere'; a 'conquering gaze from nowhere' that 'honed to perfection in the history of science tied to militarism, capitalism, colonialism, and male supremacy …

distance[s] the knowing subject from everybody and everything in the interests of unfettered power' (Haraway 1991: 188).

The astronaut, then, as heir to the dreams of American Adam is literally elevated beyond the figurative mountaintop and into a space which functions, like the wilderness, to confirm the prevailing ideology. In crude temporal terms, it is possible to claim that, as the wilderness was produced as a trope to justify colonial expansion in nineteenth-century America, so outer space was similarly produced by not only America, but much of the Western world in the twentieth century to legitimate progressive ideals and, in the particular case of the US, to reinvigorate the myth of manifest destiny that had withered since the closing of the frontier.

However, not long after the final *Apollo* mission in 1976, scepticism about the moon landings became, if not widespread, then certainly high profile. Fuelled, initially, by the publication of William Charles Kaysing's book *We Never Went to the Moon: America's Thirty Billion Dollar Swindle*, (1974) and Peter Hyams' film *Capricorn One* (1978) in which an organization not dissimilar to NASA fakes a Mars landing, the hoax accusations continue to this day (not helped by the fact that NASA recently admitted that they had mislaid 700 tapes of the original footage of *Apollo 11's* historic mission). The significance of these popular cultural productions, aside from exposing the political motivations behind the missions, is that they effectively cancelled the effect of the technological sublime by returning the entire enterprise to the level of the technological mundane: props, cameras, costumes and terrestrial broadcast technology.

Furthermore, as Stern points out, '[w]ith the thawing of the Cold War, NASA's motivation bec[ame] uncertain, the rhetoric through which it ha[d] enlisted public support and identification bec[ame] apparent and ostensibly timeless truths about the destiny of mankind gain[ed] a specific location, historically and geographically' (Stern 2000: 210).

In other words, in order for the myth to function, it is necessary for it to be seen as a project of benign world leadership, with astronauts as the vanguard of an evolutionary leap that would benefit the entire planet, rather than as the vain exploits of two nations involved in a historically unprecedented military standoff.

SIMULATED SPACE

In 1991, Istvan Csicsery-Ronay Jr edited an issue of the journal *Science Fiction Studies,* which featured an article by Jean Baudrillard in which he suggested that '[c]lassic SF was one of expanding universes: it found its calling in narratives of space exploration, coupled with more terrestrial forms of exploration and colonization indigenous to the 19th and 20th centuries' (Csicsery-Ronay 1991: 310). However when there is no more virgin ground left to the imagination, *when the map covers all the territory, something like the reality principle disappears.* The conquest of space constitutes, in this sense, an irreversible threshold which effects the loss of terrestrial coordinates and referentiality ... The conquest of space, following the conquest of the planet, promotes either a de-realizing of human space, or the reversion of it into a simulated hyperreality. (Csicsery-Ronay 1991: 311, his emphasis)

It is possible to argue, in fact, that this 'derealizing' of human space happened the moment that Yuri Gagarin, on 12 April 1961, became the first human to orbit the Earth or, in the case of the US, 5 May of the same year – the day on which Alan Shepard became the first American to journey into space. Indeed, conspiracy theories aside, and as *The Right Stuff* makes clear, space flight was always a *simulation* in the sense that, for everyone except the astronauts, it was an event that they had access to only through the media and which they experienced as passive observers who, nevertheless, were convinced that they were witnessing the expansion of the universe in classic SF terms. The astronaut was presented as American Adam, 'privy to the vantage point of God' and pioneer of a new freedom for the human race. It was the point at which much of Western civilization collectively ventured into the space only previously inhabited by the science fiction imagination, thus making the genre somewhat redundant. Utopias and their counterpart, dystopias, can only be imagined in spaces that either do not exist or that humans have not yet 'conquered' but the collective foray into outer space marked by the *Vostok* and *Mercury* projects effectively marked the point at which, as Csicsery-Ronay Jr (1991: 391) puts it, 'the Earth cease[d] to be a source of centrifugal expansion and bec[ame] the object of centripetal collapse.'

This is nowhere better explained than in Wolfe's description of Alan Shepard's 15-minute parabolic flight beyond the Earth's atmosphere.

Even if he had been ordered ... to broadcast to the American people a detailed description of precisely what it felt like to be the first American riding a rocket into space ... he could not possibly have expressed what he was feeling. For he was introducing the era of pre-created experience. His launching was an utterly novel event in American history, and yet he could feel none of its novelty. He could not feel 'the awesome power' of the rocket beneath him, as the broadcasters kept referring to it. He could only compare it to the hundreds of rides he had taken on the centrifuge at Johnsville. (Wolfe 2005 [1979]: 256)[9]

Shepard's precreated experience is not dissimilar to that of the Earthbound observers. Fostered in part by science fiction itself, in part by the technological sublime and in part by the continuing myth of American Adam, the pioneering spirit and the 'right stuff' as an idea perpetuated by the media, the 'reality' of Shepard's flight is a technologically determined construct that thrives on repetition and dissemination. Far from being a novelty, it is an experience that can be repeated and repeated through the medium of television. And each experience is pretty much the same as the last. So, in the same way that Shepard experienced his flight as merely a repetition of his experience in the flight *simulator*, so the rest of the US can re-experience the event, along with the *frisson* of emotional connection that they felt first time around. This is Baudrillard's 'simulated hyperreality' which, elsewhere, he calls 'the Perfect Crime' (Baudrillard 2000: 67); the Perfect Crime because there is no gap between the deception of the crime and 'what really happened' in which a good detective could operate to uncover the truth. The Perfect Crime, in fact, is undetectable as such and, therefore, could be said not to exist.

This is what Baudrillard wants to convey when he talks about the map covering all the territory. In 'The Precession of Simulacra', he introduces a story by Jorge Luis Borges in which a map of an Empire is so detailed, it ends up covering all the territory but, as the Empire decays, so the map is ruined until, eventually, a few shreds remain, 'still discernible in the deserts' (Baudrillard 1983: 1). Baudrillard inverts the story as an allegory for hyperreality, 'the generation by models of a real without origin or reality ... It is the real, and not the map, whose vestiges subsist here and there, in the deserts which are no longer those of the Empire, but our own' (Baudrillard 1983: 2).

SIMULACRA

For Baudrillard, the precession of simulacra is concomitant with the development of capitalism and his use of the word 'real', in this context, needs to be understood within the context of social relations and their connection to modes of production. At the beginning of his essay for *Science Fiction Studies*, he lists 'three orders of simulacra'. The first is 'natural, naturalistic simulacra: based on image, imitation and counterfeiting'. In this order, there is an acknowledgement of a real world, a world of 'nature in God's image' that can be copied but the copy will never substitute for what is real. This first order, Baudrillard (1983: 83) describes as 'the dominant scheme of the "classical" period, from the Renaissance to the industrial revolution'.

Baudrillard draws attention to baroque art and the use of stucco – a substance that could be moulded to imitate anything, 'velvet curtains, wooden corniches, charnel swelling of the flesh' (Baudrillard 1983: 88). Baroque draws attention to its own artifice and is connected to the Renaissance celebration of artistry as an expression of the divine in human creation. This is the period that ushers in a new cosmology, expressed in the use of perspective in painting, which, as Margaret Wertheim writes, 'encodes the position of the *viewing body* ... Unlike Gothic art, which aimed directly at the Christian soul, perspective gives us images specifically for the eye' (Wertheim 1999: 110–11, her emphasis). Perspective thus emphasized the centrality of the human subject and 'provided people with a powerful psychological experience of *extended physical space as a thing in itself* (Wertheim 1999: 115, her emphasis) in contradistinction to the medieval view in which 'Christians ... oriented themselves first and foremost by a spiritual compass rather than a physical one' (Wertheim 1999: 53). Hence, what begins to emerge during the Renaissance is a world picture in which human beings become 'the measure of all things' (Wertheim 1999: 132) and the rise of modern science, which promotes an understanding of the universe as accessible to human vision. The rise of the bourgeoisie and new forms of wealth consequently began to be reflected in architectural opulence. As Henri Lefebvre describes it 'façades were harmonized to create perspectives; entrances and exits, doors and windows, were subordinated to façades – and hence also to perspectives; streets and squares were arranged in concord with the public buildings and palaces of political leaders and institutions' (Lefebvre 1991 [1974]: 47). The ability to imitate the world in stucco and other substances is thus, for Baudrillard, 'aiming ... at the control of a pacified society, ground up into a synthetic deathless substance: an indestructible artefact that will guarantee an eternity of power' (Baudrillard 1983: 91).

His second order is 'productive, productionist simulacra: based on energy and force, materialized by the machine and the entire system of production'. This is the order concomitant with the system of mass production; with the exploitation of the worker under the terms of alienated labour. Essential to Marx's analysis of the social relations of production is that the workers labour under conditions that they would not tolerate if they were aware of their exploitation. Capitalist ideology, which promotes competition under the terms of abstract individualism, covers over the *real* relations of production and revolution is premised on the revelation of what the simulation of life, as well as the mass production of commodities, masks. The 'real' in this order is obscured by the simulation, rather than replaced by it.

The second order, Baudrillard tells us, is no longer concerned with imitation and finds its fullest representation in the figure of the robot which 'no longer interrogates appearance; its only truth is in its mechanical efficacy' (Baudrillard 1983: 94). The concern of first order simulacra with 'theatrical illusion' (Baudrillard 1983: 95) gives way to 'the hegemony of the robot, of the machine, and of dead work over living labour' (Baudrillard 1983: 96). And the workers, along with the commodities that they labour to produce 'become undefined simulacra one of the other' (Baudrillard 1983: 97). The architecture of this order is represented partly by Le Corbusier's 'radiant city' with its dream of rational planning and optimum efficiency, following the model of the industrial factory (see Chapter 1) but its actual manifestation is in suburban tract housing as immortalized in Malvina Reynolds' 1962 protest song *Little Boxes*, which recalls the 'clean backyards' of Ford's ideal workforce (Chapter 1), as well as the regimented blocks of state housing, like the 'tower blocks' of British council estates.

Baudrillard's third order is the order of 'simulation simulacra: based on information, the model, cybernetic play' (Baudrillard 1991: 309) in which, as Benjamin Woolley (1992: 198) describes it, 'the empire is now capable of constructing the real so that it fits in with the map'. This is the order that is, arguably, if not ushered in, then certainly marked by the advent of the space race and 'the institution of a model of universal gravitation, of satellisation, whose perfect embryo is the lunar module: a programmed microcosm, where *nothing can be left to chance*' (Baudrillard, 1983: 62, his emphasis). As Wolfe reports, when Alan Shepard, reaching the apex of his parabolic arc in the *Mercury* capsule, looked down on planet Earth, '*everything looked so small!* It had all been bigger and clearer in the ALFA trainer, when they flashed the still photos on the screen ... The real thing didn't measure up. It was *not realistic.*' Nevertheless, he was moved to comment on 'the beautiful view' (Wolfe 2005 [1979]: 261, his emphasis), not because it *was* necessarily more beautiful than the simulation but because the part that he had to play demanded it.

EVERYDAY SPACE

Understood in this way, the relationship between Baudrillard's three orders, successive technologies and what Henri Lefebvre refers to as 'the production of space' is undeniable. Like Baudrillard, Lefebvre is concerned with how successive stages of capitalist production produce our social reality but his emphasis on space is intended to demonstrate the relationship between concepts of space, the symbols that stand for particular ideologically determined understandings of space and space as it is used in everyday life. He thus differentiates between 'spatial practice, representations of space and representational spaces [which] contribute in different ways to the production of space according to their qualities and attributes, according to the society or mode of production in question, and according to the historical period' (Lefebvre 1991 [1974]: 46). What Lefebvre refers to as *spatial practice* is the 'close association ... between daily reality (daily routine) and urban reality (the routes and networks which link up the places set aside for work, 'private' life and leisure)' (Lefebvre 1991 [1974]: 38). In other words, the way that we negotiate space in our everyday lives that has repercussions at the level of social class, gender, race and sexuality. There are spaces, for instance, which are prohibited to women, not because they are designated for males only but because they are deemed 'unsafe' or are antithetical to femininity as it is constructed in a given culture.

Representations of space he associates with 'the space of scientists, planners, urbanists, technocratic subdividers and social engineers'. This is 'conceptual space' (Lefebvre 1991 [1974]: 38), 'shot through with a knowledge *(savoir)* – i.e., a mixture of understanding *(connaissance)* and ideology – which is always relative and in the process of change' (Lefebvre 1991 [1974]: 41). Representations of space find expression in architecture and urban planning which presupposes the body in both its corporeal and social aspects (see last chapter) and can be understood as both utopian and prescriptive. Hence, as Lefebvre points out, what Le Corbusier, for instance, was working towards was 'a technicist, scientific and intellectualized representation of space' (Lefebvre 1991 [1974]: 43).

Representational space is 'space as directly *lived* through its associated images and symbols' (Lefebvre 1991 [1974]: 39). This is the space with which art and psychoanalysis concern themselves. Tending to be a-historical it is, again, connected to sexuality, gender and race and is the space that is produced by, and which reflects, consciousness of the body and the way that it is spatialized, as well as religious and mythological concepts. Lefebvre refers to 'childhood memories, dreams, or uterine images and symbols (holes, passages, labyrinths) … [e]go, bed, bedroom, dwelling, house; or square, church, graveyard' (Lefebvre 1991 [1974]: 41–2).

It is important to understand that spatial practice, representations of space and representational space or what Lefebvre elsewhere refers to as the 'perceived-conceived-lived triad' (Lefebvre 1991 [1974]: 40) are interconnected and the way that we negotiate space on a daily basis; 'all subjects' according to Lefebvre, 'are situated in a space in which they must either recognize themselves or lose themselves' (Lefebvre 1991 [1974]: 35). But this recognition (and the associated loss) depends upon the way that the subject is located in space by successive modes of production. And, 'since … each mode of production has its own particular space, the shift from one mode to another must entail the production of a new space … every society produces a space, its own space' (Lefebvre 1991 [1974]: 46 and 53). 'Capitalism', according to Lefebvre, 'and neocapitalism have produced *abstract* space, which includes the "world of commodities", its "logic" and its worldwide strategies, as well as the power of money and that of the political state. This space is founded on the vast networks of banks, business centres and major productive entities, as also on motorways, airports and information lattices' (Lefebvre 1991 [1974]: 53, my emphasis).

ABSTRACT SPACE

Abstract space is thus *global* and can be seen to correspond, increasingly, with Baudrillard's space of the hyperreal. This is particularly evident in Lefebvre's example of the production of space in the contemporary mode of production, which is 'the transformation of the perimeter of the Mediterranean into a leisure-oriented space for industrialized Europe ... Economically and socially, architecturally and urbanistically, it has been subjected to a sort of neo-colonization.' As he points out, 'the use to which it has been put calls for "ecological" virtues such as an immediate access to sun and sea and a close juxtaposition of urban centres and temporary accommodation'. The Mediterranean, in this example, 'has attained a certain qualitative distinctiveness as compared with the major industrial agglomerations' in which it is set up in opposition to the stresses of the workplace and as a 'break' from daily life.

> If ... we were to accept this 'distinctiveness' at face value ... the waste and expense ... would appear as the endpoint of a temporal sequence starting in the workplace, in production-based space, and leading to the consumption of space, sun and sea, and of spontaneous or induced eroticism, in a great 'vacationland festival' ... The truth is that all this seemingly non-productive expense is planned with the greatest care: centralized, organized, heirarchized, symbolized and programmed to the *n*th degree, it serves the interests of the tour-operators, bankers and entrepreneurs of places such as London and Hamburg. (Lefebvre 1991[1974]: 58–9)

So, what Lefebvre is pointing out here is the way in which the Mediterranean is produced as a space of *leisure* and thus in opposition to work when, in fact, the obligatory yearly vacation (a non-productive space which is a sort of 'reward' for productive activity in the rest of the year) is actually more of the same. It is a controlled and hyperrealized space that feeds the forces of techno/neo-capitalism in that it promotes consumption, not of a 'real' space (and the reality of many of the spaces where we take vacations is, of course, an uncomfortable reminder of the exploitations of neo-capitalism) but of a space that, as Lefebvre says, is 'programmed' in a vast manipulation of representational spaces such as the sea which is connected to health, freedom and 'nature'.

Of course, to bring Lefebvre's argument up to date, we would have to go beyond the Mediterranean to the neocolonization of whole countries in the name of tourism and the gradual erosion of all spaces that previously represented fragments in Baudrillard's 'desert of the real'. And, with the Earth exhausted, outer space is soon to become the venue for the world's largest industry. Richard Branson's Virgin Galactic started test flying spacecraft based on Burt Rutan's SpaceShipOne in 2007 with the aim of offering the first commercial flights in 2008. Interestingly, the Web site informs us that 'the more that can be simulated beforehand, the better the real thing will be!'[10] a statement with which Alan Shepard would be unlikely to agree but that neatly encapsulates the way in which the postindustrial mode of production is driven by simulation technologies that structure experience *before it happens*. *'Nothing'*, to reiterate Baudrillard's observation, *'can be left to chance'*. Abstract space is thus the space of representational and informational technologies; television, cinema, satellites and, of course, computers, credited with the inauguration of a 'new' space, Gibson's 'consensual hallucination ... A graphic representation of data abstracted from the banks of every computer in the human system' (Gibson 1986: 67).

CYBERSPACE

'Cyberspace', according to the Progress and Freedom Foundation in 1994, 'is the latest American frontier.' '[W]e are entering new territory', declare the authors of 'A Magna Carta for the Knowledge Age', 'where there are as yet no rules – just as there were no rules on the American continent in 1620, or in the Northwest Territory in 1787.'[11] But, as David J. Gunkel points out 'the spatiality of cyberspace has been described and determined in accordance with a particular understanding ... Describing cyberspace through the words *frontier* and *new world* have had definite and often disturbing implications and consequences' (Gunkel 2001: 35 and 50). As he says, 'metaphors are always more than mere words. They are mechanisms of real social and political hegemony that have the capacity to determine the current and future shape of what they seem merely to designate' (Gunkel 2001: 51).

Thus cyberspace, like outer space, is structured in accordance with principles of entitlement and colonialism. Indeed, the corporations that increasingly dominate cyberspace are the same that dominate *world* space and that own the satellites that crowd outer space. Virgin Galactic, for instance, is part of a business empire that controls a large part of the British railway network as well as worldwide air travel, mobile communications, entertainment (predominately music and videogames), Internet access and tourism. Furthermore, the relatively low cost of access to cyberspace in the developed West is due to the deregulation of world markets, allowing the manufacture of machine parts to be distributed to corners of the world where labour is cheap and tax break incentives are offered to European and American multinationals, often by corrupt governments and thus at the expense of indigenous populations. Furthermore, as Ziauddian Sardar writes, '[c]yberspace is particularly geared towards the erasure of all non-Western histories. Once a culture has been 'stored' and 'preserved' in digital forms, opened up to anybody who wants to explore it from the comfort of their armchair, then it becomes more real than the real thing. Who needs the arcane and esoteric real thing anyway?' (Sardar 1996: 19).

Gunkel also points out that '[c]yberspace readily receives the X-Y-Z of the Cartesian coordinate system. It accepts the inscription and delimitation of the three-dimensional grid. It is, therefore, subject to the modern logic of space and spatiality' (Gunkel 2001: 36). What he is describing here is the Western mathematical logic of space, first described by Descartes in the seventeenth century when, lying in bed during an illness, he traced the progress of a fly across a tiled ceiling and developed a system for determining the location of a point in space by plotting a graph in three dimensions. Using the coordinates X, Y and Z, the same point in space can be expressed as an equation. Hence, a mapping of territory is enabled via a spatial scheme that responds to precision and calculability and can be used to direct the movement of troops as well as ordering space in terms of the rules of linear perspective.

The consequences of this are, interestingly, explored in *Star Trek: Voyager* where a Federation ship has been flung into 'uncharted' territory. Of course, the 'Delta Quadrant' is only 'uncharted' from the perspective of Starfleet. Dramatic tension derives from *Voyager's* attempts to negotiate 'safe passage' in a field distorted by the spatial logics of diverse other species. However, the premise of the series is that Captain Janeway is motivated to return her crew 'home', no matter the odds and the fact that it could take as long as 75 years. As Stern points out, 'Janeway's *Voyager*, unlike Picard's *Enterprise*, is not the benign arm of the Federation, keeping order within the known universe, but a piece of the Federation flung into the unknown where it attempts to reconstitute the familiar around itself'. Thus, in her 'unswerving focus on reaching home … Janeway insists upon Federation protocol, echoing the ways in which colonial centres were realised as such through their idealised reconstruction in the colonies.' Furthermore, Janeway insists that Starfleet's mission to explore 'where no-one has gone before' should be maintained so that, as the series proceeds, the practice of 'stellar cartography' increasingly features as a plot device as the Delta Quadrant gradually succumbs to the imposition of the Cartesian grid. Hence, 'just as England, it could be argued, was invented in nineteenth-century India, so the Federation is invented as an absent, if vital, centre in *Voyager*' (Stern 2003a: 101).

In similar terms, the consensual hallucination of cyberspace only achieves consent in terms of the same hegemonic structuring of space as applied to the wilderness and outer space and, like the impetus to explore outer space, has its genesis and initial conceptualization in technologies first developed for military training and communications.

> The dress rehearsal for the smart bombs that so consistently missed their targets in the [First] Gulf War was carried out in cyberspace … The Internet was developed as a foolproof mode of communication in case of a nuclear war and

expanded as a computer network that linked university research centres with the defence departments. Virtual reality (VR) first emerged as a safe and inexpensive way of training pilots to fly advanced military planes. (Sardar, 1996: 20)

Unsurprisingly, General Norman Schwartzkopf happily referred to the 1990–1 Gulf War (Operation Desert Storm) as 'the first Nintendo War' while the same application of technologies led Baudrillard (1995: 61) to claim that the Gulf War 'did not take place'.

VIRTUAL WAR

Baudrillard, in fact, wrote three essays examining the construction of hyperreal war through military and domestic communications technologies. The first, 'The Gulf War will not take place' was published in January 1991, just before the commencement of hostilities. 'The Gulf War: is it really taking place?' was written (and part of it published) during the events of February 1991 with 'The Gulf War did not take place' following in March, after hostilities had ceased. Of course, in one sense the Gulf War emphatically *did* take place as testified by the very real loss of life but Baudrillard's point is that the first Nintendo war was not a war as we had previously understood it but a *simulation* of war, meticulously planned in advance and without any real encounters other than the edited highlights designed for broadcast and in which 'the enemy only appears as a computerised target' (Baudrillard 1995: 62).

In the final essay, he compares the war to the kind of deception perpetrated by the space agency in *Capricorn One*. 'Just as wealth', he writes, 'is no longer measured by the ostentation of wealth but by the secret circulation of speculative capital, so war is not measured by being waged but by its speculative unfolding in an abstract, electronic and informational space, the same space in which capital moves' (Baudrillard 1995: 56). Thus, 'Iraq is ... rebuilt even before it has been destroyed' (Baudrillard 1995: 52). In other words, virtual war serves no interests other than those of capital, which moves in to colonize the defeated territory, first with the technology of virtual war and, finally, with the technology of 'reconstruction'; with fat contracts awarded to multinational companies. In Baudrillard's argument war, in fact, has the same effect as tourism in that it delivers up a spectacular virtualization of territory to be consumed by the West and, like tourism, serves the interests of 'bankers and entrepreneurs' and, of course, the US defence industry that 'wants a return on its investment by finding other uses for the technology it originally developed'. Hence, as J.C. Herz in her book *Joystick Nation* points out, 'By the age of twenty, most military personnel have been playing videogames for a dozen years ... Today's joystick jockeys, as Ronald Reagan liked to argue, are tomorrow's high-tech soldiers' (Herz 1997: 198). Similarly, Mary Fuller and Henry Jenkins find echoes of the neocolonialism of postindustrial abstract space even in such apparently innocuous games as *Super Mario Brothers* and find significant correspondences between 'the physical space navigated, mapped, and mastered by European voyagers and travellers in the 16th and 17th centuries and the fictional, digitally projected space traversed, mapped and mastered by players of Nintendo®' (Fuller and Jenkins 1994: 58). Thus,

Case Study: Videogames and the Appropriation of Space

'Space', writes James Newman (2004: 31), 'is key to videogames', a statement that makes sense not only in terms of the game play itself but also in the way that, throughout their history, they have traversed national boundaries, colonized spaces like gaming arcades, invaded the home and borrowed from technologies designed for the exploration and appropriation of other spaces; outer space and the hyperreal spaces of virtual war and tourism.

The first successful arcade videogame is credited to Al Alcorn, an electronic engineer working for *Atari*, who developed *Pong* in the early 1970s. The prototype *Pong* was installed in a bar in Sunnyvale, California called Andy Capp's and proved so popular that, when the bar's owner called Alcorn to tell him that the unit had malfunctioned, he discovered that so many quarters had been inserted into the coin slot that it had jammed. Later, in 1978, the popularity of arcade videogames became a brief threat to the Japanese economy when the release of Toshihiro Nishikado's *Space Invaders* caused a nationwide shortage of the yen.

The appeal of *Pong* is simple. It reproduces an already familiar pastime, table tennis, but without the need to master the physicality of the game. A square 'ball' bounces off 'paddles' which move up and down in response to the press of buttons and which are situated to left and right of a vertical line. The aim is to keep the ball in play for as long as possible. If a player

misses the ball with a paddle, it disappears off the screen for a moment, only to reappear in an unexpected position. The skill is in predicting the trajectory of the ball as it bounces off different parts of the paddle. Thus the hand/eye coordination skills of the real life game are retained but the movement of the body through space is simulated on screen and controlled by only small movements of the fingers (originally to press a button but later to control a joystick or press computer keys).

Although *Pong* appears to have little in common with later, more expansive games where the aim is exploration and control of virtual or simulated spaces through firepower, fighting skills, the acquisition of resources and speed, what is wholly similar is the ability to effect large changes in game space with very small movements of the body, which, as Julian Stallabrass (1996: 85) points out, is 'rather like driving a car, where the same disparity between movement and effect is apparent'. Indeed, driving simulators, like Sierra Entertainment's *Grand Prix Legends*, published in 1998, have proven to be among the most popular games and simulators are now used by driving schools before allowing novices to actually get behind the wheel of a car.

Driving simulators, however, mimic the actual conditions of driving in a city where traffic restricting laws have to be obeyed and the rules of courteous the production of space under the terms of increasingly sophisticated computing technologies both reinforces and reproduces the connections between colonialism, entitlement and technological mastery implied in the voyages of 'discovery', reinvented to invest the space race with noble ideals and inserted into the discourse of cyberspace which, despite the fact that it is presented as a purely virtual world, nevertheless has significant effects in the lived spaces of the *real* world.

---

behaviour adhered to, unlike games such as the highly successful *Grand Theft Auto* series (Rockstar Games), which encourages risky behaviour, including driving at high speed, mowing down any pedestrians who happen to get in your way and, of course, stealing cars, often by stopping them on the road and yanking the driver out of their seat. While it is often argued that the popularity of games like *Grand Theft Auto* points to their enjoyment by teenaged boys (even though games containing violence are supposedly restricted to those over 18), their appeal can be seen to lie in the way in which they permit transgressive behaviour in a space that is highly representative of what Stallabrass (1996: 89) calls 'the self under capital, subject to fragmentation, reification and the play of allegory': the city.

The space of the contemporary city is marked by increasing hierarchical division and exclusion which is apparent both at street level and in the discourses which structure urban experience. Peter Marcuse, for instance, notes that, in New York city, following the events of 11 September 2001, certain urban trends that were already becoming apparent were reinforced and escalated due to a perceived need for increased security. The decentralization of business activities, which was already taking place because globalized corporations have less need of a single, central location intensified after 11 September, creating what Marcuse (2003: 276) calls 'decentralized concentrations', which are 'secured,

walled, fortified, organized so as to be able to exclude the undesirable, the stranger, the discordant in order to attract and admit only those having business there or those from whom a profit can be made'. These 'citadels' are 'oriented to protecting business activities, often including luxury housing for their participants, even when they are not averse to providing shopping opportunities or profitable entertainment for a broader clientele' (Marcuse 2003: 277).

Conversely, the 'underside of the citadel' is what Marcuse calls 'the excluded ghetto' where those outside the globalized economy are segregated. Unlike the ghettos of the past, which were marked by poverty and racial segregation but could be said to constitute a community, united in similar low-paid and low-status employment, the residents of contemporary ghettos are excluded from mainstream employment, often by the 'emphasis on citizenship, educational qualification, and background checks applicable to more and more jobs' (Marcuse 2003: 278). The result is a city marked increasingly by electronic surveillance, 'gated' communities, social exclusion and fear of strangers. Currently, some cities in the UK are experimenting with security cameras that 'shout' at loitering teenagers and, in London, the congestion charge and other traffic-calming measures, along with a public transport system that is among the most expensive in the world, effectively prohibit travel around the city for all but the highest earners.

Furthermore, cities are becoming increasingly hyper-realized as they compete for lucrative tourist revenues. What Sarah Chaplin and Eric Holding (2002: 193) call 'the post-urban city' adopts the tactics of the cinema and invents a more extreme form of spectacle in order to compete'. '[M]any cities', they write, 'have turned to theming as a way of promoting and accentuating their USP (unique selling point)'. In other words, cities have adopted their cinematic representations and have accentuated those features that have become familiar through countless films and TV series to offer potential tourists and investors an experience that conforms to already determined expectations. This is achieved through the four strategies of 'efficiency, predictability, calculability and control' (Chaplin and Holding 2002: 189) identified by George Ritzer in his book, *The McDonaldisation of Society* (Ritzer 1996). Thus, '[t]he reified quality of the post-urban city is like the experience of dining in a fast food restaurant' with a menu which offers 'a sustainable array of attractions' which, needless to say, 'sets up a focus which often places the aspirations of the tourist above the needs of the local inhabitant'. In fact, under these conditions, local inhabitants themselves come to identify with their predetermined roles in the sense that, in order to take advantage of the experiences which the city offers, they must, in effect, become tourists themselves and thus subject to the 'crowd control, funnelling and shepherding' (Ritzer 1996: 191), which attends the tourist experience or else exclude themselves from some areas of the city altogether. Thus, post-urbanism, along with citadelization and a burgeoning excluded ghetto creates a city in which movement is increasingly curtailed and the hegemony of technocapitalism imposes an order under which the bodies that inhabit the city are, according to Elizabeth Grosz (1995: 108), 'representationally reexplored, transformed, contested, reinscribed'. We are subject to the 'play of allegory', under the terms of which we recognize ourselves only as extras in a succession of movies where the roles become increasingly limited.

Hence, games like *Grand Theft Auto* offer the pleasure of transgressing the restrictions of the contemporary city but under the assured conditions of a preprogrammed scenario that not only mimics a movie but gives the player a starring role. And, as Kate O'Riordan (2001: 229) points out, 'game space is inserted into the architecture of television ... an imaginary space in which we are culturally acclimatized to viewing images that reflect certain aspects of reality.' Because the city itself has become a hyperreal theme park that increasingly borrows from its screen representations, the opportunity to temporarily 'inhabit' screen space through an avatar, while enacting a transgressive scenario offers a simulation of freedom that, while affectively acute, is nevertheless enacted under conditions of safety (like immersion in *Star* Trek's holodeck – but with the safety controls firmly *on*). Furthermore, although games in the *Grand Theft Auto* series present a series of tasks to be completed and pit the player against an array of adversaries, they also provide an experience similar to flight or driving simulators where the sheer thrill of driving dangerously can be experienced without the necessity to complete a task against the clock. The sense of freedom is thus compounded. The space of the city is not only offered up as a playground where the stringent rules of access and engagement under the terms of technocapitalist posturbanism have been suspended but the requirement to achieve in terms of a specific agenda, characteristic of the 'self under capital', where the rewards of labour are understood in terms of 'freedom' and 'choice' can be avoided. Alternatively, if you do choose to pit your skills against the game, and accrue points and promotion to the next task, you experience the thrill of briefly inhabiting a meritocracy where your skills really *are* recognized and you really *do* benefit from competition.

That this is an illusion hardly needs pointing out. Indeed, for Stallabrass, the 'self under capital' is precisely what is simulated by videogames that 'force a mechanization of the body on their players ... Games demand that the players hone their skills to make the body a machine, forging from the uncoordinated and ignorant body of the acolyte an embodiment of the spirit of the game' (Stallabrass 1996: 89). In other words, the desire to explore, to transgress boundaries, to move at speed and to elude the forces of law and order is harnessed to a strict regime of bodily control in which the only true achievement is effective manipulation of the computer interface controls; precisely what is required for the service-industry jobs that promise access to the citadels of the contemporary city. Ironically, one of the qualifications for jobs in the European Union is currently the European Computer Driving Licence.

And, of course, in a far more deadly 'play of allegory', these same skills are required of what Kevin Robins and Les Levidow (1995: 107) refer to as the 'cyborg soldier ... constructed and programmed to fit integrally into weapons systems.' In contemporary war, '[k]illing is done "at a distance," through technological mediation, without the shock of direct confrontation. The victims become psychologically invisible. The soldier appears to achieve a moral dissociation; the targeted "things" on the screen do not seem to implicate him in a moral relationship' (Robins and Levidow 1995: 106).

What also became apparent during the 'Nintendo war' was the way in which the close relationship between videogames and television could be exploited to ensure participation of the home audience. As Robins and Levidow (1995: 109) point out, '[t]he Gulf War was "total television" an entertainment form that merged military and media planning', replete with images that 'evoked an audience familiarity with video games, thus offering a vicarious real-time participation'.

Tuning my TV to BBC News 24 during the US-led invasion of Iraq in 2003, I was confronted with a view of the battlefield from a camera mounted on the gun turret of a British army tank. As it panned the field, searching for targets, I became, for that moment, complicit in its inexorable mission to target, aim and fire. The precision with which it accomplished this produced an undeniable sensation of achievement. This, then, is the play of allegory at its most inventive

and deadly. It should thus come as no surprise that the US military has, for some time, been offering a free, downloadable videogame called *America's Army: Virtual Army Experience*, which offers the opportunity to 'execute a simulated mission in the war on terror'.[12] The implication, that the 'right stuff' can be identified in cyberspace, also encodes the suggestion that anyone with a high score tempted to sign up for the *real* army, has achieved the necessary moral dissociation and sufficient immersion in the space of the hyperreal to be oblivious to the difference between pixellated space and the very real, historically determined and economically contested spaces in which the theatre of war actually takes place. As Robins and Levidow report:

> In the five months preceding the January 1991 attack on Iraq, the US war machine devoted laborious 'software work' to mapping and plotting strategic installations there. The concept of 'legitimate military target' extended from military bases and the presidential palace, to major highways, factories, water supplies, and power stations. The basic means of survival for an entire population were reduced to 'targeting information'. Enemy threats — real or imaginary, human or machine — became precise grid locations, abstracted from their human context. (Robins and Levidow 1995: 107–8)

What is remarkable here is how this 'software work' produces a space that emulates the way that videogames map and encourage the production of what Shoshona Magnet (2006: 143) calls 'gamescape'. The concept of gamescape, as Magnet explains it, requires that we understand gamespace as produced according to the same cultural strategies that have constructed 'landscape' as 'a place to escape ... combining entertainment with fantasy hideaways' (Magnet 2006: 148). As Magnet points out, in the contemporary idea of landscape '[v]ision plays an increasingly central role' (Magnet 2006: 147), offering up the space as 'part of the cultureless natural world' (Magnet 2006: 149). The terrain presented to view is, like the wilderness, offered up as sublime, empty, ripe for colonization and, perhaps more pertinently, mapping. 'Maps', according to Magnet 'regularly contain blatant distortions with an eye to promoting one-sided geopolitical agendas' and are 'a form of discourse that help to neutralize the unequal distribution of power and resources' (Magnet 2006: 153). As discussed above, maps function to impose a grid on the landscape that allows the possibility of travel to specific points, or an overview of specific resources, while permitting a totalizing perspective.

In the game that Magnet analyses, Pop Top Software's *Tropico*, the map 'makes it easier for the player to engage in oppressive behaviour' (Magnet 2006: 153). *Tropico* is an adventure game that, like Maxis' *Sim City* series and 'god' games like Lionhead Studios' *Black and White*, provides a populated space that the player must manage from a position of power; mayor (*Sim City*), evil or benign god (*Black and White*) or, in the case of *Tropico*, 'tourist-ruler become dictator ... You as presidente must study the Tropico map and decide where to build — a project much like that of other real life rulers who make decisions based on cartography ... The player-dictator visually reads the gamescape to control it' (Magnet 2006: 147 and 149).

As Michael Hardt and Antonio Negri have argued, under the conditions of contemporary global capitalism, the rules of modern warfare, drawn up on the basis of conflicts between nation-states, are inapplicable. As they point out, 'the sovereignty of nation-states is declining and instead at a supranational level is forming a new sovereignty, a global Empire' (Hardt and Negri 2005: 7). On the other hand, 'nations are absolutely necessary as elements of global order and security' (Hardt and Negri 2005: 23), not least because nations mark out power hierarchies and function as repositories of oppositional ideologies, 'otherness' and identifiable and hyperrealized tourist destinations. In what Hardt and Negri call 'nation building', 'nations

can be destroyed and fabricated or invented as part of a political program ... Such nation building resembles less the modern revolutionary birth of nations than it does the process of colonial powers dividing up the globe and drawing the maps of their subject territories' (Hardt and Negri 2005: 23).

Videogames like *Tropico*, *Sim City*, and *Black and White* reproduce the 'software work' that enables the process of nation building where even to be a dictator or an 'evil' god has an apparently benign aspect — the development of a thriving population with housing, sanitation, healthcare, recreation and work. As Magnet points out, in *Tropico*, '[i]t is easy to imagine your avatar "presidente" in the role of an International Monetary Fund (IMF) banker or U.S. puppet government official coming in to fix the "unruly" problems of the locals through oppressive governance and micromanagement' (Magnet 2006: 151). The production of gamescape thus mirrors the production of space under the terms of what Hardt and Negri call 'a *general global state of war*' (Hardt and Negri 2005: 5, their emphasis) in which war has become 'the primary organizing principle of society' (Hardt and Negri 2005: 12), such that 'daily life and the normal functioning of power has been permeated with the threat and violence of warfare' (Hardt and Negri 2005: 13), which, I would add, is normalized on the basis of cyberspatial rules of engagement. 'In the culture of the simulacrum' write Mark C. Taylor and Esa Saarinen, 'every war is a war game. Both the event and the pseudo-event are staged on the video screen' (Taylor and Saarinen 1994: cyberwar 1). Equally, I would add, every video game is, in some sense, a simulation of the appropriation of space. While, it may be argued, many board games that had been part of the culture for a long time before computers allowed us access to cyberspace, have similar aims, the crucial difference is that video games are designed for cyborgs. Our complete immersion in the hyperreal space of the simulated event makes the distinction between game worlds and the 'real' world very flimsy indeed.

CHAPTER SUMMARY

- The myth of outer space, like that of the untamed wilderness, functions to establish a connection between technological mastery and colonial supremacy.
- According to Henri Lefebvre, culture *produces* space according to different orders of socio-economic organization.
- Contemporary culture is characterized by the production of *abstract* space, which contributes to the determination of what Jean Baudrillard terms the 'hyperreal'.
- Cyberspace is an aspect of abstract space produced by communications and information technologies, which succeeds the wilderness and outer space as the 'new frontier'.

6 TECHNOAESTHETICS

In pre-Second World War Germany, the Nazis mounted a huge exhibition of so-called 'degenerate art' (*Entartete Kunst*), which opened in Munich on 18 July 1937. The aim was to ridicule the *avant garde*. Several now well known and well respected artists including such luminaries of late modernity as Marc Chagall, Max Ernst, Wassily Kandinsky, Paul Klee and Piet Mondrian, among many others, were included and '[p]ictures were displayed in a mad jumble, without frames, as if arranged by fools or children without any sense of reason, high and low, just as they came, furnished with inciting titles, explanations or filthy jokes' (Grunberger 1974: 536). To reinforce the desired effect, an exhibition of the 'new German art', approved by Hitler, was mounted in the close vicinity.

The modernist *avant garde* was at odds with National Socialism because its specific aim was to challenge the classical aesthetic with its reference to balance and harmony and representation of ideal forms. Renaissance 'artists, designers and architects', writes Christopher Crouch, 'ultimately looked to the past for inspiration. Their aim was to recreate a golden age, to take the remnants of the classical world and to reconstitute them into a coherent cultural structure' (Crouch 1999: 15). In similar terms, the Third Reich or 'Thousand-Year Empire' alluded to the thousand-year rule of the Holy Roman Empire. Thus National Socialist Realism evoked the classical representational forms of the Renaissance and, when not depicting Hitler himself, portrayed idealized representations of the German 'Volk' and glorified the body of the ideal Aryan type.

Art was important to Hitler, not only because he was (or aspired to be) an artist himself but because he understood the power of art to represent ideas. The modernist aesthetic of the late nineteenth and early twentieth centuries has, as R.L. Rutsky points out, 'often been defined ... in terms of its relation to technology (Rutsky 1999: 8, see Chapter 1, this volume). But, despite the fact that, for Hitler, technological development was the cultural expression of a superior race and the Nazi vision could be understood as that of 'an aestheticized technological state' (Rutsky 1999: 9), the technique of abstraction spoke too insistently of dangerous ambivalences and insecure identities. The modernist *avant garde* was concerned less with aestheticizing technology and more with producing what has been called a 'machine aesthetic', which was expressed both in the forms of mass production and the incorporation of the displacements of time and space effected by machines. The challenge to Renaissance perspectival technique that this produced (see last chapter) evoked the possibility of conflicting points of view and confronted the viewer with uncertainty and dissolution of the self. The kind of ambivalence that it expressed was clearly at odds with the absolutes required by National Socialism. Nevertheless, as Rutsky suggests, there was a tendency within modernism towards reconciling classical aesthetics with the technological, 'even among the left avant-gardes' (Rutsky 1999: 9) and the work of the Italian Futurists, although, in general, non-representational was influenced by an explicitly fascist ideology.

FUTURISM

'We will sing of the great crowds agitated by work, pleasure and revolt', wrote Filippo Tommaso Marinetti in 'The Founding and Manifesto of Futurism', first published in *Le Figaro* on 20 February, 1909. And he continues:

> the multi-colored and polyphonic surf of revolutions in modern capitals: the nocturnal vibration of the arsenals and the workshops beneath their violent electric moons: the gluttonous railway stations devouring smoking serpents; factories suspended from the clouds by the thread of their smoke; bridges with the leap of gymnasts flung across the diabolic cutlery of sunny rivers: adventurous steamers sniffing the horizon; great-breasted locomotives, puffing on the rails like enormous steel horses with long tubes for bridle, and the gliding flight of aeroplanes whose propeller sounds like the flapping of a flag and the applause of enthusiastic crowds.[1]

The Futurists, as their name implies, wanted to reinvigorate Italy by turning away from the past and celebrating the new technologies that were making dramatic changes to social and cultural life at the turn of the twentieth century. 'The Italy of the future', write Caroline Tisdall and Angelo Bozzolla, 'meant youth, speed, the beauty of the motorcar and the aeroplane' (Tisdall and Bozzolla 1977: 9). Anticipating Marshall McLuhan's announcement of the 'global village' (2001 [1967]: 63) in the late 1960s, they were committed to separating the production of art from 'the sheltered life of the cultured intellectual' (Tisdall and Bozzolla 1977: 8) and using the new means of mass communication to reach a wider audience. Marinetti

> argued that motion, speed, simultaneity, and process are the shaping elements of modern experience. To represent contemporary reality, art should depict objects in motion. Movies and dance are truly modern art forms because they move.

Painting is inherently static, but it can suggest motion through distortion of the image and techniques like the simultaneity of Marcel Duchamp's famous *Nude Descending a Staircase* [see Chapter 1, this volume]. Poetry can express the new aesthetic by speaking directly of machines and motion, and it can enact its subject by choppy diction, short lines, rapid and kaleidoscopic sequences of images and phrases, and passages in which several texts are understood as occurring at the same time. (Hardison 1989: 122)

Marinetti was a friend of Mussolini and Futurist politics, in general, tended towards anarcho-libertarianism, which was, nevertheless, coupled with an intense nationalism: '[t]he fatherland', wrote Marinetti, 'is the psychic and geographical awareness of the power for individual betterment' (Marinetti 1991: 157) '[W]ar', they announced, 'is the only hygiene of the world' (Marinetti 1991: 70) and they supported female suffrage only because they believed that women with the right to vote would 'involuntarily help us to destroy that grand foolishness, made up of corruption and banality, to which parliamentarianism is now reduced' (Marinetti 1991: 81). Nevertheless, as Andrew Murphie and John Potts point out, Antonio Gramsci 'saw the Futurists as cultural revolutionaries, praising their destruction of rigid traditions and values'. As they suggest, 'by absorbing the properties of the machine into their art, they built a prototype that is still being used by artists. Technology and technological processes could now be both the subject and material of art' (Murphie and Potts 2003: 46).

Thus, despite the fact that Walter Benjamin, in his famous essay 'The Work of Art in the Age of Mechanical Reproduction', quotes Marinetti's glorification of the aesthetics of war in support of his contention that mankind's 'self-alienation has reached such a degree that it can experience its own destruction as an aesthetic pleasure of the first order' (Benjamin 1972 [1936]: 244), the Futurists are important for inaugurating a new aesthetic for a new century in which '[t]he face of the world as it had been known for centuries was changing daily' (Tisdall and Bozzolla, 1977: 7).

MECHANICAL REPRODUCTION

But, to return to Benjamin, his essay was singularly important in supplying an analysis of the effects of mass production technologies on the reception of art and the political implications of the process of reproduction. Benjamin, a Jew and founding member of the Frankfurt School, writing in the year before *Entartete Kunst*, was keenly aware of the impetus behind fascism's confrontation with the *avant garde*. '[T]heses about the developmental tendencies of art under present conditions of production ...', he writes, 'brush aside a number of outmoded concepts, such as creativity and genius, eternal value and mystery – concepts whose uncontrolled (and at present uncontrollable) application would lead to a processing of data in the Fascist sense' (Benjamin 1972: 220). What he is referring to here is precisely the kind of art that Hitler approved; the kind that would produce an aesthetic response confirming a politics of authority and demanding a recognition of the possibility of transcendent genius because it evokes values associated with its emulation of the relics of triumphant empire. When he refers to 'present conditions' we need to remember that he was writing at a time of increasing mass production in the field of the arts and entertainment and he is primarily concerned with exploring the recontextualization of art as both reproducible (as opposed to unique) and as a commodity for mass consumption, rather than art like Cubism or Futurism which, as he puts it, 'appear as deficient attempts of art to accommodate the pervasion of reality by the apparatus ... [T]hese schools did not try to use the apparatus as such for the artistic presentation of reality, but aimed at some sort of alloy in the joint presentation of reality and apparatus' (Benjamin 1972: 252, n20). A truly radical art, for Benjamin, is one that uses the 'apparatus' (or technology) to cut through the structures of accepted reality and challenge the bourgeois concepts of authorship and authenticity.

His argument proceeds from a similar premise to that of Roland Barthes in his essay 'The Death of the Author' (1989) in which he argues that meaning has been fixed in literary criticism by according the author an intention or specific meaning based on his or her biography, location in historical time and/or cultural moment. This fixing of meaning through a technique of penetration in which the text is forced to offer up its 'secrets' is political in the sense that it accepts as truth not only the facts of the author's own life but ideologically determined readings of history which the text is held to exemplify or categorically establish. Writing, in this formulation, is understood as 'an operation of recording, notation, representation, "depiction"' (Barthes 1989: 120). The text finds its 'origin' in the author and his or her historical and cultural moment and thus an understanding of this origin is required in order for the text to be read. Previous cultural and literary theorists (Matthew Arnold for example) had insisted that the 'masses' should therefore be educated to read certain texts because, without the necessary education, their meaning would be obscure. But, '[w]e now know', writes Barthes, 'that a text is not a line of words releasing a single 'theological' meaning (the 'message' of the Author-God) but a multi-dimensional space in which a variety of writings, none of them original, blend and clash' (Barthes 1989: 121). What he means here is that meaning in a text is situational. Different readings are produced by different people depending upon their *own* cultural and historical location, not that of the author.

Barthes' essay paved the way, not only for new forms of literary criticism but for more complex interpretations of, for instance, Shakespeare's plays, which have influenced their restaging in contemporary settings and their rewriting as screenplays for films like Gus van Sant's *My Own Private Idaho* (1991), which weaves together the story of a narcoleptic street hustler (River Phoenix) with an updated interpretation of the figure of Prince Hal in Shakespeare's *Henry IV, Part 1* (Keanu Reeves) and which has become a classic of gay cinema. The film not only uses bowdlerized dialogue from the original play but uses it to make a powerful statement about the social effects of Reaganomics in 1980s America. A Barthesian reading of the film itself may produce an analysis that understands the reference to Shakespeare as a critique, not only of the cult of 'genius' to which he undeniably belongs but of the ideology of abstract individualism from which the cult proceeds, which pervades his work and which is also the structuring ideology of the American dream, here associated with poverty, violence and homophobic disavowal. But, at the same time, the bowdlerized Shakespearean language and Van Sant's directorial technique refer also to Benjamin's disquisition on the potential of film technology to close the distance that imparts 'aura' to a work of art. Shakespeare is brought down, in the context of what is essentially a road movie, from the echelons of high art, literally, to street level. This disallows the illusion that what we are witnessing is a transparent enactment of reality.

THE AURA

Film, for Benjamin, could lead to 'a tremendous shattering of tradition' by not only 'substituting a plurality of copies for a unique existence' but by 'permitting the reproduction to meet the beholder ... in his own particular situation' (Benjamin 1977: 223). Although these processes can be applied to all mass productions of art objects, Benjamin designates film as '[t]heir most powerful agent' due to the fact that it 'is completely subject to [and] founded in, mechanical reproduction' (Benjamin 1977: 232). Comparing film to the theatre, for instance, he notes that, in the theatre, the audience is in the presence of actors whereas, in the cinema, it is in the presence of technology or what he calls 'mechanical contrivance' (Benjamin 1977: 231). Indeed, the completed film, 'comprises certain factors of movement which are in reality those of the camera' (230).

We can understand what he means here by considering a theatre set, complete with props and scenery, that is in full view of the audience before the play begins. The props are static and, after the first glance, somewhat uninteresting until they are brought to life by the presence of actors moving around the stage. The play does not exist without the actors, no matter how important the props are to an understanding of the performance. Indeed, many plays emphasize this point by doing away with props altogether. Film, on the other hand, often relies entirely on the movement of the camera through the scenery and some of the most important, and captivating scenes minimize the presence of the actors. This is particularly true of road movies where an aerial shot of a car on a lonely road may be the only clue to human presence. Indeed, it could be argued (and often has been) that the landscape (and, particularly, the American landscape) itself is the 'star' in such movies and is certainly the source of much of the aesthetic appeal of films like *My Own Private Idaho* and *Thelma and Louise* (Ridley Scott 1991). In such scenes, there is no *acting*, as such. The car, in fact, could be driven by anybody.

From this we can understand that part of the aesthetic of the theatre depends upon the 'aura' of the performance, a term that, for Benjamin, is connected to the *presence* of a work of art, as well as its location in history and tradition and the 'cult value' that attaches to it as representative of a mystique, whether religious (as in, for instance, the paintings of Fra Angelica) or secular; associated with antiquity, obscurity and authenticity. The mystery of the Mona Lisa's smile, for instance, is as much a part of her aura as the fact that the painting is the authenticated work of an acknowledged 'genius' of the Renaissance, Leonardo da Vinci, and the facts and speculation about its history and the intention of the artist. The original painting has never been too easy to view (at one point it was really too high on the wall for easy viewing) but art lovers continue to flock to the Musée du Louvre in Paris. While Benjamin would never advocate the destruction of such works and, indeed, a certain sense of nostalgia for the aura tends to pervade his essay, he is excited by the potential for mechanical reproduction to cut through their mystery and provoke an aesthetic response that has less to do with reverence and more with accessibility. '[I]t enables the original', he writes, 'to meet the beholder halfway, be it in the form of a photograph or [in the case of music] a phonograph record' (Benjamin 1977: 222–3).

The withering of the aura is thus a necessary stage in the politicization of the aesthetic. Futurism was undeniably political but Marinetti and his cohorts were not interested in bringing art to the masses. Rather, they were concerned with producing an aesthetic that would provoke a response to the potential of the new technologies for renewal of the 'fatherland' through war and the glorification of youth and speed. Benjamin, on the other hand, is concerned with the sense in which the aura sustains attitudes of reverence and esteem based on provenance and respect for tradition. Art that can be photographed and reproduced indefinitely closes the distance required for these attitudes and, in 'meeting the beholder halfway' allows questions to be raised as to the value of authenticity and the function of ideology in sustaining privileges such as access to art and the ability to criticize it. To return to film, then, he is impressed by the fact that the presence of the technology detracts from the aura of the acting performance. '[T]he film actor', he writes, 'lacks the opportunity of the stage actor to adjust to the audience during his performance … aura is tied to his presence; there can be no replica of it' (Benjamin 1977: 230–1). A good actor (like a politician) can gauge audience response and adapt accordingly and can thus be assured of retaining power. In the cinema, the audience takes 'the position of a critic, without experiencing any personal contact with the actor. The audience's identification with the actor is really an identification with the camera' (Benjamin 1977: 230) and power is returned to the beholder. This is why, Benjamin notes, 'film responds to the shriveling [sic] of the aura with an artificial build-up of the "personality" outside the studio. The cult of the movie star, fostered by the money of the film industry, preserves not the unique aura of the person but the "spell of the personality," the phony spell of a commodity' (Benjamin 1977: 233).

He is presaging here his Frankfurt School colleagues, Theodor W Adorno and Max Horkheimer who, in *Dialectic of Enlightenment,* first published in 1947, introduced the concept of 'the culture industry' (Adorno and Horkheimer 1997: 120) to describe the mass production of entertainment and its effect on how art is received and understood. 'Interested parties', they write, 'explain the culture industry in technological terms. It is alleged that because millions participate in it, certain reproduction processes are necessary that inevitably require identical needs in innumerable places to be satisfied with identical goods' (Adorno and Horkheimer 1997: 121). However, they present a penetrating argument for understanding the culture industry as primarily concerned with manufacturing the needs to be satisfied so that the object of consumption is less about the acquisition and appreciation of art as a commodity and more about the confirmation of, and identification with, a predetermined subjectivity.

IDEOLOGY AND AESTHETICS

This is an argument that is, of course, familiar to contemporary students and academics in that identification through consumption and the commodification of art and daily life formed the basis of much cultural criticism from the latter part of the twentieth century. But, like Benjamin, Adorno and Horkheimer were writing under the shadow of fascism and although, at times, they appear to be in disagreement with him, their concerns are similar in that they are keenly aware of the connection between ideology and aesthetics and how this contributes to the production of propaganda. Nevertheless, while Benjamin was writing just prior to the beginning of the Second World War, Adorno and Horkheimer had lived through it and had witnessed the machinations of Nazi propaganda from the relative safety of California, following their escape from Nazi Germany but where, also, the culture industry could be said, at the time, to be most highly developed. Television, at this time, was in its infancy but radio and the movies were extremely popular and it is to these technologies that Adorno and Horkheimer turn their attention.

What is perhaps most interesting in their argument is their contention that the culture industry *because* it is an industry requires a standardized product and thus must predetermine the response to it. In part, they are concerned with the effects of advertising and the collusion between different branches of the culture industry such that '[t]he culture industry as a whole has molded men as a type unfailingly reproduced in every product' (Adorno and Horkheimer 1997 [1944]: 127). But, overwhelmingly, what they are interested in is the connection between this and the content of the product, or the way in which

> [a]musement under late capitalism is the prolongation of work. It is sought after as an escape from the mechanized work process, and to recruit strength in order to be able to cope with it again. But at the same time mechanization has such power over a man's leisure and happiness, and so profoundly determines the manufacture of amusement goods, that his experiences are inevitably after-images of the work process itself. The ostensible content is merely a faded foreground; what sinks in is the automatic succession of standardized operations. What happens at work, in the factory, or in the office can only be escaped from by approximation to it in one's leisure time. (Adorno and Horkheimer 1997 [1944]: 137)

This is a reiteration of an argument that Adorno had originally presented in 'On Popular Music' (Adorno 1994 [1941]), which discussed the structure of pop songs and the way in which they were received by the masses. Identifying the whole genre with what we would probably now call 'easy listening', he deplores its lack of complexity in contrast to what he called 'serious music' (Adorno 1994: 197, Beethoven is his example) and describes it as 'rigid and mechanical' (Adorno 1994: 200) and 'musical automatism' (Adorno 1994: 199). But before we accuse Adorno of musical snobbery, we need to take into account his concern with the effects of the consumption of popular music on the possibility for the workers to recognize their alienation. Because popular music is 'standardized' (Adorno 1994: 200) both in its method of production and in the structure of individual songs, it 'keeps the customers in line by doing their listening for them' (Adorno 1994: 203). In other words, the scheme or formula of a song that has been well received is repeated in successive 'hits' but with slight variations, not only in the structure of the song (which generally follows the format: verse, chorus, middle eight or bridge and reprise) but in elements that lend themselves to marketing (image of the performer, lyrical content, subgenres and identification of particular styles within the standardized scheme).

PSYCHOTECHNOLOGY

Adorno deplores the enjoyment that people get from listening to popular music because what they are, in fact, enjoying is their own oppression. Or, in Adorno's words, they succumb to 'a process of masochistic adjustment to authoritarian collectivism.' '[L]isteners', he writes, 'are ready to replace dreaming by adjustment to raw reality ... they reap new pleasure from their acceptance of the unpleasant' (Adorno 1994: 207). People adapt to 'machine music' (Adorno 1994: 208) because the pleasure they experience when listening to it is derived from the assurance that it offers that there is no alternative to the system under which they labour. If they can derive pleasure from a standardized and repetitive product that, even when they grow tired of it, is quickly replaced by another which doesn't deviate too radically from the familiar format and which appears to be a product of the same industrial machinery to which they are an appendage and which acts as 'social cement' (Adorno 1994: 206) in that it ossifies relationships both in and outside of the factory or office, then they have no need to approach the more difficult listening experience of music which challenges preconceived ideas and is experienced for its own sake, and as a totality, rather than as a fetishized commodity. Thus, Adorno can claim that, 'there is justification for speaking of a preestablished harmony ... between production and consumption of popular music. The people clamor for what they are going to get anyhow' (Adorno 1994: 206).

Although many of Adorno's ideas seem somewhat anachronistic to contemporary readers, his fundamental argument, that art that succumbs to the 'cult of the machine' (Adorno 1994: 208) serves authoritarianism and induces conformity makes a great deal of sense in terms of its potential as propaganda. It does not take a leap of faith to understand that art that discourages critical engagement and that promotes a sense of security serves to reinforce established ideas. Thus, 'the mechanical repetition of the same culture product has come to be the same as that of the propaganda slogan. In both cases the insistent demand for effectiveness makes technology into psychotechnology, into a procedure for manipulating men' (Adorno and Horkheimer, 1997 [1944]: 163), something that the Nazis knew only too well. Goebbels 'officially forbade art criticism in November 1936' and '[a] principal accusation against the Jews within Nazi Germany was that they were urban, intellectual, bearers of a destructive corrupting "critical spirit"' (Sontag: 2001 [1975]: 88).

While there may seem to be a contradiction here between Benjamin's cautious welcoming of mechanical reproduction as a means of at least challenging the aesthetic of wholeness, immutability, tradition and distance which fascist ideology demands and which is concentrated in the 'aura' and Adorno and Horkheimer's exposure of the same technique as promoting a compliant response, what they have in common is an understanding that 'aesthetic modernism, despite its awareness of modern technological reproducibility and complexity, remains haunted by the spirit of utopia, by the desire for wholeness' (Rutsky 1999: 45). Thus, as Susan Sontag demonstrates in her analysis of the work of the Nazi film director Leni Riefensthal, the potential which Benjamin saw in the technique of film production is often mitigated by the culture industry itself which is able to mobilize psychotechnology in the service of salvaging the aura. Referring, principally, to Riefensthal's two epics of Nazi glorification *Triumph of the Will* (1935) and *Olympia* (1938), Sontag shows how, in the effacing of the history of their production, both under the Nazis and in the publicity that progressively effected the de-Nazification of Riefensthal's work long after the war had ended, both the films, and Riefensthal herself, emerge as mythologized paeans to the art of filmmaking. Writing in 1975, Sontag points out that

> it is generally thought that National Socialism stands only for brutishness and terror. But this is not true: National Socialism – more broadly, fascism – also stands for an ideal or rather ideals that are persistent today under other banners: the ideal of life as art, the cult of beauty, the fetishism of courage, the dissolution of alienation in ecstatic feelings of community; the repudiation of the intellect; the family of man (under the parenthood of leaders). These ideals are vivid and moving to many people, and it is dishonest as well as tautological to say that one is affected by *Triumph of the Will* and *Olympia* only because they were made by a filmmaker of genius. Riefensthal's films are still effective because, among other reasons, their longings are still felt. (Sontag 2001 [1975]: 96)

Indeed, Benjamin may have had Riefensthal's films in mind when he wrote that '[t]he violation of the masses, whom Fascism, with its *Führer* cult, forces to their knees, has its counterpart in the violation of an apparatus which is pressed into the production of ritual values' (Benjamin 1972: 243). *Triumph of the Will*, for instance, purports to be a faithful recording of the 1934 National Socialist Party Congress but, in fact, as Sontag reports, the Congress itself was 'from the start conceived as the set of a film spectacle' with Riefensthal 'in on the planning of the rally ... [T]he historic event serv[ed] as the set of a film which was then to assume the character of an authentic documentary' (Sontag 2001 [1975]: 79 and 83). It is not so much that we cannot, with a little analysis, discern the possible disjuncture between the sequences of the rally itself and the 'overpopulated wide shots of massed figures alternating with close-ups that isolate a single passion, a single perfect submission' (Sontag 2001: 87) which could have been shot at any time and anywhere and spliced into the film later, but that paying attention to the artifice betrays the aesthetic sublimation of the longings to which Sontag refers. In other words, we ignore the way in which the technology of film can manipulate the content to produce an emotional response because of our longing to have certain values confirmed in art.

PRE-DIGESTED CULTURE

It is these same longings that, arguably, construct responses to contemporary Hollywood film and which mark the distinction between the more challenging cinema of the *avant garde* and mainstream 'blockbusters' whose appeal is in their presentation of conflicts which are resolved by a hefty application of neo-liberal values. When Adorno and Horkheimer wrote, in 1944, that '[t]he description of the dramatic formula ... as "getting into trouble and out again" embraces the whole of mass culture from the idiotic women's serial to the top production' (Adorno and Horkheimer 1997 [1944]: 152), they could have been describing any period of cultural production up until the present day. Nor is the formula restricted to drama. In 2005, a French made documentary called *March of the Penguins* enjoyed considerable box office success due to its presentation of a 'heartwarming love story from the coldest place on Earth'. As the Emperor penguins waddle 70 miles across Antarctica to return to their breeding ground, '[c]omparisons between humans and these flightless, seagoing birds are unavoidable', writes Joe Williams in the St Louis Post-Dispatch, 'not only for the comical diligence of their walk but for what happens after they reach their destination. In the same spot at which they were all born, the penguins seek out an individual mate to produce and nurture an offspring.'[2]

Comparisons, of course, are perfectly avoidable, if only because of the assumptions made about the mating habits of humans, let alone penguins, but what is at stake here is a presentation of struggle and its resolution in the context of the myth of romance and heterosexual normality which invokes 'nature' (see Chapter 3) to reconfirm established values. Furthermore, identification with the emotional context of the film is encouraged by articles such as the one in the St Louis Post-Dispatch and by the advertising posters which promise 'a delightful, wholesome experience for the family'.

The culture industry thus produces a product that, in Adorno's description, is 'predigested'. In the case of music it is 'already listened to for them' not only because the product is standardized and familiar but because it is 'pseudoindividualized'

(Adorno 1994 [1941]: 203) through marketing, packaging, reviews and, of course, advertising which Adorno and Horkheimer consider to be indistinguishable from propaganda. 'Advertising', they write, 'becomes art and nothing else, just as Goebbels – with foresight – combined them' (Adorno and Horkheimer 1997 [1944]: 163). In other words, there is little to choose between the techniques and effects of art, advertising and propaganda. Indeed, advertising may employ challenging images and make use of the language and iconography of dissidence but this is how pseudoindividualization works. The artistry masks the fact that it is predigesting the product for an audience that prides itself on its sophistication.

POP ART

The period in which Adorno and Horkheimer were writing ushers in the collapse of the distinctions between so called 'high' art and mass culture which, for Fredric Jameson is a 'fundamental feature of all the postmodernisms' (Jameson 1991: 2): art, music, philosophy, architecture, the novel, film and poetry. Comparing Vincent Van Gogh's painting of a pair of peasant boots with Andy Warhol's *Diamond Dust Shoes,* he finds that 'Van Gogh's footgear' speaks to the viewer with 'immediacy', while he is 'tempted to say that [*Diamond Dust Shoes*] does not really speak at all' (Jameson 1991: 8). Jameson, in fact, agrees with Heidegger that 'Van Gogh's painting is the disclosure of what the equipment, the pair of peasant shoes, *is* in truth' (Jameson 1991: 8), which is to say that the work of art performs, hermeneutically, to structure associations between the artefact that it depicts and the world in which the boots function in the field of labour. Equally, Jameson suggests, the use of colour and the care with which the boots are studied and depicted performs a kind of 'Utopian gesture' (Jameson 1991: 9), which suggests the possibility that the labour that they represent may itself be transformed into a thing of beauty.

Warhol's shoes, on the other hand, are a 'random collection of dead objects hanging together on the canvas like so many turnips, as shorn of their earlier life world as the pile of shoes left over from Auschwitz' (Jameson 1991: 8). We may get the impression here that Jameson doesn't like Warhol's work very much but his tone betrays a fascination with the way in which Warhol strips the shoes of any context. They, in fact, seem to block the hermeneutic gesture which Van Gogh's painting invites: 'it is as though the external and colored surface of things – debased and contaminated in advance by their assimilation to glossy advertising images – has been stripped away to reveal the deathly black-and-white substratum of the photographic negative which subtends them' (Jameson 1991: 9).

Warhol, as is now well known, began his working life as a commercial artist, working in the magazine publishing and advertising industries. He was thus, from the start, deeply immersed in the culture industry and his best known work references the style and technique of magazine reproduction. 'My image', he said in 1962, 'is a statement of the symbols of the harsh, impersonal products and brash materialistic objects on which America is built today. It is a projection of everything that can be bought and sold, the practical but impermanent symbols that sustain us' (Buchloh 1989: 52).[3] Warhol's style, which Charles E. Stuckey characterizes as 'art-about-commercial-art' (Stuckey 1989: 6) makes, if not a virtue, then certainly a feature of the process of mechanical reproduction itself. Famously, he announced that '[p]aintings are too hard. The things I want to show are mechanical. Machines have less problems. I'd like to be a machine' (Stuckey 1989: 9). Unsurprisingly, the famous loft studio that he occupied from 1963 was called 'The Factory'. Consequently, the Warhol aesthetic relies upon repetition and the techniques of reproduction, such as silkscreen printing, which demands a response to the subject matter wholly conditioned by awareness of the process that has created it. For instance, in the giant repetitions of images of famous stars like Elizabeth Taylor, Marilyn Monroe, Elvis Presley and Jackie Kennedy, the technique evokes the repeated exposure, through the machinations of the culture industry, that imparts 'aura' to celebrity while demanding acknowledgement of the technologies involved: the camera and printing press. Furthermore, the larger than life reproductions, themselves referring to the originals that Warhol clipped from magazines, enlarge and exaggerate the slight imperfections which occur with repeated printings and are equally reminiscent of the successive frames that make up the moving image of film and the giant faces of closeups on the movie screen.

Crucially, Warhol's method also involved relinquishing the actual production of his artworks to teams of assistants and often even the selection of subject matter and the disposition of the works in the gallery were left to friends, colleagues and curators. Warhol thus deconstructs the concept of the artist as originator and author of his work, a gesture that alludes to Marcel Duchamp's exhibition of manufactured goods or 'readymades' as art but, unlike Duchamp, Warhol was concerned, primarily, with the process of reproduction rather than the product. Nevertheless, the genre of 'Pop' art to which Warhol belongs has in common with this period of Duchamp's work an aesthetic that refuses to comply with the notion of 'genius'. 'Pop', he said, 'comes from the outside', rather than, 'the hard, gemlike flame of creativity said to generate art for art's sake' and thought to be 'made from the *inside*, the inside of the creator' (Rosenthal, 1989: 42).

In Warhol, the commodity becomes the subject of art (not only celebrities but Campbell's soup cans and Coca-Cola bottles, among other familiar items, were subjected to his technique) while the process of creating art emulates the process of commodity production and, crucially, elicits the technology of manufacture as both technique and aesthetic. Thus, the tools and materials of art production, it is suggested, can be manipulated by anyone and not just the specialist trained in the techniques of painting and drawing.

INDUSTRIAL MUSIC

Nor was this democratization of art production confined to the visual arts. In the late 1940s, French radio broadcaster Pierre Schaeffer pioneered *musique concrète,* which manipulated both musical and 'real world' sounds using the then newly developed tape recording technologies, thus creating music out of 'found' sounds rather than composing for traditional instruments. The famous BBC Radiophonic Workshop, best known for originating the theme to the science fiction TV programme *Dr Who,* was set up by the British Broadcasting Corporation in 1958 specifically to study the possibilities of creating music by tape manipulation and the techniques of *musique concrète* formed the soundscape for much of the progressive rock of the 1960s and 1970s and were adapted by the early 'industrial' music producers like performance art collective *COUM Transmissions*, which later spawned the industrial music group *Throbbing Gristle.*

Industrial music, perhaps more so than progressive rock, was in opposition to the culture industry and concerned to subvert the musical automatism of chart hits and formulaic pop. It was also, as *Throbbing Gristle* founder Genesis P. Orridge explained in a 1991 interview, 'inventing an anti-musak'. Musak is a musical form pioneered by the Musak Corporation of America, which deliberately created an environment conducive to repetitive labour and mall shopping with the intention to 'disguise stress, to control and direct human activity in order to generate maximum productivity and minimum discontent' (Rushkoff 1994: 210). Among *COUM Transmissions'* performances in 1974 was *Marcel Duchamp's Next Work* which 'consisted of twelve replicas of Duchamp's *Bicycle Wheel* (1913) – a bicycle wheel attached upside-down to a stool – arranged in a circle. These were played by volunteers as if they were musical instruments' (Ford 1999: 45). This performance is described by Simon Ford as 'a homage to, and a negation of, Duchamp's selection and presentation of an everyday object – a bicycle wheel – as a work of art. Whereas Duchamp rendered a mass-produced object useless by transforming it into art, COUM transformed this same art object back into a utilitarian object, in this case a musical instrument' (Ford 1999: 46).

Throbbing Gristle, whose sound was described by one reviewer as suggesting 'the dreams of complex industrial machines, the heartbeat of the London underground [and] the random noise generated by racing back and forth across a short wave radio dial at night' (Ford 1999: 7.24) used home-made synthesizers and sampling machines, which produced similar effects to the Futurist Luigi Russolo's Noise Intoners or *Intonarumori* as described in his 1913 'Art of Noises' manifesto. These were designed to reproduce the noise of machines and the city, break the 'limited circle of pure sounds' and explore the potential in the 'combination of the noises of trams, backfiring motors, carriages and bawling crowds'.[4]

MACHINE AESTHETICS

Hence, in the musical machine aesthetic, the technologies of sound making and the technologies of everyday life and work are inextricably linked, whether reproduced as noises in a performance soundscape or repurposed as musical instruments. Charles Mudede, writing about the repurposing of the turntable in the production of hip-hop, describes it as 'enstrangement' or the defamiliarization of 'something that has been smothered by habit' (Mudede 2004: 73). As Paul Gilroy points out, 'black expressive cultures' (Gilroy 1987: 134) have always encoded 'a powerful antipathy to the commodity form' expressed, not only in song lyrics but, perhaps more potently, in 'the critique of the economy of time and space which is identified with the world of work and wages from which blacks celebrate their exclusion. In these patterns of consumption, the night time is the right time. The period allocated for recovery and reproduction is assertively and provocatively occupied instead by the pursuit of leisure and pleasure' (Gilroy 1987: 210).

Furthermore, referring to hip-hop in particular, he points out that, in its development in the spaces of 'urban poverty where real instruments are an expensive luxury but where record players are commonplace, the everyday technology of consumption has been redefined and become an instrument with which music can be produced. Records are deprived of the authority and reverential treatment appropriate to a fixed and final artistic statement' (Gilroy 1987: 211). 'Real Hiphop', writes Mudede, 'does not sample real sounds ... but samples copyrighted music. The hiphop DJ does not shape raw sound into a form recognized as music, but shapes information into a sonic series recognized as music' (Mudede 2004: 72). More recently, the mixing board and dedicated computer programs like Ableton Live have supplanted the turntable at the point of production but sampling, the essence of the 'scratch',[5] remains the *sine qua non* of all contemporary dance musics. 'Because the scratch is based on a recording', writes Mudede, quoting David Goldberg, 'it becomes the manipulation of information and not just the vibrational properties of air' (Mudede 2004: 73). Music created with repurposed technology is thus both a quintessentially urban form and, like pop art, a mode of postmodern aesthetic production that uses the products of the culture industry in such a way that their significance in the economy of cultural production is critiqued and destabilized.

Case Study: Digital Reproduction and Everyday Arts: From Walkman to iPod

In Jon Courtenay Grimwood's science fiction novel *RedRobe* (Grimwood 2000), the central character, Axl Borja, has a soundchip implant in his brain that provides a suitable musical accompaniment to his experiences, bypassing the active selection of a soundtrack to everyday life, originally made possible by the introduction of the Sony Walkman in the 1980s. When Axl's chip is disconnected, 'when doors shut they just slam' (Grimwood 2000: 9). Thus, Grimwood extrapolates from Walkman technology to suggest a future in which music is not only an intensely private experience but one which thoroughly aestheticizes the everyday, providing a 'soundscape' of coded musical affects.

The Sony Walkman, the first mass market personal listening device, was introduced in 1979 and 'eventually sold 340 million units' (Levy 2006: 127). Although portable transistor radios that used a single earplug had been on the market for some time, what the Walkman allowed was a truly *personal* experience in that cassette tape technology allowed users to select their own music which they could rewind, fast forward and replay any number of times. But perhaps the true innovation of the Walkman was the lightweight headphones which enabled faithful stereo reproduction that produced a cocoon of sound, allowing an individual to 'aurally check out of the environment and withdraw into a private universe while technically present in the "real" one' (Levy 2006: 125). 'As you walked around', writes Simon Levy, 'the music you were listening to transformed itself into a *sound track*, reshaping your perception of the crappy world you were otherwise stuck in' (Levy 2006: 138, his emphasis). Thus, the Walkman experience is largely conditioned by intertextuality, by the filmic soundtrack that aestheticizes and conditions responses to the urban environment. The 'crappy world' is transformed into the

kind of montage produced by film editing which, like a film, is sutured by sound.

This close association between music, the city and film is unsurprising, given that the way we experience the city is largely conditioned by cinema. Writing in 1960 Siegfried Kracauer, described the experience of the cinema and the city as mutually defining. For him, the power of film editing is in the 'psychophysical corres-pondences' evoked by 'more or less free-hovering images of material reality'; images that intimate 'emotions, values, thoughts'. Consequently, '[t]he implication is that the flow of life is predominantly a material rather than a mental continuum' (Kracauer 1960: 171). When Kracauer refers to the 'flow of life' he intends to evoke the illusive continuity of perception that characterizes film spectatorship, what he refers to as the 'solidarity of the universe' or 'spatial continuum', which allows the spectator 'the feeling of being omnipresent'. This same sense of 'kaleidoscopic sights mingl[ing] with un-identified shapes and fragmentary visual complexes' he also associates with the city street (Kracauer 1960: 72). Thus, as David B. Clarke explains it 'the camera's penetration of reality entails a transformation in the perception of the cinemagoer, and does so in a manner consonant with the experiences offered by the flicker-ing, virtual presence of the city' (Clarke 1997: 10). Unsurprisingly, Michael Bull has reported that Walkman users often imagine themselves as characters in films (Levy 2006: 123 and 381n) and, in *RedRobe*, Axl Borja's soundtrack is partly derived from his experiences as a child soldier in a war broadcast as reality TV.

The city, of course, has its own soundtrack, what Shuhei Hosokawa refers to as 'the tone of urban life in general' (Hosokawa 1984: 166). Much of this 'tone' is the acoustic representation of the grid imposed by urban planning, road design, laws which restrict the movement of different people and vehicles, and the unwritten social laws under which we negotiate our status in the urban environment as well as the ever present sounds of information and communications technologies. If I stop typing for a moment and listen to the sounds outside my home (I live in the inner city), I can hear police sirens, doors slamming, the faint sounds of a television or radio, the ringtone from someone's mobile phone as they pass my window and their voice when they answer it, a car horn, the rattle of what is obviously a heavy goods vehicle negotiating the speed ramp further down the street and, underneath it all, the drone of traffic with, occasionally, the distinctive sound of a diesel engine. These sounds provide a 'text' that I can 'read'; an aural semiotics, which I decode, half unconsciously, in order to locate myself in space and time. The sounds contextualize my environment but they also contextualize *me* in the sense that I respond to their familiarity and their indication of the social and economic structure of which I am a part. Luigi Russolo's *Art of Noises* and Throbbing Gristle's industrial music were attempts to decontextualize and aestheticize these sounds by bringing them into the context of performance but, for Hosokawa, the Walkman 'decontextualises the given coherence of the city-text, and at the same time, contextualises every situation which seemingly does not cohere with it' (Hosokawa 1984: 171).

What Hosokawa is suggesting here is that the act of walking through the city enclosed in a private sound track is, itself, a kind of performance which can 'construct and/or deconstruct the network of urban meaning' (Hosokawa 1984: 178). What he calls the 'secret theatre' (Hosokawa 1984: 177) of the Walkman

is conditioned, primarily, by the 'walk act' from which '[a]ll expressive corporal practices, especially dance, theatre, certain sports, derive'. 'The walkman', he says, 'connects it with music' (Hosokawa 1984: 175) but not, as with dance and theatre, in a dedicated public space or prearranged venue but in the space of the wearer's own body. The Walkman 'intrudes inside the skin' and 'the order of our body is inverted, that is, the surface tension of the skin loses its balancing function through which it activates the interpenetration of Self and world ... Through the walkman ... the body is opened; it is put into the process of the aestheticisation, the theatricalisation of the urban – but in *secret*' (Hosokawa 1984: 176–7). Nevertheless, this is a shared secret. The opening of the body permits admittance to 'the secret garden of the walkman in which people communicate with one another through the form – not the content – of the secret' (Hosokawa 1984: 178).

Therefore, what Hosokawa is proposing is that, while the Walkman can subvert the city text on an individual level, those who gain admittance to the secret garden are, in fact, brought together in a subversive performance. This claim is echoed by Iain Chambers who questions whether the Walkman is 'a political act'. 'It is certainly', he suggests 'an act that unconsciously entwines with many other micro-activities in conferring a different sense on the *polis*. In producing a different sense of space and time, it participates in rewriting the conditions of representation: where 'representation' clearly indicates both the iconic or semiotic dimension of the everyday *and* potential participation in a political community' (1997: 142).

The suggestion here is that the Walkman is a technology that was, in its time, if not, like the turntable, intentionally repurposed then certainly a catalyst producing unintended and potentially political consequences. Interestingly, the cofounder of Sony, Akio Morita, was initially concerned that the Walkman would produce 'isolationist issues' (Levy 2006: 132) and ensured that early Walkmans were provided with dual headphone jacks and a 'hot line' button that allowed two listeners to share the music and communicate with each other but these enhancements were soon abandoned because it became clear that nobody was using them. If Hosokawa and Chambers are correct, the 'Walkman effect' is not in the sharing of the music itself but in the sharing of an aesthetic experience that transcends the boundaries of 'taste', which, as the sociologist Pierre Bourdieu has shown, marks the stratification of social class in the contemporary capitalist world order.[6]

It doesn't matter *what* you are listening to but, rather, the conditions, provided by the Walkman, under which you are experiencing the listening. Walkman listening also, in this formulation, has elements in common with the performance of black expressive cultures in that it promotes a shared and knowing destabilization of the practices that mark out the divisions between public and private, work and leisure. And, of course, most people listening to Walkmans did not purchase tapes of complete albums or predefined compilations but made their own by selecting tracks from vinyl records (or, later, CDs) or dubbing from a prerecorded onto a blank tape — a practice that was, technically, illegal.

When Apple's iPod hit the market in 2001 it came with a sticker that said simply 'don't steal music' but the status of music as a commodity was already under attack. Initiated by hiphop DJs, digital sampling had already 'challenged conventional assumptions about authorship and copyright and thus compromised corporate interests' (Haupt 2006: 108). 'Corporate interests' here comes down to the four major conglomerates who currently control global music production and distribution: Universal Music Group, Sony BMG Music Entertainment, EMI Group and Warner Music Group. With the invention of the Moving Picture Experts Group 1, Layer 3 (MP3) codec in 1988

and the spread of home computers, it became possible for individuals to share music online, thus potentially bypassing the traditional chain of distribution from producer to consumer, threatening the profits of the big four and musicians' royalties (although, as Adam Haupt points out, copyright holders are more often corporate entities than artists themselves).

The first successful peer-to-peer file sharing service on the internet, Napster, offered, according to Haupt, 'a similar kind of challenge to the major labels that digital sampling in hip-hop had in earlier years' (Haupt 2006: 116) but, in 2000, Napster was successfully sued by the Recording Industry Association of America on behalf of the record labels. What emerged in its wake was a slew of sites using Gnutella, an open source software enabling file sharing but without a central database. If the record companies want to sue, they now have to target individual downloaders and, although some high-profile cases have emerged, in general, music sharing on the Internet is beginning to prove John Perry Barlow's assertion that 'information wants to be free'. Despite the fact that Apple's iTunes Music Store has been touted as 'a revolutionary legal solution to digital piracy', as Gabrielle Cosentino points out, the figures prove that 'most iPod owners use it to store, and possibly even share, unlawfully downloaded files' (Cosentino 2006: 187 and 188). Furthermore, '[t]he technical characteristics of the iPod allow users to easily swap files, carry them around, organize them in personal collections, and play them in public venues' (Cosentino 2006: 198).

Thus, the MP3 revolution has effectively added an element of subversive illegality to membership of the secret garden which is further enhanced by implicit associations with drug culture. 'Without altering one's chemical composition', writes Levy, 'the iPod does change your head' (Cosentino 2006: 124) and he reports that, following the success of the Walkman, 'Sony itself would come to the conclusion that two impulses — both associated, by the way, with the effects of drugs — were behind the lure of personal audio: escape and enhancement' (Cosentino 2006: 136). Cosentino implicitly concurs when he refers to the ubiquitous 'white lines' of iPod earbud wires 'noticeable across the population of Manhattan' (Cosentino 2006: 185).

However, these utopian associations tend to mask the fact that what the iPod, in fact, represents is a hegemonic shift in which dominance of the market, and thus the loyalty and acquiescence of the consumers, is shifting from the music producers and distributors to the hardware and software developers. As Cosentino points out:

> Apple's brand has [always] been built on the co-optation of countercultural visual and linguistic signs, to evoke a utopian, liberating, and empowering view of technology, aesthetically translated into an original style of product design. The most striking quality of the iPod, or its 'aura' ... stems in fact from its unique design. As the traditional physical support of music (LPs, tapes, or CDs) dissolve into the immaterial, infinitely replicable digital substance of music files, the aura of the work of art moves from the content to the medium — in this case, the playback device ... By evoking universal values such as imagination, nonconformity, freedom, and stylishness, Apple presents itself as a company based on the ethos of empowering people through technology, thus pushing the brand-customer relation beyond mere commerce into the realm of representation and identity. (Cosentino 2006: 193–4 and 195)

Thus, by evoking Benjamin, Cosentino is suggesting that Apple's 'lax ... policy towards intellectual property' (Cosentino 2006: 203) and appearing to turn a blind eye to the fact that its customers *are* effectively, stealing music is not so much implicit support for liberating music from the constraints of commodification as a carefully developed business strategy attentive to the manipulation of subcultural semiotics. While the aura of the work of art, and thus its marketability, detaches from the music itself, it reattaches to the playback device through the aesthetics of industrial design supported by an appeal to subcultural capital.[7]

As Haupt points out, while hip-hop originally challenged the ownership of music through sampling, in which '[t]he integrity of the "original" music text as a coherently branded commodity item [was] "violated" during the process of recontextualization/(re)composition' (Haupt 2006: 111), recuperation of the form as a new commodity was swift. As he writes, '[w]ithin what has now become "mainstream" rap music, sampling is by and large no longer a subversive practice that threatens corporate interests or offers direct/parodic political challenges to hegemonic representations ... [O]ne key element of hip-hop, rap, has been co-opted/recuperated by key record labels to be repackaged — devoid of counter-hegemonic content — as a highly saleable commodity' (Haupt 2006: 112 and 114). By comparaison, in the shift from Walkman to MP3 technology, the counterhegemonic potential of the secret garden has been coopted as a marketing strategy as part of a move which has the potential to break the monopoly of the big four but which may see companies like Apple claim the space that they vacate. Already, Apple has started to sell 'limited edition' iPods preloaded with music in deals with musicians like U2 and Bob Dylan, thus potentially replacing the record company in the corporate hierarchy.[8] The difference is, of course, that, unlike a CD, the iPod can be wiped and reloaded but, as Cosentino (2006: 203) reports, Apple has already successfully claimed copyright violations against an artist that tried to sell a modified U2 iPod on eBay.

Furthermore, although the iPod may retain the potential of the Walkman to deconstruct the sound-text of the city, through iPod advertising, the city itself fights back with a visual assault calculated to reconnect the effect with the image of the product. 'Conspicuous investments', writes Cosentino, 'have ... been poured on the famous iPod "silhouette" campaign. The advertising campaign, showing black silhouette over monochrome backgrounds, has ... become a hallmark of urban visual landscape, both in the U.S and across international markets' (Cosentino 2006: 195). What Cosentino doesn't mention is that the black silhouettes of anonymous iPod users with the ubiquitous white product standing out in stark relief encodes the suggestion of an exclusive community, connected by the 'white lines' of the earbud wires.[9] And, it is perhaps no accident that the silhouettes are black and thus evoke the dissident aesthetic associated with hip hop and other black musics. Thus the iPod colonizes the secret garden and does so by strategically inserting its signifiers into the spatial continuum, rendering the 'walk act' a reaffirmation of brand loyalty rather than a subversive performance.

What the iPod does provide is a sense of individual empowerment through what Michael Bull calls 'accompanied solitude'. In his study of iPod use, Bull finds that the aestheticization of the street through an individual soundtrack is 'non-interactive, in the sense that others are blissfully unaware and unaffected by the aesthetic impulse' (Bull 2005: 350). In fact, Bull's respondents report casting other street users as 'extras' in their own personal movie. Furthermore, although Walkman users reported similar effects, Bull comments that an added attraction of the iPod is the power conferred on the user by having their entire music collection at their disposal and the opportunity to suit music to shifting moods and/or spaces. 'The world beyond the music being played through the iPod', he writes, 'becomes a function of the desire of the user and is maintained through time through the act of listening. The world is thus brought into line through acts of privatised, yet mediated, cognition' (Bull 2005: 351). 'Bringing the world into line', although individually empowering, would seem to suggest that what the iPod offers is a fantasy of neoliberalist individuation in which control of the street, and other street users enables an illusion of power *over* the body, self and environment rather than power *to* effect

change through a collective deconstruction of the text of the post-Fordist city. Indeed, Sean Cubitt has suggested that headphone listening, in itself, promotes a hyperindividualist aesthetic.

> Transmitted through air, sound occupies and creates an environment. Transmitted directly to the ear ... that space is reduced to an optimal (and imaginary) point midway between the ears: the Cartesian theory of the pineal gland as central control point in the brain where, hierarchically, all perceptions attain consciousness ... Such a Cartesian soundscape ... not only returns us to a residual dualism of mind over sensorium, not only reduces the experience of sound from a bodily to a purely auricular event, but also remodels the sound space as individuated ... Far from symbolising a dichotomy between the urban nomad (Chambers 1996) and the urban solipsist (Hosokawa 1984), the walkman [or iPod] is the precise material descriptor of their synthesis in the synergetic and corporate hyperindividual as machine ensemble. (Cubitt 1998: 103, 104)

On the other hand, these criticisms tend to obscure the major difference between public and private, mobile music, which is that the secret garden or theatre is just that – *secret*. Collective acts of public listening have significance, as Rey Chow points out, in terms of '[g]igantic emotions' that are 'the emotions of reverence, dedication, discipline and nostalgia, all of which have to do with the preservation of history as it ought to be remembered' (Chow 1997: 136). While Chow is writing within the context of Chinese culture, her analysis of certain types of public music as loudly proclaiming the rightness of official culture and its associated history has resonances in the din of conflicting muzak in the shopping mall and the playlists of radio stations which confirm the ascendancy of corporate entertainment in the West. Writing about the Walkman, Chow suggests that it is a 'form of listening that is a decisive break from the past ... The 'miniaturizing' that does not produce a visible body — however small — that corresponds with 'reality' leads to a certain freedom. This is the freedom to be deaf to the loudspeakers of history' (Chow 1997: 136). Thus, Chow disagrees with Adorno's analysis of popular music in America as 'a training course in ... passivity'. Portable audio devices allow it instead to be 'a 'silent' sabotage of the technology of collectivization with its own instruments' (Chow 1997: 140). If Chow is correct, the iPod generation may be the vanguard of a movement which takes its aesthetic cues from the random and infinitely mobile soundscape of the iPod 'shuffle' rather than the conformist dictates of consumer culture.

CHAPTER SUMMARY

- The arts of modernity and, by extension, postmodernity are characterized by a response to the effects of machine technologies on social life as well as the possibilities of the production of art *by* the machine.
- Walter Benjamin believed that mechanical reproduction could democratize aesthetics and make art accessible to the majority.
- What Theodor W Adorno and Max Horkheimer called the 'culture industry' is the mass production of popular arts, which are, for them, indistinguishable from propaganda and that thus function to maintain the ruling ideology.
- The use of 'repurposed' technologies in art and music draws attention to the role of the machine in mass production and subverts its intended function.

7 TECHNOLINGUISTICS

The technology that structures social life necessarily effects changes in modes of expression, allowing us to manage the conceptual shifts which new modes of work and leisure introduce. Technological change introduces neologisms into language, which accrue significance in terms of the way they are inserted into the complex structures of culture. 'Cyberspace', for instance, a word invented by a science fiction writer who had never used a computer, gained currency as a description for a mode of experience that was beginning to defy previous concepts of space and communication (see Chapter 5). Similarly, when, in 1900 Marconi sent the first message (actually one letter, 'S') in Morse Code from England to Canada, he initiated the 'wireless telegraph'. In 1906, Reginald Fessenden experimented with what he understood to be a 'wireless telephone' but which was really the first rudimentary radio broadcast and 'wireless' became the descriptor for such broadcasts, as well as the equipment that facilitated them. Although, in the US, 'radio' supplanted 'wireless' in the 1920s, the former term was retained in the UK until well into the century. The term fell out of use until the early twenty-first century when it was revived to describe short range networking by computers. Thus, between the inception of the term and its reintroduction, several reconceptualizations take place in which meaning is derived, not from the technologies themselves (they are all, in literal terms, without wires in the sense that they do not require a direct connection from sender to receiver) but from the cultural context in which they operate.

SEMIOTICS

The study of language as a system in which terms derive meaning from their relationship to other terms at a given point in time was initiated by Ferdinand de Saussure, a Swiss linguist whose *Course in General Linguistics* (1916) was influential in initiating the 'linguistic turn' that dominated cultural analysis through much of the twentieth century. Saussure's contribution to linguistics was to point out that words achieve meaning through difference rather than correspondence. In other words, there is no direct relationship between a word and what it refers to. Any sound, or visual sign could be used to distinguish what we mean to say (and, indeed, different languages have very different sounds for similar ideas or concepts). To explain this, Saussure divided what he calls the 'sign' into the 'signifier' (the sound or other indicator) and the 'signified' (the concept or idea to which it refers). He was able to demonstrate that the relationship between signifier and signified is arbitrary and that signs largely derive meaning from what they are not. When we hear a word we unconsciously measure it against other, similar sounding words and also against other words that refer to things that are similar to it in some way. For instance, in my example above, 'wireless' would, at one point in the history of its use, have been differentiated from 'telephone' and, later (but probably only in Britain after the Second World War) also from 'television' and 'gramaphone' (or record player). When 'wireless' was supplanted by 'radio', the technology did not change in any dramatic way. One signifier had merely replaced another indicating a subtle shift in meaning associated with the impact of broadcast technology on the culture in which it was consumed.

Saussure thus pointed the way towards an understanding of language as largely determining the way that we experience reality in the sense that, to continue with my example, the world in which 'radio' is an intelligible part of reality is specific to a particular culture at a particular point in time. Indeed, the so-called Sapir-Whorf hypothesis, attributable to the American linguist Edward Sapir and his student, Benjamin Lee Whorf, goes further. According to Whorf, '[w]e cut nature up, organize it into concepts, and ascribe significances as we do, largely because we are parties to an agreement to organize it in this way – an agreement that holds throughout our speech community and is codified in the patterns of our language. The agreement is, of course, an implicit and unstated one, *but its terms are absolutely obligatory*; we cannot talk at all except by subscribing to the organization and classification of data which the agreement decrees' (Whorf 1956: 213–14, his emphasis). If language expresses our reality and we 'cannot talk at all' outside the terms of the agreement, then this implies that there is no reality that is independent of language. Sapir, in fact, went so far as to say that '[t]he worlds in which different societies live are distinct worlds, not merely the same world with different labels attached' (Sapir 1956 [1929]: 69). Of course, this begs the question of how exactly the 'agreement' is formulated and under what terms a particular use of language can be said to receive legitimation.

The theorist most closely associated with formulating a reply to this question is Roland Barthes who, in 1956 wrote that 'it is human history which converts reality into speech' (Barthes 2000 [1956]: 94). Barthes developed Saussure's system of semiology to demonstrate that meaning is made not only through the conjunction of signifier and signified but also through a second order level of signification that he called 'metalanguage' or 'myth' (Barthes 2000 [1956]: 100). Saussure's first order of signification, in which a signifier is arbitrarily attached to a signified to form the sign, he referred to as 'denotation' (Barthes 2000 [1961]: 197) to indicate that this describes merely the 'empty' (Barthes 2000 [1956]: 108) formal structure of language. 'Connotation' (Barthes 2000 [1961]: 198), on the other hand, describes the reception of the word or image in its 'full' (Barthes 2000 [1956]: 108) significance in which its meaning is ideologically determined.

MYTH

The fact that Barthes originally coined the terms 'denotation' and 'connotation' in an essay on *The Photographic Message* is instructive. Other 'analogical reproductions of reality – drawings, paintings, cinema, theater', he maintains, are received with a second order of signification that he calls '*style*' (Barthes 2000 [1961]: 196), which is the assumption that we bring to their viewing of some sort of intention on the part of the artist to offer a comment on what they depict. A photograph, on the other hand (and it is press photographs he is referring to, rather than those produced with a specific artistic intention) professes to be 'a mechanical analogue of reality' (Barthes 2000 [1956]: 197) or a faithful recording with no intention other than to portray 'truth'. We thus ascribe to a particular technology the ability to transparently represent the world when, in fact, as Barthes demonstrates, this is an ideological move *in itself*. The connotation of the word 'photograph' in its 'empty', formal meaning (at least at the time that Barthes was writing) is simply the result of the action of light on presensitized paper, which is developed with the application of chemicals. The connotation is the power that we ascribe to the image, the 'full' meaning of which is derived from living in a culture in which alienation creates the desire to experience unmediated reality and in which technology, the tool of alienated labour, is nevertheless imbued with the power to secure truth.

I will return later to a fuller discussion of the structuring of language in technocratic capitalism but first it is necessary to explore the way in which the *content* of the photograph is also subject to second order signification. Put simply '[d]enotaton is *what* is photographed, connotation is *how* it is photographed. 'Connotation' writes John Fiske, 'is the human part of the process, it is the selection of what to include in the frame, of focus, aperture, camera angle, quality of film and so on' (Fiske, 1982: 91). And this 'human' part is never innocent in itself but is determined by ideological constructs.

Consider, for instance, the difference between photographs of the British Royal Family and minor celebrities. Because the Royal Family carries connotations of respect and authority, its members will tend to be photographed in ways that reflect their status. Minor celebrities, on the other hand, particularly if they are female, are rarely photographed other than in compromising situations. While the Queen may be shot in soft focus to minimize the ravages of age, young celebrities are subjected to 'revealing' harsh focus framing which points up their 'imperfections' unless, of course, they are modelling for a fashion magazine, in which case they will be enhanced by artistic framing and strategically placed lighting to establish the desirability of the clothes. It is revealing that, despite the fact that the manipulation made possible by contemporary digital techniques is widely understood, press photographs that confirm widely held beliefs are still held to be authentic reproductions of reality. Thus the technology of the camera, although itself connoting, in certain contexts, authenticity and transparency, functions to sustain the coding of its subjects in terms of ideological representations.

This, then, is what Barthes means by *myth*. There is no fabulation or hidden meaning attached to a press or celebrity photograph. Its meaning, in fact, is clear and well defined but *only* within the context of a community of language speakers for whom the second order signification is meaningful. In my example, both the Queen and the minor celebrity are subject to a gender-biased ideology that demands that women conform to codes of behaviour deemed appropriate in terms of age and social class. The reason that we are interested in minor celebrities who appear to transgress these codes is that these transgressions serve to confirm what is understood to be 'normal' or 'natural'. Thus Barthes is at pains to point out that '[t]his is why myth is experienced as innocent speech: not because its intentions are hidden – if they were hidden, they could not be efficacious – but because they are naturalized' (Barthes 2000 [1956]: 118). Thus when Barthes writes that 'myth is type of speech', what he intends to convey is that language is conditioned by ideology.

TECHNOLOGICAL RATIONALITY

This is why novels like *Brave New World* (1932) can construct a political philosophy for imagined worlds that is largely conveyed through changes to everyday language. Huxley communicates his critique of modernity through strategically nuanced expressions and recontextualized terms to produce a technologically determinist metalanguage for a future world in which Henry Ford is worshipped as a prophet and 'mother' and 'father' are terms of abuse. Here is a typical passage: 'Our Ford – or our Freud, as, for some inscrutable reason, he chose to call himself whenever he spoke of psychological matters – Our Freud had been the first to reveal the appalling dangers of family life' (Huxley 1977 [1932]: 52).

In Huxley's England of the future, production-line techniques have been applied to *re*production, not only as an efficient means of producing replacement workers but, by means of a system of modified cloning and a technique of infant conditioning called 'hypnopaedia', a guaranteed 'happy' workforce who, as Huxley himself pointed out in his preface to the 1946 edition 'do not have to be coerced, because they love their servitude' (Huxley 1977: 14). The system is sustained and naturalized by the language, which attaches the connotations of Christian mythology to Fordism and, in doing so, promotes a totalitarian ideology in which psychoanalysis has become a science of adjustment to a rigid caste system, guaranteed to produce carefully calculated armies of 'sane men, obedient men, stable in contentment' (Huxley, 1977 [1932]: 55) and dedicated to consumption as a way of life.

If *Brave New World* sounds chillingly prophetic it is perhaps because Huxley recognized, as did Herbert Marcuse, that technological rationality promotes what he calls a 'functionalization of language' (Marcuse, 1991 [1964]: 86) in which 'discourse and communication make themselves immune against the expression of protest and refusal' (Marcuse, 1991 [1964]: 90). In what he calls 'The Language of Total Administration', '[m]agical, authoritarian and ritual elements permeate speech and language' (Marcuse, 1991 [1964]: 85). Language is subject to 'operational redefinitions' (Marcuse, 1991 [1964]: 98), which block dialectical thought by fixing concepts in terms of functionality.

This is perhaps best explained with reference to my case study for Chapter 4, which discussed the meaning of death in technocapitalist cultures, in which the logical extension of the application of medical expertise to preventative healthcare has meant that death itself is seen as a form of failure; a result of inattention to care of the self, rather than an inevitability to which all bodies must eventually succumb. Thus, 'death' has been operationally redefined as something avoidable rather than inevitable but *only* in terms of those 'technologies of the self' (Foucault 1988: 16) that police subjectivity in contemporary cultures.[1] In fact, suicide, a crime that deprives the spirit of transcendence in Christian mythology, has, in my discussion of the technique of cryonic suspension, effectively been coopted by a new mythology of transcendence that relies upon notions of correct investment and the kind of language associated with the sale of insurance policies. Life, in this sense, has been operationally redefined as something to be *earned*.

Marcuse (1991 [1964]: 89) himself gives the example of an advertisement for a 'Luxury Fall-Out Shelter' which he finds in a November 1960 edition of the *New York Times*. As he says, 'no language should be capable of correctly joining luxury and fall-out' (Marcuse 1991 [1964]: 90) but, at the height of the Cold War, the threat from technologies of mass destruction could be deflected by, once again, attention to technologies of the self where failure to survive a nuclear attack is recast as failure to invest in the necessary protection. Rather than protest against the proliferation of nuclear devices, the population is encouraged to estimate the risk in terms of consumer choice. Thus, the language 'controls by reducing the linguistic forms and symbols of reflection, abstraction, development, contradiction; by substituting images for concepts.' This is further demonstrated in Carol Cohn's discussion of 'technostrategic' language in nuclear defence discourse (see Chapter 3, this volume). 'Speaking the expert language', she points out, 'not only offers distance, a feeling of control, and an alternative focus for one's energies – it also offers escape – escape from thinking of oneself as a victim of nuclear war' (Cohn 1987: 706). 'But', Marcuse points out, 'this kind of discourse is not terroristic … One does not "believe" the statement of an operational concept but it justifies itself in action – in getting the job done, in selling and buying, in refusal to listen to others, etc.' (1991 [1964]: 103).

SCIENTISM

As Marcuse demonstrates, operational concepts do not emerge spontaneously nor are they simply the result of the exploitation of anxieties by capital's need for new markets but are generated in accordance with the principles of what we would now call 'scientism'. Scientism is generally represented as a worldview that privileges scientific method as the guarantor of truth and it is thus held to be in opposition to other worldviews, which privilege, for example, religious explanations. Michael Shermer has famously stated that '[s]cientism is a scientific worldview that encompasses natural explanations for all phenomena, eschews supernatural and paranormal speculations, and embraces empiricism and reason as the twin pillars of a philosophy of life appropriate for an Age of Science'.[2] However, as I will demonstrate, it is more productive to understand the term as referring to the selective production of knowledge under the terms of operational rationality.

Neil Postman suggests that scientism can be understood in relation to three related ideas. First, that 'the methods of the natural sciences can be applied to the study of human behavior'. Second, 'that social science generates specific principles which can be used to organize society on a rational and humane basis' and third, 'that faith in science can serve as a comprehensive belief system that gives meaning to life' (Postman 1993: 147), which he traces to 'the nineteenth century hope that the assumptions and procedures of natural science might be applied without modification to the social world, to the same end of increased predictability and control' (Postman 1993: 159–60). Postman wants to suggest that the social sciences cannot be called sciences, strictly speaking, because they only enable us to tell stories about the state of the social world at any given historical moment; they do not actually *discover* anything. But this is to assume that the natural sciences have a greater claim to truth because their practitioners, in Postman's words, are 'researchers without bias or values, unburdened by mere opinion' (Postman 1993: 158). This, as my previous chapters have demonstrated, is not necessarily the case (see particularly Chapter 2).

Marcuse, on the other hand, casts the problem in terms of the elimination of what he calls 'transitive meaning' (his emphasis) in social research. '[A]ll cognitive concepts', he writes, '... go beyond descriptive reference to particular facts. And if the facts are those of society, the cognitive concepts also go beyond any particular context of facts – into the processes and conditions on which the respective society rests, and which enter into all particular facts, making, sustaining, and destroying the society' (Marcuse 1991 [1964]: 106). In other words, a statement about a particular social condition actually has meaning in the context of social conditions in general and the historical forces which have shaped them, but social research requires that the problem is cast in terms of what Marcuse calls 'the fallacious concreteness of positivist empiricism' (Marcuse 1991: 107). He gives the example of a worker complaining to a researcher that 'wages are too low', a statement which has a transitive meaning in terms of the exploitation of labour under the terms of capitalist economics, which is translated as 'B's present earnings ... are insufficient to meet his current obligations' (Marcuse 1991: 110), which restricts the problem to a particular case. The study can then proceed on the basis of examining employer/employee relations in an isolated context: 'Once the personal discontent is isolated from the general unhappiness, once the universal concepts which militate against functionalization are dissolved into particular referents, the case becomes a treatable and tractable incident' (Marcuse 1991: 111).

The importance of Marcuse's argument is in the emphasis that he places on the way that functionalization restricts meaning in linguistic utterances. Language becomes the vehicle for the transmission of an ideology that privileges empiricism as the guarantor of statements about the world. Every time we read in a newspaper or hear a broadcast journalist state that 'studies have shown that ...', we fall prey to the hegemony of scientism in which we acquiesce to the 'facts' because we cannot argue with them; they have been functionally determined to the extent that they cannot be proved to be false. Or, as Marcuse explains it

> the criteria for judging a given state of affairs are those offered by (or, since they are those of a well-functioning and firmly established social system, imposed by) the given state of affairs. The analysis is "locked"; the range of judgement is confined within a context of facts which excludes judging the context in which the facts are made ... and in which their meaning, function, and development are determined. (Marcuse 1991: 116)

TECHNOLOGY AND LITERACY

It would seem, then, that the language of scientism largely creates the reality that it intends to study. Or, alternatively, that empiricism in the social sciences demands a conceptual framework in which signification becomes ossified around a central idea or philosophy so that the range of alternative ideas becomes severely restricted. Indeed, this is the criticism central to most poststructuralist theory, which is associated with the linguistic turn in philosophy – essentially, a turn away from metaphysics (the nature of what exists in the world) to epistemology (how knowledge is made and understood). It follows that the way that we express what we come to know is of vital importance in the way that that knowledge is constructed and disseminated and, because so much of our communication is mediated by technologies, any use of language needs to be considered within the context of its mode of transmission.

The close connection between language, communications technologies, subjectivity and cultural forms is the concern of Marshall McLuhan in his now famous books *The Gutenberg Galaxy* (1962) and *Understanding Media* (1964). McLuhan's concept of the 'global village' is now accepted as a prescient understanding of the potential for communications technologies to implode conventional, modernist notions of time and space, as has now been realized with the growth of the Internet. But his fundamental concern is with the effect of technological extensions of the human sensorium, primarily, in *The Gutenberg Galaxy* with the effect of the printed word on systems of meaning and communication and the consequent shift from language as experienced aurally and as primarily received through vision.

'Schizophrenia', according to McLuhan, 'may be a necessary consequence of literacy.' What he means by this is that writing can separate thought from action. The development of literacy and the elevation of reason thus gives birth to the 'detribalized individual' (McLuhan 1995: 117) whose thoughts are communicated at a distance and translated through a technological medium: the phonentic alphabet. 'Only the phonetic alphabet', writes McLuhan, 'makes a break between eye and ear, between semantic meaning and visual code; and thus only phonetic writing has the power to translate man from the tribal to the civilized sphere, to give him an eye for an ear ... "Civilization" must now be used technically to mean detribalised man for whom the visual values have priority in the organisation of thought and action' (McLuhan 1995: 122). Thus the concept of the abstract individual is communicated, as an idea, through the technology of writing while, at the same time, it fosters 'habits of individualism and privacy' through 'extension and amplification of ... visual power'.

In other words, literacy brings about not only a change in culture but a change in the way that language is used and understood. If we accept, with McLuhan, that orality is essentially tribal and collective whereas literacy promotes privacy and separation, then it follows that the way that language means, and thus how we understand ourselves, cannot be separated from its mode of communication. Literacy ushers in a new conceptual world determined by the translation of words into visual symbols. Furthermore, in early Christianity, as Michael Heim points out, 'the cult of the book was … the cultivation of a transcending state of mind, of a distanced and composed contemplative attitude' (Heim 1987: 175). Thus '[t]he literate man or society develops the tremendous power of acting in any matter with considerable detachment from the feelings or emotional involvement that a nonliterate man or society would experience' (McLuhan 1997 [1964]: 79). 'Literacy', writes Heim, 'is as much an expression of the way a person inhabits the world as it is an instrument within the world of human concerns' (Heim 1987: 167–8).

The alphabet, for McLuhan, is a 'hot' medium, and printing doubly so, in that their assault on the sense of sight is intense and speedy, providing for a kind of information overload. 'Any hot medium', he writes, 'allows of less participation than a cool one, as a lecture makes for less participation than a seminar, and a book for less than dialogue' (McLuhan 1997 [1964]: 23). Similarly, poetry could be said to be a 'cool' medium, while a technical manual is 'hot'. McLuhan's famous pronouncement that 'the medium is the message' (McLuhan 1997: 7) refers to 'the change of scale or pace or pattern' that any new technological medium 'introduces into human affairs' (McLuhan 1997: 8) so that the change from a 'hot' to a 'cool' medium as the primary mode of communication can be understood as an event highly charged with political consequences. As he warns 'any medium has the power of imposing its own assumption on the unwary' such that, in the developed West, the linear and sequential form of typography has dominated what we understand as rationality. '[W]e have confused', he says, 'reason with literacy, and rationalism with a single technology' (McLuhan 1997: 15). The consequence is that 'literate man is quite inclined to see others who cannot conform as somewhat pathetic' (McLuhan 1997: 17).

In fact, the ability to negotiate and manipulate typographic technology had, until very recently, been equated with intelligence. It is perhaps no accident that the identification of dyslexia as a form of medical condition that is responsive to new techniques of literacy has emerged at the same time as new information and communications technologies have problematized the assumption of linearity as the natural progression of the process of thought. Hypertext, the system of textual links which structures cyberspaces like the Internet, not only confounds the linear narrative but also affects the 'classic author/reader distinction', which, as Benjamin Woolley (1992: 153) points out, 'is looking less and less valid'. People affected by dyslexia (and its associated condition, dyspraxia) are unable to orient themselves within the logic of linear text or, in some cases, within the spaces of the Cartesian grid (see Chapter 5). But hypertext enables the reader to control what s/he reads and in what order, not only within a single document but across a myriad of documents in different locations. It becomes possible to suggest that the identification of dyslexia is contingent upon the privileging of a particular mode of reading and spatial orientation that, in cyberspace, simply does not exist. Also, there are as many narratives as there are readers so that hypertext becomes a technological realization of Roland Barthes' 'Death of the Author' (see last chapter).

INCORPORATED PRACTICES

Consideration of conditions like dyslexia also brings into focus the discrepancy between the body considered as 'information' (see Chapter 4) and the necessity of understanding how 'incorporated' practices are involved in the production of language both as speech and in writing and the use of typographic technologies. As N. Katherine Hayles suggests, the orientation of the body in space and time and the habitual practices that enable cultural negotiation and which can be understood as precognitive (like copy typing, which is a 'habit' of the body rather than a purely cognitive process) cannot be separated from the way that language means.

Hayles illustrates how incorporated practices affect language with reference to the metaphors that we use which refer to the orientation of a 'normal' (upright) body in space with words like 'up', 'down', 'bottom' and 'top' signifying success, failure, dominance and submission. As she suggests, when we can understand 'the bottom of the ladder' to mean that the aim is to reach the top, then similar metaphors underpin what must be achieved by the completion of the reading process. Furthermore, as Christopher Land (2005: 455) explains it, '[g]rounded in writing, language develops linearly'. Consequently, dyslexia, or indeed any disorientation towards the processing of linear and sequential reasoning, presented as a series of marks on a page, can be understood as a condition that exposes the link between the structure of written language, the technologies that determine that structure, and the normalization of the human subject. This, equally, confirms Hayles' (1999: 206–7) point that 'when people begin using their bodies in significantly different ways, either because of technological innovations or other cultural shifts, changing experiences of embodiment bubble up into language, affecting the metaphoric networks at play within the culture'.

To illustrate her point, Hayles subjects William Burroughs' novel *The Ticket That Exploded* (1962) to a close reading from which emerges a significant analysis of the linguistics of technologically mediated bodies. For Burroughs, 'the word is a parasite with material effects' (Hayles 1999: 215); language is 'a virus' (213) that not only codes bodies but *produces* them. Burroughs was writing at a time when tape recording was impacting on Western culture and, as Hayles demonstrates, his writing develops an understanding of subjectivity as essentially formed through recording and repetition and of tape recording as a technology which mimics and reinforces the envelope of sounds which contain bodies in approved cultural forms while, at the same time, allowing for disruptive play that problematizes the notion of fixed identity.

Because we are currently inhabiting a cultural moment in which the disruptive and transformative properties of the virus challenge assurances of both bodily coherence and the structure of information, we are well placed to understand the correspondence that Burroughs sets up between technologies that manipulate language and the structuring of identity through practices of inscription (reading, writing, speech) that are both internal and external to the body.

Consider, for example, the way that 'junk' email attempts to disrupt the feedback loops through which email client programs recognize 'friendly' mail. The battle to protect the integrity of our personal mailboxes is fought on the field of the words that constitute our 'private' worlds. Junk filters allow messages that correspond to the names in our personal address books and regularly used subject lines while the code that attempts to disseminate the junk uses a similar technique. Junk mail that 'gets through' can then come to seem like a personal violation. Because we use email to sustain our social networks and maintain our connections in cyberspace, it has become a technology through which we constantly rehearse our self definitions: our selves are produced and reproduced through acknowledgement by others. The intrusion of junk mail has several effects. It not only penetrates our defences but interpellates us both as consumers and as fragile subjects, vulnerable to incursion. Most junk mail is trying to sell us something and uses a carpet bombing technique to reach the small but significant proportion of people who will be vulnerable to its message. Whether we respond with annoyance or interest, we are nevertheless acknowledging the determination of our identity by the dominant culture. The responses, 'yes, this is me and I must buy this product' and 'this is not me and I must secure myself against further incursion' are equivalent in that they are both attempts to figure a coherent self in the face of a linguistic assault that attempts to fragment it. The suggestion is always one of incompleteness that must be fought (in a never-ending battle) on a terrain provided in advance.

This is why the Marxist philosopher, Louis Althusser (1971: 172), claims that we are 'always already' subjects of the dominant order. Althusser follows the post-Freudian psychoanalyst, Jacques Lacan, in understanding subjectivity as given in language. From the moment that we learn to speak, we enter what Lacan calls the 'symbolic order' (Macey, 1994: xxv), which is self-regulated by the incorporation of norms, beginning with gender difference (language that applies to the gender that you understand yourself to be, measured against what is given as its opposite), which then conditions all other linguistic oppositions. Both Lacan and Althusser were attentive to Saussure's structural linguistics but what Althusser achieves is a way of demonstrating how we are trapped into linguistic patterns that constantly reproduce inequalities. In a sense, we reproduce our own oppressions every time we open our mouths to speak.

PLAY BACK AND SPONTANEITY

Burroughs understood this only too well. As Hayles (1999: 213) demonstrates, in *Ticket That Exploded*, he is concerned with the incorporation of language and its effects on the materiality of the body but also with the correspondence between tape recording and the way that the body is infected by 'the surrounding, culturally constructed envelope of sounds and words'. There are similarities here with Michel Foucault's argument that the body is a discursive production and that our experience of our own bodies is never separable from everything that can be said (and therefore thought) about bodies at any given historical moment. But the crucial difference is that while, for Foucault, 'technologies of the self' are incorporated practices for maintaining (or attempting to maintain) what is given as optimal embodiment and which may or may not include recourse to material technologies (like cosmetic surgery), for Burroughs, technologies like tape recording are always already incorporated in that they are produced *out of* the body while also being part of the 'culturally constructed envelope of sounds and words'.

As Walter Ong (1982: 79) reminds us, in the *Phaedrus*, Plato has Socrates say that writing, 'is inhuman, pretending to establish outside the mind what in reality can be only in the mind' and similar objections were raised when print technology was introduced to Western culture and in the early days of computing. But 'intelligence is relentlessly reflexive, so that even the external tools that it uses to implement its workings become 'internalized', that is, part of its own reflexive process ... Technologies are not mere exterior aids but also interior transformations of consciousness, and never more than when they affect the word' (Ong 1982: 81 and 82). In other words, there is a continual loop of feedback between the technologies through which we externalize ideas expressed as language and the way that those conceptualizations of the world are internalized as 'play back', having been transformed by both the mode of their dissemination and the discourses that structure its reception within the culture.

It is this 'play back' that interests Burroughs in that tape recording is an externalization of the sounds made by the body and an analogue of our subvocalizations, 'the internal monologue that provides a narrative sense of personal, subjective continuity which we think of as "our self"'.

> These subvocalizations simultaneously come from outside, hence the notion that they are a viral infection, and constitute an inside: the subject 'I'. They are external in at least two senses. On one hand they are often constituted by fragments and snippets picket up from conversations, the daily press, books, radio and television. Alternatively they might be generated in response to an external authority, as … when one's passport or papers are out of order. In such situations one incessantly runs excuses and explanations round and round, rehearsing the potential encounter with 'control'. (Land 2005: 453)

Burroughs' technique with tape (and he did actually employ the technique in tape recordings that he made from the late 1950s through the late 1970s) is similar to the 'cut up' technique that he employed in his writing. As he writes in 'The Cut Up Method of Brion Gysin', '[y]ou can not will spontaneity. But you can introduce the unpredictable spontaneous factor with a pair of scissors.'[3] By cutting up, folding and re-arranging text, the narrative continuity of 'self' is disrupted. The cut-up, like hypertext, is dyslexic in that it disconnects linear sense and makes new and surprising associations. Indeed, by doing violence to an authorized artefact, the technique demands that we recognize how inscription practices authorize and institute norms that affect, not only our sense of self, but our conceptualizations of the material world from which it receives its definition. Burroughs used tape recorders to 'record a particular message, which would then be rewound and forwarded to an arbitrary point when something else, a snippet of speech, white noise from the radio, music or street sounds, would be layered over the original recording' (Land, 2005: 460).

If tape is manipulated in this way, then, to borrow McLuhan's terms, it is transformed from a 'hot' to a 'cool' medium. In fact it becomes very cool indeed, in the sense that, as Ong (1982: 91) explains it, '[i]f you put the word 'part' on a sound tape and reverse the tape, you do not get 'trap', but a completely different sound, neither 'part' nor 'trap'. It is not meaning*less* in that it is still an externalized body sound but it does not carry meaning in the conventional sense. It invites us to *make* meaning, rather than succumb to structures of meaning which reinscribe our bodies as producers and recorders of the dominant order. 'On the one hand', writes Hayles, 'magnetic tape allows sound to be preserved over time; in this respect it counters the ephemerality of sound by transforming it into inscription'. But

> [o]n the other hand, inscriptions can be easily erased and reconfigured; in this sense, it reproduces the impermanence of sound. Burroughs was drawn to both aspects of the technology. The inscription of sound in a durable medium suited his belief that the word is material, whereas the malleability of sound meant

that interventions were possible, interventions that could radically change or eradicate the record. (Hayles 1999: 217)

As with the cut-up, Burroughs' technique with recorded sound is designed as a strategy to both confound technolinguistic determinism and 'to expel the language parasite from the body' (Lydenberg, 1987: 133), a strategy that, as Robin Lydenberg notes, parallels the attack on '[t]he logocentric system, based on the belief in an epistemological and moral supremacy of voice, presence, identity and truth' (Lydenberg, 1987: 136), which forms the basis of poststructuralist thought.

DECONSTRUCTION

Deconstruction, for instance, a mode of reading that problematizes the way that meaning is distinguished in linguistic systems, takes as one of its concerns the way in which speech is accorded priority over writing in Western discourse. According to Jacques Derrida, writing, under the terms of Western metaphysics, is understood as coming after speech in that it is seen as an attempt to represent speech and as a substitute for speech in that speech entails the idea of presence (the speaker and the person to whom s/he is speaking being, literally, in each other's presence). But presence here can be seen to have a more complex relation to meaning in that it is thought in opposition to absence. Because absence denotes lack; presence becomes associated with plenitude – with 'full' meaning or direct access to thought.

Absence/writing thus becomes the inferior term in the binary speech/writing. Derrida refers to the privileging of thought over its representations (for example, in writing) as 'logocentrism' (Derrida 1997 [1974]: 12) and this term describes not only the elevation of thought/reason in post-Enlightenment philosophy but the assumption of a 'centre' (Derrida 2001 [1967]: 352) or determining essence that can fix meaning in such a way as to guarantee that language will express truth.

This appeal to an authoritarian 'outside' is demanded by structuralist semiotics in that, as Derrida demonstrates, although the relationship between signifier and signified is understood to be arbitrary, here again, the signified (concept or what is thought) is privileged over the signifier, understood as a mark or inscription. Saussure cannot privilege the 'inside' of thought and/or speech, without reference to the 'outside' understood as writing. The oppositional hierarchy is necessary for Saussure to make his argument in the first place. But deconstruction has another 'move' to make, which, while recognizing a hierarchy, simultaneously overturns and confounds the structure that makes the hierarchized terms intelligible. That is to say, both the desire for and the impossibility of fixing meaning coexist and this can be demonstrated by returning to Saussure's contention that signs can only be said to have meaning in terms of their difference from other signs. Put simply, if signs mean only in a negative sense, then there can be no positives in language. Language is never identical to itself but always defers meaning (or truth) in the play of what Derrida calls 'différance', a neologism that he coins to indicate that the structure of language is such that it means both in terms of difference and continual deferment. The example often given is of looking up a word in the dictionary which leads you to another word which, when you look it up, leads yet to another word, and so on. If you think of the term 'wireless' with which I started the discussion of language in this chapter, you will be thinking of it in terms of what it means for you *right now*. Like all signifiers, it only means in terms of its difference from other signifiers but, in order for it to have a fixed meaning, true for all time and in all situations, it would have to be not different from anything at all! The term 'différance' itself demonstrates this in that it is a 'nonword' in the lexicon of everyday speech (it sounds exactly like difference) but, even when written down, the concept that it refers to is one that presents us with an insurmountable difficulty when we try to fix its meaning. Thus, what deconstruction is interested in is undermining the certainties of language in order to demonstrate the way that logocentrism works to substantiate a particular form of truth at any given moment. Put simply, what seems 'logical' is only so because there *is* no transcendent truth. Niall Lucy gives a good demonstration when he writes about trying to type 'différance' using word-processing software:

> in order to write differance I have to fight against the software I am using to write this, which has been programmed in such a way that differance registers only as a 'mistake' that has to be 'corrected'. No sooner have I written differance than it disappears, its place having been taken by difference. I then have to go back to difference (to where differance was) and change the 'e' to an 'a'. Every time I want to write differance I have to override the automatic software commands, or I have to write over what has been written into the program, a program that has been designed to 'process' words. Included in that design, clearly, is the recognition of what does *not* count as a 'word' – such as differance. Hence the software I am using is perfectly logocentric. (Lucy 2004: 25–6)

Lucy's battle with his word processor while trying to type 'differance' is, on the level of natural language, a demonstration of the operation of deconstruction and its ability to expose the way that the logic of signification restricts thought. But on the level of machine code (and, to a greater or lesser extent, the other languages that intervene between it and the natural language that appears on the screen), a different logic operates – one that depends on only one difference, that between 0 and 1, which are themselves integers representing the flow of electrons as they are counted either in or out of electronic 'gates'. Word processing is thus, itself, a technology that has demonstrably changed the way that we understand how language means. As Michael Heim has pointed out 'natural language and thinking in natural language are simply incompatible with the binary digits used on the level of machine-language' (Heim 1987: 132). Furthermore, the phenomenon of word processing (or any other software with a user interface) is what he calls 'self-masking' in that '[d]issimulation is internal to the phenomenon because informational systems, unlike mechanical systems in general, are largely opaque, their function not being inferable from the underlying, chiefly invisible substructure' (Heim 1987: 131). We thus tend to think

Case Study: Data Processing and Symbolic Power Structures

At the end of Jean-Luc Godard's 1965 science fiction dystopia, *Alphaville*, an extraordinary scene shows a long corridor of undifferentiated rooms, populated by bodies in extreme states of disorientation. People grope blindly at blank walls, move in circles or crawl along the floor. The logic of negotiating a simple corridor seems to elude them and the closed doors offer no avenues for escape. Only one person is moving in a straight line, Lemmy Caution (Eddie Constantine), the private detective straight out of a comic book, who has come from the 'lands without' to liberate the people of Alphaville from the dastardly clutches of *Alpha 60*, a computer to which they have become enslaved. In its death throes, *Alpha 60* relinquishes control of the people who, rather than awakening to a new world of liberation, succumb to disorientation and meaninglessness. Simple tasks like moving in a straight line or opening a door become impossible because the logic that structured the reality of their world no longer operates to control signification. The world has lost meaning and bodies can no longer function within it. In true science-fiction comic-book fashion, Lemmy Caution destroys *Alpha 60* by asking it to solve a riddle and rescues the scientist's beautiful daughter by teaching her to say 'I love you'.

In a 1966 review of the movie for *Film Quarterly*, John Thomas refers to it as 'the ultimate Message Movie' which is 'equally, the ultimate Meaningless Movie' (Thomas 1966: 48). the 'message' is that the world cannot exist without poetry, cold logic destroys love and the rational efficiency of technocracy can only lead to totalitarianism. But the message is delivered through a series of disconnected and often confusing scenes, which Thomas describes as 'the very poetry that Godard, speaking through Lemmy Caution, offers as Alphaville's salvation'. Thus, the story is little more than a rewrite of countless pulp science fiction novellas and the movie has little to say on the level of narrative that is not better expressed in other media, but the structure of the movie itself functions as a deconstructive device which overturns and challenges meaning, even as it is expressed. Or, as Thomas explains it, '[e]ach member of the audience has his own Alpha 60 in operation when he sits through a movie, and it is into this computer that Godard feeds a visual poetry designed to destroy it' (Thomas 1966: 49).

This 'visual poetry' was partly achieved with the use of a handheld camera, which Godard took into the streets of Paris, often filming at night with only streetlighting for illumination. The city itself is wholly of informational systems only in terms of *what* they enable to be produced (text, statistics, music, video etc.), rather than *how* they enable it.

Lucy's word processor is only 'perfectly logocentric' because he has not yet discovered how to manipulate the program to permit 'differance' as part of its internal dictionary, as I have done to enable the writing of this chapter. In other words, the colonizing of speech, thought and action by the logic of data processing is a function of the technolinguistic structuring of power relations, rather than an inherent effect of the machines themselves.

---

defamiliarized and flickering lights are often employed to disturb the coherence of a scene. At one point, the black-and-white film reverses to negative and scenes are often intercut with unrelated or abstractly related images (like e = mc², flashing in neon). Just as Alphaville's 'unassimilables' (people unable to conform) are hounded to suicide or executed in a bizarre ritual involving a swimming pool and synchronized swimming, so the film presents the viewer with unassimilable images that cannot be contextualized within the logic of the narrative. The apparent seamlessness of traditional narrative film is thus exposed and explored, which has the effect of foregrounding the technological artifice of which cinema is composed. Indeed, at one point in the film, Lenny Caution is shown around a theatre where unassimilables are executed as they 'watch a show', suggesting that Godard is offering a very pointed critique of the normative function of entertainment media.

Thus the function of Godard's technique, and indeed of much *avant garde* cinema, is similar to that of the cut-up or Burroughs' experiments with tape recording in that the effect is such that the relationship of the body to discourse is exposed and destabilized. The scene where the bodies of the inhabitants of Alphaville are seen to founder and become dislocated from their environment when they are disconnected from *Alpha 60* thus gains significance as an analogue for the dislocation of the body when it is severed from the 'culturally constructed envelope of sounds and words'. If cinema itself can be understood as responsible for disseminating the viral infection that is the word, a parasite having very real effects at the level of the body, then the silencing of *Alpha 60*'s omnipresent and grating voice becomes analogous to the disruption of the 'internal monologue which is nothing other than the story the self tells to assure itself that it exists', which Burroughs 'propose[d] to stop ... by making it external and mechanical, recording it on tape and subjecting the recording to various manipulations' (Hayles, 1999: 211).

Like *HAL9000* in Stanley Kubrick's *2001, A Space Odyssey*, originally released three years after *Alphaville*, *Alpha 60* demonstrably signifies as a metaphor for Marcuse's 'Language of Total Administration'. Both are *speaking* computers whose voices are significant as much as for how they sound as for what they say. *HAL*'s is cloyingly 'pleasant' whereas *Alpha 60*'s is grating and monotonous (apparently Godard employed a man who had lost the use of his vocal chords and had learned to speak from his stomach) but both are 'mechanical', omnipresent and cannot be silenced other than by 'death' (they, in effect, have no 'off' switch). It is significant, also, that *HAL9000* has the biggest speaking part in the film, reflecting 'his' total power in terms of the mission with which he is entrusted (the astronauts aboard the *Discovery* are bland puppets, completely controlled by *HAL*).

Similarly, *Alpha 60* speaks and what he says becomes reality for the inhabitants of Alphaville, to the extent that their 'bible', which is actually a dictionary, has to be constantly updated to reflect the new conceptual universe mandated by the computer's manipulation of logic. The word 'love', of course, is banned, poetry is outlawed and, in Alphaville, as one of *Alpha 60*'s technicians tells Lemmy Caution, '[n]o one ever says 'why'; one says 'because'. In the life of individuals, as in the life of nations, everything is cause and effect'. Thus, in the operationally rational universe controlled by *Alpha 60*'s circular logic, nothing is left to be interrogated. Effects are shown to have predetermined causes and anything anomalous is simply eliminated. 'Everything has been said', intones *Alpha 60*, 'provided words do not change their meanings and meanings their words.' The elimination of poetry thus ensures the eradication of ambiguity, metaphor and interpretation. *Alpha 60* is, in McLuhan's terms, technology 'heated up' to exclude any possibility of imagination. Hence, as Natasha von Braun (Anna Karina) tells Caution, '[n]o one's lived in the past, or will live in the future'. The past cannot exist because it carries memory and the future cannot be imagined. Without memory or imagination, it is suggested, the inhabitants of Alphaville are enslaved in a technolinguistically determined and perpetual present.

That Godard implies that this necessarily has effects at the level of the body is particularly interesting for an analysis of technolinguistics in the computer age. In fact, a contemporary reading of *Alphaville* can usefully explore *Alpha 60* as representing the social and cultural effects of Mark Poster's (1990: 94) 'superpanopticon' to

which I briefly referred in Chapter 1. Although *Alphaville* predates the kind of participatory surveillance enabled by the superpanopticon, the imagination of an omnipresent computer that restricts and manipulates language and thereby controls the habits and constitution of bodies resonates suggestively with Poster's contention that 'the Superpanopticon imposes a new language situation that has unique, disturbing features'.

Essentially, the encoding of information in databases, to be effective, requires the elimination of ambiguity. Anyone who has worked as a data entry clerk will know that only a limited number of categories are available and the decision as to which type of information is entered in any given category is governed by preset rules, which reflect the aims of the organization that has gathered the data. In fact, the programming of databases is governed by a capitalist ideology that understands information as a commodity and is thus structured to make the building of the database as fast and efficient as possible while maximizing the saleability of the data. At its most innocuous, this enables the identification of trends that will show, for instance, that people in a certain income bracket favour particular brands of beer and allow the advertising of the product to be adjusted to suit their lifestyles (which is also identified by the collation of information across several databases). However, data mining and warehousing (see Chapter 1) has more pernicious implications where more sensitive information is concerned. Poster gives the example of an individual having a code entered against his or her name which encodes the information 'subscriptions to communist periodicals' (Poster 1990: 96). In the current political climate, communism is considered less of a threat than terrorism so, to update Poster's example, we could substitute 'frequent viewer of Web sites associated with terrorist organizations'. 'Here', as Poster (1990: 96) points out, 'the category itself is politically charged'.

But different Web sites will be precoded to reflect the degree of perceived threat and will be matched with other information such as ethnic origin, which marks the individual concerned as a threat to national security, whether or not they *themselves* would ever actually contemplate taking part in terrorist activity. This is a particularly sensitive area for academics who are often involved in research involving issues like terrorism, pornography and anticapitalist politics as part of their remit to interrogate cultural trends. There is every possibility, for instance, that my research into the global surveillance system Echelon (see Chapter 1), most of which was accomplished via the Internet, has been registered on a database held by my service provider. The issue here is not whether my service provider is interested in, or intends to sell, this information but the mere fact that it exists entails the possibility that it may be matched with other information which may identify me as an 'unassimilable' at some point in the future. Whether or not my paranoia here is justified, what this example serves to illustrate is that 'why' is not a word in the vocabulary of databases. Or, as Poster points out

> [t]he electronic information gathering that constitutes databases, for all its speed, accuracy and computational power, incurs a tremendous *loss* of data' and he contends that 'the database imposes a new language on top of those already existing and that it is an impoverished, limited language, one that uses the norm to constitute individuals and define deviants ... [T]he structure or grammar of the database *creates* relationships among pieces of information that do not exist in those relationships outside of the database. In this sense databases constitute individuals by manipulating relationships between bits of information.' (Poster 1990: 94–6)

Like the inhabitants of Alphaville, we are defined by the symbolic logic of computing, which reduces the possibilities for ambiguity in language and thus produces discourses that constrain subjectivity and normative principles that affect our habits and comportment. We are constrained to live in a continual present in which constant self-surveillance prohibits the possibility of imagining a radically different future and where memory is eliminated by the ubiquity of statistically determined 'facts'.

Furthermore, as Poster points out, the 'normalizing gaze of the Superpanopticon' doesn't so much invade privacy as constitute 'an additional self', composed entirely of data culled from shopping habits, credit card transactions, medical records, records of public transport use and computer log files, which 'may be acted upon to the detriment of the "real" self without that "real" self ever being aware of what is happening' (Poster 1990: 97–8). In similar terms, as Hayles points out, 'Burroughs's project [was] ... to rewrite or erase the "pre-recordings," and to extricate the subject from the parisitic invasion of the "Other Half"' (Hayles 1999: 213), understood as '"the word" ... a separate organism attached to your nervous system' (Hayles 1999: 212). Thus, Burroughs' 'Other Half' and Poster's 'other self' are both adjuncts to the body that are produced out of the dissemination of the word virus by technology and which control the parameters of what Lydenberg (1987: 140) calls 'the logocentric body' which she describes as 'an artificial construct of some complexity [which] has disguised itself as nature'. The aim of 'Burroughs and other radical thinkers', then, is to 'deconstruct the logocentric body, to liberate a new plural body without limits' (Lydenberg 1987: 141).

With this in mind, it seems that what Burroughs hoped to achieve with the cutting and splicing of words on tape Godard gestures towards with his technique of destabilizing a familiar narrative with unassimilable images and sounds. As Thomas notes, '[c]hief among the images that create the texture of this film is a flashing light [which] is as characteristic of modern civilization as anything else you might name, and particularly appropriate to Alphaville, where direct sunlight is rarely seen' and he concludes that 'what is important is that the image is *there*, and is its own justification ... These patterns of flickering light *are* the movie, what else in it is of greater importance?' (Thomas 1966: 49). Thus a strong argument can be made for reading *Alphaville* as a text that deconstructs the logocentric body by imaging a characteristic of postmodern civilization: the '*flickering signifiers*' that Hayles identifies as created by information technologies, 'characterized by their tendency toward unexpected metamorphoses, attenuations and dispersions [and which] signal an important shift in the plate techtonics of language' (Hayles 1999: 30, her emphasis).

Following Donna Haraway, Hayles uses the word 'informatics' to describe the complex network of relations in which bodies, language, culture and information technologies are entwined and out of which they are all produced. 'In informatics', she writes, 'the signifier can no longer be understood as a single marker, for example an ink mark on a page. Rather it exists as a flexible chain of markers bound together by the arbitrary relations specified by the relevant codes.' In other words, the way in which words (and, of course, images and sounds) are processed by computers makes them insubstantial and somewhat immaterial. A book is a 'thing' which is present in itself but, in cyberspace, books exist as highly transformable patterns of information. A good example is Wikipedia, the online encylopaedia, which has no single author but is constantly expanded and updated by any number of anonymous 'authors' in any number of locations. Wikipedia's interface presents the information it contains as words on a screen but

> for the computer, the relevant signifiers are electronic polarities on disks. Intervening between what I see and what the computer reads are the machine code that correlates alphanumeric symbols with binary digits, the compiler language that correlates these symbols with higher-level instructions determining how the symbols are to be manipulated, the processing program that

mediates between these instructions ... and so forth. A signifier on one level becomes a signified on the next higher level. Precisely because the relation between signifier and signified at each of these levels is arbitrary, it can be changed with a single global command. (Hayles 1999: 31)

Indeed, it is precisely because of this arbitrary relationship that an artefact like Wikipedia, which itself destabilizes concepts like 'author' and 'book', is able to exist. And, in as much as it can be said to 'exist' it does so as an ever shifting pattern of information, both at the level of machine code, compiler languages and processing programs *and* at the screen interface where I can read that Denis Diderot, co-editor of 'perhaps the most famous early encyclopedia ... viewed the ideal encyclopedia as an index of connections. He realized that all knowledge could never be amassed in one work, but he hoped the relations among subjects could be.'[4] Diderot would perhaps have been impressed by the hypertextual nature of Wikipedia where linear, alphabetical order is abandoned in favour of a complex network of connections which changes constantly as new editors manipulate the content. Unlike *Alphaville's* 'bible', Wikipedia does not attempt to fix the boundaries of what can be known and expressed. In fact, it does not recognize the boundary as a condition of its existence.

Hayles suggests that flickering signifiers require us to substitute the binary pattern/randomness in place of presence/absence where '[r]andomness is the contrasting term that allows pattern to be understood as such' (Hayles 1999: 33). As in Derrida's critique of Saussure's linguistic system, in which absence can be read as the condition of presence, rather than its inferior opposite, so in Hayles' system of flickering signification pattern only emerges because randomness is embedded in the system. In my Wikipedia example, pattern, emerging out of randomness, is its defining feature. There is no 'plan' to the editing of Wikipedia, no central control that determines who can edit or in what time frame and no 'publication date'. All that is needed is the will on the part of individuals to contribute, a user friendly interface and, perhaps most importantly, the machine that makes it possible in the first place.

This, as Hayles demonstrates elsewhere, makes the crucial difference in understanding how computers force us to re-evaluate previous ideas about the way that we make meaning from language. The binary speech/writing becomes redundant in the era of computing in which a third term 'code' must be added if we are to understand the importance of our interactions with electronic texts. Code, fundamentally, is the only thing that computers understand. And it is a very precise language. As Hayles demonstrates, there can be no ambiguity at the level of machine code.

> The translation from binary code into high-level languages, and from high-level languages back into binary code, must happen every time commands are compiled or interpreted ... Because all these operations depend on the ability of the machine to recognize the difference between one and zero, Saussure's premise that differences between signs make signification possible fits well with computer architecture. (Hayles 1999: 45)

Hayles points out that what becomes important here is Derrida's charge that when, on a conceptual level, Saussure separates signifier and signified, he leaves open the possibility of a 'transcendental signified' (Hayles 1999: 47) which will provide the authority for meaning to be intelligible by guaranteeing that the conjunction between sound (or word) and concept does not suffer from the implication that their pairing is, in fact, arbitrary and contingent. In other words, '[i]n Derrida's view, Saussure's definition of the sign undercuts the metaphysics of presence in one sense and reinforces it in another' (Hayles 1999: 46–7). But, '[i]n the worldview of code, it makes no sense to talk about signifiers without signifieds. Every voltage change must have

a precise meaning in order to affect the behavior of the machine' (Hayles 1999: 47). And voltages are very real. They are *material* and cannot be reduced to the abstractions that Saussure needs to propose his theory. And this non-ambiguous materiality is what provides the conditions for the revolutionary potentials of flickering signifiers

With this relationship in mind, Wikipedia and all that it offers for rethinking the concept of the book and authorship can be extended into rethinking language and communication. As Hayles (1999: 49) points out, '[c]ode has become arguably as important as natural language because it causes things to happen.' In fact, in the contemporary world, it causes the most important things in our lives to happen, from how we earn our money to how we conduct our personal relationships. It is the language that we use, from day to day and from moment to moment in our interactions with machines and thus with each other. On some level, we *all* understand code because it is the only language that the machines that we depend on intimately respond to. 'Code is not the enemy', writes Hayles, 'any more than it is the savior'. Rather it is 'increasingly positioned as language's pervasive partner' (1999: 61) and what we must take into account if we are to counter the technolinguistic determinacy increasingly written into our daily lives. This, perhaps, is what Godard recognized when he made a film about technology with an almost banal narrative, which used the techniques of his craft to turn it into poetry. The flickering signifiers of *Alphaville* deconstruct the deterministic logic of the narrative to question the linearity that is written into our understanding of text, as well as the logocentrism that determines meaning in language. This, Hayles is suggesting, is also the promise of code. In simple terms, this means that it offers opportunities for creative hacking but, in a more complex sense, we can use our understanding of code to question the hegemony of data processing and the way in which, as in Burroughs' analysis of tape recording, it produces who we are.

CHAPTER SUMMARY

■ As demonstrated in the work of Ferdinand de Saussure and Roland Barthes, the meanings derived from language are contingent and ideologically determined.

■ The way in which language means is inseparable from its mode of communication.

■ The language of 'scientism' in the social sciences restricts meaning to operationally functional concepts.

■ Technologies that reproduce language affect concepts of identity and embodiment and can be manipulated to expose the impossibility of fixed meanings.

CONCLUSION

In April 2003, Prince Charles, the son of the reigning British monarch, requested that the Royal Society urgently discuss the 'threat' of nanotechnology, raising 'the spectre of the "grey goo" catastrophe in which sub-microscopic machines designed to share intelligence and replicate themselves take over and devour the planet.'[1] The Prince was not taken particularly seriously and was accused of being unnecessarily alarmist and of dealing in science fiction rather than 'true' science. Yet, as Colin Milburn points out in his essay for N. Katherine Hayles' *Nanoculture: Implications of the New Technoscience* (Milburn 2004), the boundary between science fiction and science writing in what he calls the nanotech 'technoscape' is very permeable indeed. The 'dense discourse network' (Milburn 2004: 109), which produces the idea of nanotechnology and insinuates its potential, as Milburn demonstrates, not only includes science fiction texts but, as he suggests, at the current stage of nanotech research '[n]anotechnology *is* science fiction' (Milburn 2004: 120, my emphasis) and '[t]he tactics of separating nanotech from the science fiction with which it is complicit fail on every level' (Milburn 2004: 121). This is not to say that the proposed benefits (or otherwise) of nanotechnology are unrealizable but that the scientific imaginary and the science-fictional imaginary are inseparable in that they both emerge from within a culture that cannot imagine a future *other than* in terms of technology and its application.

As I suggested in Chaper 1, science fiction does not so much predict the future as project the social impact of burgeoning technologies, which are mapped onto future or alternative worlds and this, at least according to Milburn's argument, is also the business of science writing. As Donna Haraway has pointed out, the scientist 'reads for a living' (Haraway 1991: 207) and it is the texts that promote future scenarios of benefit both to the pursuit of profit and to our concepts of what counts as a move in the direction of allieviating the burdens of human existence, which resonate strongly enough to produce marketable results.

For instance, as I pointed out in the case study for Chapter 2, the genetic modification of food crops was, in part, an attempt to mitigate the disaster produced by the 'green revolution', which had caused alarm across both the developed and developing world, but it was also prompted by the genomics industry and the burgeoning knowledge of gene sequencing that was to culminate in the mapping of the human genome, which, itself, was largely informed by the myth of human perfectibility and the drive to eliminate the causes of illness, disease and, finally, death. In other words, none of our technologies is realized without the understanding that it, in some way, fulfils a collective desire. Technologies enter the world through a process informed by ideologies which structure what we mean by things like 'nature', 'life', 'person', 'body', 'animal' and 'machine' and these meanings affect our responses to what is a viable subject for scientific enquiry and how the effects of scientific research are incorporated into the culture.

What this suggests is that, like the clones that I introduced in Chapter 3, the life of technoscientific artefacts is, to an extent, always already determined, even before such artefacts can be said to exist. But, as I pointed out, clones are monsters with lives of their own. Every attempt to accommodate them to the ethics of the existing world order is doomed to failure because the world into which they will emerge has already been changed. The contest, then, is over how that change is to be managed. As Milburn puts it, 'nanotech's narratives of the "already inevitable" nanofuture ask us *even now* to reeavalute the foundations of our lived human realities and our expectations of the shape of things to come' (Milburn 2004: 114, his emphasis) but it is the terms under which this reeavaluation takes place to which we need to attend.

As my case study for Chapter 4 makes clear, 'the "already inevitable" nanofuture' of which cryonics is very much a part looks, from one point of view, like the promised land – a utopia in which the idea of life will no longer be circumscribed by the inevitability of death. But, on the other hand, this is to assume that life without death is meaningful or, in a more mundane sense, that a future world will welcome the addition of resurrected twenty-first century cryonauts whose expectations of what a future world will be like were formed within a particular culture and in a particular time. Cryonics, in fact, is very much science fiction at the present time in that self-selecting cryonauts commit themselves to a future in which it is understood that technology, and nanotechnology in particular, will be fully realized in the triumph of the liberal humanist individual, a trope of many SF scenarios which fail to imagine the decline of Western culture or that the posthuman will be anything other than the final dominance of reason over the decay of the body.

And scientists are deeply implicated here. How could they not be? Technologies that attract the big money are those that resonate with progressive ideals, as applied to both the social world and the human body. For scientists not to consider their most lucrative source of funding would be to write themselves out of a job. Thus nanotech pioneers like Eric Drexler and Ralph C. Merkle 'are deeply involved in the idea of freezing and preserving human bodies … Merkle is a director of the Alcor

Life Extension Foundation [and] Drexler is on the scientific advisory board of the Alcor Foundation and has written extensively about cryonics' (Milburn 2004: 127). Furthermore, the companies that have made the biggest investment in nanotech to date are those involved in the manufacture of anti-ageing products aimed squarely at the lucrative market sustained by 'new' femininities that police the gender divide by perpetuating the myth of attainment through maintenance of a youthful female body. Thus, if nanotechnology is science fiction, it is highly unimaginative and attuned only to a future which perpetuates the inequalities of the cultural moment in which it is currently being produced.

Nevertheless, the boundaries that technoscience is invested in maintaining for the sake of its continuing dominance are, paradoxically, threatened by the very technologies that it produces. As Milburn argues, nanotechnology borrows, rhetorically, from science fiction even as its exponents try to argue that it is 'real' science and 'envisions the components of the body and mechanical objects as indistinguishable, and, subsequently, utilizes the biological machine *as the model* for the nanomachine, achieving a terminal circularity' (Milburn 2004: 125, his emphasis). Nor, as I have pointed out, is this 'terminal circularity' confined to nanotechnololgy. *All* technologies propose that they will serve 'our' needs when, in fact, the 'we' that is implied is profoundly changed even before we have incorporated any given technology into our lives. Although, on one level, this can be construed as a claim that technology *determines* our lives, on another it can serve as a reminder that the essential human, to which technology is a mere adjunct, is a myth that sustains our belief that technoscience is benign because it is produced out of objective reasoning. Essentialism is what enables the claim that the ability to reason is something that can be attributed only to those that exhibit certain predetermined characteristics and what produces hierarchies of 'types', applied to both the natural and human worlds. Consequently, the people and other organisms that suffer most are those pushed to the bottom of the hierarchy.

Because the paradoxes that technoscience tries so hard to avoid become more apparent as technology literally invades our bodies, so the possibilities for a resistant politics, which may shape a more egalitarian world, become more acute. When Donna Haraway argues for '*pleasure* in the confusion of boundaries and for *responsibility* in their construction' (Haraway 1991: 150) she is demanding that we recognize the potential inherent in technologies that exert 'strong symbolic influence over the way we conceptualize the world and ourselves' (Milburn, 2004: 123) and grasp the opportunity that they offer to reconstruct that world according to new metaphors of existence, rather than enable the effort to fit them into a pre-existing scenario, which benefits only those individuals, corporations and governments invested in retaining power.

One of the boundaries most acutely troubled is that between art and science which, as I demonstrated in Chapters 6 and 7 becomes permeable at the point at which technology invades the cultural sphere, affecting modes of expression and lending new shapes to symbolic power structures. As my discussion of the Nazi art exhibition *Entartete Kunst* and Leni Riefensthal's films makes clear, the manipulation of art forms is of crucial importance to the maintenance of political regimes and it can be seen to be equally important in the formulation of resistant strategies. So, while Jean-Luc Godard's film, *Alphaville*, uses the technology of cinema itself to suggest a poetic resistance to technolinguistic determinism, Rey Chow proposes that personal listening devices may disrupt the soundscape of conformity that structures Chinese culture and, I have suggested, the no less pervasive musaks of Western consumerism. Both these technologies are very much products of the techno-capitalist world order but both can be understood as boundary artefacts, which, to borrow Milburn's term, may enable the construction of an alternative technosphere attuned to the democratizing of art which Walter Benjamin imagined in 'The Work of Art in the Age of Mechanical Reproduction'. This is not only 'art for all' but art that appropriates the means of production to promote interventionist discourses; in Haraway's words 'seizing the tools to mark the world that marked [us] as other' (Haraway 1991: 175).

Finally, we need to be attentive to the spaces where the technosphere is constructed: the laboratory, the popular press and, perhaps most promisingly, the Internet where, increasingly, the formation of culture takes place. As I suggested in Chapter 5, both the wilderness and outer space have been colonized by being written into the *telos* of Western individualism and cyberspace is dominated by the ever expanding pornosphere and the military-industrial complex. But, the portals to cyberspace are many and, as I pointed out in Chapter 7, the language of electronic processing and hypertext can confound the linear narratives required by technoscientific determinism. It is a space where Haraway's task of 'recoding communication and intelligence to subvert command and control' may become a real possibility.

Science differs from myth or religion in the fact that, although it offers explanatory stories about the world, it does so within the context of applicability. It lends itself to the production of very real artefacts with real and positive effects in the world. Thus, it is possible to suggest that there is no 'pure' science or, put another way, that the cognitive effects of science are structured within a nexus that includes both the worldview in which its results are interpreted and the practical applicability of those results. The purpose of studying technoculture is to provide ourselves with a vocabulary with which we can articulate the ways in which science *becomes* culture and argue for the results of its application to be responsive to the social worlds that it produces and that inform its production.

GLOSSARY

Actor network theory: Body of theory attributed to, among others, Bruno Latour and Donna Haraway, which particularizes matters of concern in social ecology in order to focus on the network of actors, both human and non-human, which have to be taken into account in order to effect change

Aura: Walter Benjamin's term for art that retains its authority through being associated with distance, mystique, authenticity and the cult of genius

Autopoiesis: Literally, 'self-producing'. Used to describe the way in which organisms sustain themselves in continual interaction with their environment

Avatar: Term which describes the virtual body which inhabits **cyberspace**

Body without organs (BwO): Terms coined by Gilles Deleuze and Felix Guattari to describe the political potential of understanding bodies in terms of **autopoiesis**

Cryonics: Technique of preserving bodies at the point of death for reanimation at a time when a cure is available

Culture industry: Term coined by Theodor W. Adorno and Max Horkheimer to describe mass culture and its political effects

Cybernetics: Body of knowledge inaugurated by Norbert Wiener, which understands the actions of both people and machines as based on a circular processing of information between organism and environment

Cyberspace: Term coined by the novelist William Gibson to describe information space as created by computer networks

Cyborg: Term used by Donna Haraway to describe the breakdown of boundaries between humans, animals and machines under the terms of contemporary **technocultures**

Data mining: Describes the technique by which computers search databases at high speed to retrieve consumer profiles or security information

Deconstruction: Method attributable to Jacques Derrida, which exposes the insecurity of meaning in language

Embushelment: Term coined by Steve Fuller to describe the difference between the discourse of scientific expertise and the kind of science that feeds the popular imagination

Enframing: The sense in which, according to Martin Heidegger, people and things are understood in relation to instrumentality (*see* **standing-reserve**)

Episteme: Term coined by Michel Foucault to describe the connections between scientific knowledge and cultural institutions in any given period of time (*compare with* **paradigm**)

Extrapolation: Term that describes the imagination of the future based on estimations of the course of currently existing social and technological trends

Fordism: Term that describes the rationalization of labour as implemented by Henry Ford

Futurism: Early twentieth-century Italian art movement that glorified speed and industrial technology

Hyperrreality: Term coined by Jean Baudrillard to describe the construction of reality by the commodity form

Informatics: Term attributable to Donna Haraway, which describes the network of power relations in the information economy

Knowledge economy: Describes the marketing of information as a commodity in global capitalism

Logocentrism: Term derived from **deconstruction**, which refers to the logic that imparts truth to statements under the terms of modernist discourse

Metalanguage (myth): Term coined by Roland Barthes to describe the second order of signification in which ideology informs meaning (*see* **semiotics**)

Metanarrative: Term coined by Jean-François Lyotard to describe stories about the world which legitimate what comes to be accepted as 'truth'

Modernity: Historical epoch dominated by the pursuit of truth through the scientific method

Nanotechnology: Engineering of cellular 'automata' to effect structural changes in an organism

Network society: Term coined by Manuel Castells to describe the organizational form of global capitalism in which network structures replace hierarchical organization in both businesses and communities

Panopticism: Term used by Michel Foucault to describe the implicit surveillance that conditions populations to police their behaviour

Paradigm: Term coined by Thomas Kuhn to describe a period of time in which scientific knowledge is dominated by a specific set of ideas, before pressure from anomalies forces it to give way to a new paradigm

Pop art: Term that describes the kind of art associated with Andy Warhol, which aestheticizes the process of mechanical reproduction

Post-normal science: Term coined by Ziauddin Sardar to describe the bridging of the gap between public concerns and scientific expertise (*see also* **actor network theory** and *compare with* **embushelment**)

Posthuman: Disputed term that stands for both the emergence of the transcendent human (*see* **transhumanism**) and the critique of humanism proposed by theoretical figures such as Donna Haraway's **cyborg**

Postmodernism: Historical epoch in which uncertainties about the future predicted by Enlightenment rationalism are expressed in art and culture

Psychotechnology: Term coined by Theodor Adorno and Max Horkheimer to describe the use of entertainment technology to produce a product that is indistinguishable from propaganda

Repurposing: The appropriation of technology to create new musical or visual experiences

Romanticism: Late eighteenth- and early nineteenth-century movement that lamented human alienation from nature in the pursuit of technological progress

Scientism: The belief that the scientific method is applicable to all problems, including social problems (*see* **technological rationality**)

Semiotics: Theory, attributable to Ferdinand de Saussure, which explores the way in which meaning is derived from language

Spectacle: Term coined by the *Situationist International* to describe the cultural effects of commodity capitalism

Standing-reserve: Term coined by Martin Heidegger to describe an understanding of nature which sees it only as a resource for technology

Superpanopticon: Term coined by Mark Poster to describe a more highly developed form of **panopticism**, which relies on the ability of computers to store, sort and retrieve large quantities of data (*see* **data mining**)

Technocapitalism: Term coined by Steven Best and Douglas Kellner to describe the way that contemporary global capitalism is enabled by and dependent on information and communications technologies

Technocracy: The politics of a **technologically determined** culture

Technoculture: The interdependence of technology and culture

Technological determinism: The idea that technology determines social life, rather than the other way around

Technological rationality: Term coined by Herbert Marcuse to describe 'common sense', which understands all problems as solvable by technological means (*see* **scientism**)

Technological sublime: Term coined by Fredric Jameson to describe the fascination with technology and its connection with power in contemporary cultures

Transgenics: Term that describes the practice of genetically engineering organisms

Transuranics: Any element with an atomic number greater than Uranium (92), which are engineered rather than produced in nature

Transhumanism: Belief that technology will eventually provide the means to transcend the human condition

QUESTIONS FOR ESSAYS AND CLASS DISCUSSION

INTRODUCTION

1. What is the role of technology in defining the historical period referred to as modernity?
2. In what sense can machines be said to affect our understandings of who we are?
3. What is 'technocapitalism' and how does it structure contemporary social conditions?
4. What is the connection between the personal computer and Fredric Jameson's 'Third Machine Age'?
5. How do technologies facilitate forms of surveillance?

TECHNOSCIENCE AND POWER

1. What is scientific 'objectivity' and how can it be contested?
2. What is the difference between Kuhnian 'paradigms' and Foucaultian 'epistemes'?
3. Discuss the concept of expertise and the way in which it is valorized.
4. What are the local effects of the global demand for new technologies?
5. What are the social effects of technoscientific power structures?

TECHNONATURE/CULTURE

1. What are the historical conditions that have produced our ideas of 'nature'?
2. What is 'human nature' and how is it identified?
3. In what sense can technoscience be said to have policed the boundary between nature and culture?
4. How does nature figure our relationship to animals and machines?
5. What is Romanticism and how do its ideas permeate contemporary culture?

TECHNOBODIES

1. What are the effects of understanding bodies as distinct from minds?
2. What, according to Michel Foucault, is a 'disciplined' body?
3. How do digitial technologies destabilize concepts of corporeality?
4. What are 'marked' bodies and how are they produced in technoscientific discourse?
5. What are 'cyborg' bodies and how are they theorized?

TECHNOSPACES

1. How has space travel affected the way that we orient ourselves in Earth space?
2. What is abstract space and how is it connected to technocapitalism?
3. What is the significance of maps and how do they affect how we understand technospaces?
4. What is the connection between technology and colonialist geographies?
5. What are the social relations of cyberspace?

TECHNOAESTHETICS

1. How does art mediate the divide between technoscience and everyday life?
2. How might we apply Walter Benjamin's discussion of mechanical reproduction to contemporary ideas about art and technology?
3. What is 'psychotechnology' and how does it operate?
4. What are the aesthetics of cyberspace?
5. How does digital reproduction affect our responses to film and photography?

TECHNOLINGUISTICS

1. How do technologies mediate our social interactions and how is this expressed in language?
2. How does the language of technoscience affect the discursive production of identities?
3. What is 'scientism' and what is its connection to language?
4. In what way do technologies work to stabilize/destabilize meaning?
5. What is the connection between 'natural' language and machine code?

NOTES

Chapter 1 Introduction: Technology and Social Realities

1. See http://www.time.com/time/time100/builder/profile/ford3.html.

2. In this sense, Marxism could be said to promote a passive technological determinism and, indeed, historical materialism has been criticized by, among others, Mikhail Bakunin for privileging a narrow, developmental view of social change that requires the application of scientific expertise to an understanding of prevailing conditions and thus the necessity for a vanguard party of intellectuals or what Bakunin calls 'gentleman metaphysicians ... who consider it their mission to prescribe the laws of life in the name of science' (http://www.marxists.org/reference/archive/bakunin/works/1873/ statism-anarchy.htm#s1). For Marx, '...men, developing their material production and their material intercourse, alter, along with this their real existence, their thinking and the products of their thinking' (Marx and Engels 1947: 47) but, for Bakunin, 'men' only designates a small and elite cadre of experts.

3. From a speech given at the anniversary of the *People's Paper*, 1856.

4. Indeed, beginning with social Darwinism in the mid- to late nineteenth century and, more recently, sociobiology and some branches of contemporary evolutionary psychology, the idea of the competitive individual has been supported by biologists and social scientists who have extrapolated from animal behaviour (and the idea of the 'selfish gene' as proposed by Richard Dawkins). However, the early twentieth-century Russian anarchist, Peter Kropotkin, mounted a direct attack on Social Darwinism also based on observations of animal behaviour but coming to very different conclusions (see *Mutual Aid: A Factor of Evolution*, http://dwardmac.pitzer.edu/Anarchist_Archives/kropotkin/mutaidintro. html). For a feminist argument against the findings of sociobiology see Evelyn Reed's *Sexism and Science*. Also see Hilary and Steven Rose (eds.) *Alas Poor Darwin: Arguments Against Evolutionary Psychology*.

5. See Gilbert Ryle, *The Concept of Mind*.

6. This term was first popularized by James Burnham in his 1940 book *Managerial Revolution* where it was used to refer to management ideologies that promoted the interests of company managers above those of shareholders, workers and so forth, resulting in the kind of insider dealing which led to the 2001 'Enron scandal'. I am using it in a more general sense to apply to any system in which technique constructs the ideology of both company management and social systems. See glossary.

7. A similar argument underpins Murray Bookchin's (2004: 81) concept of 'technology for life', which forms part of his argument for what he calls 'post-scarcity anarchism' (Bookchin 2004: 2). Bookchin criticizes traditional socialism as 'a beehive of industrial activity, humming with work for all' (Bookchin 2004: 48) when, in fact, technology could liberate us from work altogether. However, he emphasizes that it should necessarily be a *decentralized* technology for life 'tailored to the community and the regional level' (Bookchin 2004: 81), which would, he thinks, eliminate the need for bureaucracy and

esoteric expertise. Ultimately, he is arguing against control of production by the state and the kind of excesses seen in the Marxist command economies of, for example, the former Soviet Union.

8. http://www.bopsecrets.org/CF/graffiti.htm.

9. See Joseph Stigliz's *Gobalization and its Discontents*

10. iDA Singapore, http://www.ida.gov.sg/idaweb/media/infopage.jsp?infopagecategory=ncbarchivemediareleases.mr:media&versionid=4&infopageid=I1046.

11. *Wired* magazine, issue 1.04, September/October, 1993, http://www.wired.com/wired/archive/1.04/gibson.html.

12. Many thanks go to Greg Grey who, unlike myself, is a driver, for this very pertinent observation.

13. Millennium Development Goals, http://www.developmentgoals.org/, updated September 2004.

14. Guardian Unlimited, 'Brown takes global poverty campaign to Rome', Friday, 9 July 2004, http://www.guardian.co.uk/globalisation/story/0,7369,1257982,00.html.

15. War on Want, 'The global divide, globalisation, work and world poverty' (pamphlet), emphasis in original.

16. *Asian Labour News*, 'Singapore: Migrant workers and wage arrears', 2 March 2004, http://www.asianlabour.org/archives/001071.php.

17. Part III, *The Shadows in The Cave*, BBC2, Wednesday, 3 November 2004. See http://news.bbc.co.uk/1/hi/programmes/3970901.stm.

18. Datawatch, http://www.datawatch-europe.com/mch/datamining.html?g=dm.

19. See Duncan Campbell's 'Interception 2000' report at http://www.fas.org/irp/eprint/ic2000/ic2000.htm#_Toc448565514 and Armin Medosch's article 'A Very Private Affair' for Metamute at http://www.metamute.com/look/article.tpl?IdLanguage=1&IdPublication=1&NrIssue=21&NrSection=10&NrArticle=296&ILStart=4.

20. Barlow, John Perry, 'The Economy of Ideas' in *Wired* magazine, Issue 2.03, March, 1994 http://www.wired.com/wired/archive/2.03/economy.ideas_pr.html.

21. Tania Branigan, 'Great Firewall of China', *Guardian Unlimited*, http://www.guardian.co.uk/g2/story/0,,1349283,00.html.

22. US Department of Health and Human Services Administration for Children and Families, 'Child Maltreatment 2002' (published 2004), http://www.acf.dhhs.gov/programs/cb/publications/cm02/summary.htm.

Chapter 2 Technoscience and Power

1. *News. Telegraph*, 13 April 2003, http://www.opinion.telegraph.co.uk/news/main.jhtml?xml=/news/2003/04/13/nhonda13.xml&sSheet=/news/2003/04/13/ixhome.html.

2. See http://public.web.cern.ch/Public/Welcome.html.

3. See http://www.antiwar.com/spectator/spec280.html.

4. See http://andrejkoymasky.com/mem/holocaust/ho07.html.

5. *Double Helix: The DNA Years*, BBC4, 28 April and 29 April 2004.

6. See http://www.stanford.edu/dept/HPS/BirthOfTheClinic/biohome.htm.

7. Skin Product Creams the Competition http://www.sun-sentinel.com/features/health/sfl-bal-te.aging17jun17,0,2376849.story?coll=sfla-news-science.

8. See articles on gender and hypercapitalism at http://www.opengender.org.

9. Actually, Patriot did not 'work' as effectively as Bush's speech suggests. As Chris Hables Gray points out 'while Patriots hit 41 of 42 Scuds that were fired at over Israel, they only destroyed the warhead 44% of the time' and may, in fact, have caused more damage than they prevented (Gray: 1997: 46).

10. See http://www.betterhumans.com/News/news.aspx?articleID=2003-02-28-3.
11. 'GM Food Risk to Humans "Very Low"', http://www.newscientist.com/article.ns?id=dn3959.
12. See http://www.monsanto.co.uk/elsewhere/elsewhere.html.
13. See http://www.squat.net/caravan/ICC-en/KRRS-en.htm.

Chapter 3 TechnoNature/Culture

1. For a fuller discussion of the masculine bias of technoscience and an analysis of Tiptree's work see Debra Benita Shaw, *Women, Science and Fiction: The Frankenstein Inheritance*.
2. Famously, the physicist Alan Sokal invited 'anyone who believes that the laws of physics are mere social conventions ... to try transgressing those conventions from the windows of my apartment. I live on the twenty-first floor' (Sokal and Bricmont 1997: 249n).
3. Embryonic stem cells are 'totipotent'. This means that they have the ability to become any type of organ, which is why they can, potentially, be used to heal damaged adult organs. It was originally thought that, once they lose this ability, they remain differentiated and their totipotency cannot be 'switched back on'. Dolly proved that this was not the case. Therefore, people who had argued for the embryo not being a 'person' until such time as the cells had differentiated (thought originally to happen at 14 days) and had used this as an argument for abortion, effectively lost the argument.

Chapter 4 TechnoBodies

1. See http://www.stelarc.va.com.au/index2.html.
2. It is interesting to note that, in the period that Pfeil is discussing, Springsteen's music (in songs like *Glory Days* and *The River*) relentlessly attacks nostalgia. Although this might be said to somewhat invalidate Pfeil's argument, the fact remains that his reading of Springsteen's *body* captures a cultural moment in which its representations are accruing new meanings as they are affected by prevailing socio-economic discourses.
3. *The Story of The Genome Project*, http://www.abc.net.au/science/slab/genome/story.htm.
4. See http://www.viewingspace.com/genetics_culture/pages_genetics_culture/gc_w03/kac_webarchive/gfp_bunny_page/gfp_bunny.htm.
5. The symbolic order is what the psychoanalyst Jacques Lacan proposes that we enter into when we learn language. The binary differentiations that distinguish us first, as belonging to one or other gender and which we then understand as the rule that applies to all language, become part of our psychic orientation. The symbolic order encodes the rules of the culture into which we are born and determines our self-understanding in relation to it. See Slavoj Žižek, *Looking Awry. An Introduction to Jacques Lacan through Popular Culture*.
6. See http://www.show-and-stay.co.uk/sinatra-music.html.
7. Moore's Law is attributed to Gordon Moore, the co-founder of computer chip company Intel. He wrote an article for *Electronics* magazine in April, 1965 in which he stated 'The complexity for minimum component costs has increased at a rate of roughly a factor of two per year.' In other words, the number of transistors on a silicon chip has increased while the cost has been held down. Most commentators agree that, taking all factors into account, chip complexity has continued to increase and will continue to do so, with no appreciable effect on cost.
8. See http://www.alcor.org/FAQs/faq03.html#rich.
9. The Turing Test, which is designed to test whether a computer is able to use language in the same way as a human, was first described by Alan Turing in 1950. A human engages in conversation (using a keyboard method) with two others that he or she cannot see, one of which is a computer. If the judge cannot tell the difference, the machine is deemed to have passed the test.

Chapter 5 TechnoSpaces

1. 'President Bush Announces New Vision for Space Exploration Program', http://www.whitehouse. gov/news/releases/2004/01/20040114-3.html.
2. Meriwether Lewis and William Clark led an expedition to chart the lands acquired from the French in what is known as the Louisiana Purchase. The expedition, also known as the Corps of Discovery, took place between 1804 and 1806 and travelled overland across more than 8,000 miles.
3. The space shuttle *Columbia* exploded 39 miles above the Earth, scattering debris over most of east Texas and Louisiana and killing all seven members of the crew.
4. See http://www.telegraph.co.uk/news/main.jhtml?xml=/news/2003/02/03.
5. See http://english.pravda.ru/society/2003/04/04/45590_.html.
6. See http://psychiatrictimes.com/p030402.html.
7. Our preoccupation with discovering life on Mars can, in this context, be read as motivated by anxieties that, like America when it was first 'discovered', the planet may harbour inhabitants with a prior claim to the territory.
8. See http://en.wikipedia.org/wiki/Prime_directive.
9. It is worth pointing out that Shepard's experience was somewhat of an anomaly. For instance, Mette Bryld and Nina Lykke (1999: 111) recount the response of Scott Carpenter, another of the original seven Mercury astronauts, 'who went up hoping to be let in on a "great secret" [and] became so swept away by the sublimity of the experience of orbiting Earth that his over-composed astronautic self gave way to an emotional, erratic identity' to the extent that one 'disgusted NASA official' listening to Carpenter's 'anguished cries during re-entry' was moved to ask 'whether the astronaut thought he was changing his sex'.
10. See http://www.virgingalactic.com/.
11. See http://www.alamut.com/subj/ideologies/manifestos/magnaCarta.html.
12. See http://www.americasarmy.com/.

Chapter 6 TechnoAesthetics

1. See http://www.cscs.umich.edu/~crshalizi/T4PM/futurist-manifesto.html.
2. See http://www.stltoday.com/stltoday/entertainment/reviews.nsf/movie/story/FE3CB4CF5FBC83 3F86257037003289ED?OpenDocument.
3. Originally in 'New Talent USA', *Art in America* 50(1): 42 published in 1962.
4. See http://www.obsolete.com/120_years/machines/futurist/art_of_noise.html. More recently, city sounds have formed a component of the performances of 'illbient' artists like DJ Spooky. See http:// www.djspooky.com/.
5. A technique that involves manually moving a vinyl recording rythmically backwards and forwards on a turntable while manipulating the crossfader on a mixing desk.
6. See Pierre Bourdieu, *Distinction: A Social Critique of the Judgement of Taste*
7. For a discussion of subcultural capital see Sarah Thornton, 'The Social Logic of Subcultural Capital' in *The Subcultures Reader*.
8. Levy (2006: 183) reports that Howard Stringer, CEO of Sony America, expressed the opinion that Apple should share its profits from the iPod (rather than just the songs sold by the iTunes store) because 'the iPod wouldn't exist without the songs sold by labels like Sony' .
9. See the 'Apple Dreamland' at St George's subway station in downtown Toronto at http://www. macminute.com/2004/03/11/toronto.

Chapter 7 TechnoLinguistics

1. According to Foucault (1988: 18), technologies of the self 'permit individuals to effect by their own means or with the help of others a certain number of operations on their own bodies and souls, thoughts, conduct, and way of being, so as to transform themselves in order to attain a certain state of happiness, purity, wisdom, perfection, or immortality.'
2. Shermer, Michael, 'The Shamans of Scientism' in Scientific American.com, June 2002, http://www.sciam.com/article.cfm?articleID=000AA74F-FF5F-1CDB-B4A8809EC588EEDF.
3. See http://www.ubu.com/papers/burroughs_gysin.html.
4. See http://en.wikipedia.org/wiki/Encyclopedia.

Conclusion

1. 'Brave New World or Miniature Menace: Why Charles fears grey goo nightmare', http://education.guardian.co.uk/higher/sciences/story/0,12243,945672,00.html.

ANNOTATED GUIDE FOR FURTHER READING

Badmington, N. (ed.) (2000), *Posthumanism*, Basingstoke: Palgrave. An edited volume that brings together a collection of writings which help to situate the idea of the posthuman in history and critical theory. The introduction offers a very helpful reading of the concept.

Bukatman, S. (1993), *Terminal Identity: The Virtual Subject in Post-modern Science Fiction*, Durham, NC: Duke University Press. A well known book that interrogates subjectivity in contemporary cultures through an analysis of science fiction novels, films and comics.

Cooper, S. (2002), *Technoculture and Critical Theory: In the Service of the Machine*, London: Routledge. A good resource for supplementing knowledge of some of the theorists referred to in this volume including Heidegger, Benjamin, Lyotard and the Futurists.

Flanagan, M. and Booth, A. (eds) (2002), *Reload: Rethinking Woman and Cyberculture*, Cambridge, MA: MIT Press. A comprehensive collection of essays and short stories that analyses the constructions of gender in cyberculture.

Friedel, R. (2007), *A Culture of Improvement: Technology and the Western Millennium*, Cambridge, MA: MIT Press. A very comprehensive history of technology, which shows how the concept of improvement has influenced the development of technoculture.

Gray, C.H. (ed.), (1995), *The Cyborg Handbook*, London: Routledge. A well known and wide ranging collection of essays which helps to situate the concept of cyborg subjectivity both historically and in diverse fields of cultural production. With an introduction by Donna J. Haraway.

Green, L. (2002), *Technoculture: From Alphabet to Cybersex*. London: Allen & Unwin. A good introduction with chapters specifically dealing with contemporary technologies and their intersections with popular culture, gender and work.

Heffernan, N. (2000), *Capital, Class and Technology in Contemporary American Culture*. London: Pluto Press. An analysis of postmodernism that focuses on the connections between economics and technology in postwar America.

Law, J. and Mol, A. (eds) (2002), *Complexities: Social Studies of Knowledge Practices*. Durham: Duke University Press. A collection of case studies that address the practice of science and the development of technologies in diverse global situations, which help to elucidate the complexities of doing science in the contemporary world.

Loader, B., Pace, N., Schuler, D. and Bell, D.J. (2004), *Cyberculture: The Key Concepts*, London: Routledge. A handy A–Z guide to the concepts and neologisms of contemporary cyberculture.

Misa, T.J. (2004), *Leonardo to the Internet: Technology and Culture from the Renaissance to the Present*. Baltimore, MD: Johns Hopkins University Press. A history of technology over five centuries which examines the complex relationship between culture and technology and also includes case studies.

Nayar, P.K. (2004), *Virtual Worlds: Culture and Politics in the Age of Cybertechnology*, London: Sage Publications. An interesting analysis of the age of information technology from its genesis in the late twentieth century. Contains discussions of body modification and the erotics of cyberspace.

Oudshoorn, N. and Pinch, T. (2003), *How Users Matter: The Co-Construction of Users and Technology*. Cambridge, MA: MIT Press. A collection of essays which demonstrates how technology is sold to users and how users shape technological development.

Penley, C. and Ross, A. (eds) (1991), *Technoculture (Cultural Politics)*. Minneapolis: University of Minnesota Press. A very well known collection of case studies with a useful introduction which examines the problematics of technoculture.

Robbins, K. and Webster, F. (1999), *Times of the Technoculture: From the Information Society to the Virtual Life*, London: Routledge. An analysis of the politics of contemporary technocultures, which discusses the history of the 'information revolution' and the ethics of the incorporation of information and communications technologies into such diverse fields as the military and education.

Sheehan, J.J. and Sosna, M. (eds) (1991), *The Boundaries of Humanity: Humans, Animals, Machines*, Berkeley: University of California Press. A useful collection of essays, which demonstrate how the idea of what it means to be human has been challenged throughout the history of Western culture.

Spufford, F. and Uglow, J. (eds) (1996), *Cultural Babbage: Technology, Time and Invention*. London: Faber & Faber. A collection of case studies with an emphasis on nineteenth- and early twentieth-century science and technology.

Sutton, D., Brind, S. and McKenzie, R. (eds) (2007), *State of the Real: Aesthetics in the Digital Age*. New York: I.B Tauris & Co. Ltd. A collection of essays analysing how art, cinema and photography problematize notions of reality in digital culture.

Turkle, S. (1995), *Life on the Screen: Identity in the Age of the Internet*, New York: Simon & Schuster. A well known and very useful introduction to the way in which our interactions in cyberspace are changing our conceptions of self.

TV/FILMOGRAPHY

Alphaville, une étrange aventure de Lemmy Caution (1965), Jean-Luc Godard: Athos Films, Chaumiane, Filmstudio.

Blade Runner (1992), Ridley Scott: Blade Runner Partnership, The Ladd Company, Run Run Shaw, Shaw Brothers.

Capricorn One (1978), Peter Hyams: Associated General Films, Capricorn One Associates, Incorporated Television Company, Lew Grade.

Code 46 (2003), Michael Winterbottom: British Broadcasting Corporation, Revolution Films.

The Day After Tomorrow (2004), Roland Emmerich: Twentieth Century-Fox Film Corporation, Centropolis Entertainment, Mark Gordon Productions, Lions Gate Films.

Dr Who (1963–1989 + 2005– present), British Broadcasting Corporation.

M*A*S*H (1972-83), Twentieth Century Fox Television.

March of the Penguins (2005), Luc Jacquet: Bonne Pioche, APC.

The Matrix (1999), Andy and Larry Wachowski: Groucho ll Film Partnership, Silver Pictures, Village Roadshow Pictures, Warner Bros. Pictures.

Metropolis (1927), Fritz Lang: Universum Film (UFA).

Minority Report (2002), Stephen Spielberg: Cruise/Wagner Productions, Blue Tulip Productions, DreamWorks SKG, Ronald Shusett/Gary Goldman, Twentieth Century Fox Film Corporation.

Modern Times (1936), Charles Chaplin: Charles Chaplin Productions.

My Own Private Idaho (1991), Gus van Sant: New Line Cinema.

Olympia (1938), Leni Riefensthal: International Olympic Committee, Olympia Film, Tobis Filmkunst.

Star Trek: The Next Generation (1987–1994), Paramount Television.

Star Trek: Voyager (1995-2001), Paramount Television

Talk to Her (2002), Pedro Almodovar: El Deseo SA, Antena 3 Televisión, Good Machine, Vía Digital.

The Terminator (1984), James Cameron: Herndale Film Corporation, Cinema 84, Euro Film Fund, Pacific Western.

Terminator Three: The Rise of the Machines (2003), Jonathan Mostow: C-2 Pictures, Intermedia Films, IMF Internationale Medien und Film GmbH & Co. Produktions KG, Mostow/Lieberman Productions.

Terminator Two: Judgement Day (1991), James Cameron: Canal+, Carolco Pictures, Lightstorm Entertainment, Pacific Western, T2 Productions.

Thelma and Louise (1991), Ridley Scott: Metro-Goldwyn-Mayer (MGM), Pathé Entertainment, Percy Main.

Triumph of the Will (1935), Leni Riefensthal: Leni Riefenstahl-Produktion.

REFERENCES

Aarseth, E.J. (1997), *Cybertext: Perspectives on Ergodic Literature*, Baltimore, MD: The Johns Hopkins University Press.

Adorno, T.W. (1994), 'On Popular Music' in Storey, J. (ed.), *Cultural Theory and Popular Culture: A Reader*, London: Pearson Education.

Adorno, T.W. (2000), 'Nature as "Not Yet"' in Coupe, L. (ed.), *The Green Studies Reader: From Romanticism to Ecocriticism*, London: Routledge.

Adorno, T.W. and Horkheimer, M. (1997 [1944]), *Dialectic of Enlightenment*, trans. Cumming, J., London: Verso.

Agar, N. (2002) *Perfect Copy: Unravelling the Cloning Debate*, Duxford: Icon Books.

Aldiss, B. with Wingrove, D. (1988), *Trillion Year Spree: The History of Science Fiction*, London: Grafton.

Ali Brac de la Perriere, R. and Seuret, F. (2000), *Brave New Seeds: The Threat of GM Crops to Farmers* trans. Sovani, M. and Rao, V., London: Zed Books.

Althusser, L. (1971), *Lenin and Philosophy and Other Essays*, New York: Monthly Review Press.

Aronowitz, S. (1988), *Science as Power*, Minneapolis: University of Minnesota Press.

Balsamo, A. (1996), *Technologies of the Gendered Body: Reading Cyborg Women*. Durham, NC: Duke University Press.

Barthes, R. (1989), 'The Death of the Author' in Rice, P. and Waugh, P. (eds), *Modern Literary Theory: A Reader*, London: Arnold.

Barthes, R. (2000), *A Roland Barthes Reader*, ed. and intro. by Susan Sontag, London: Vintage.

Batchelor, R. (1994), *Henry Ford: Mass Production, Modernism and Design*. Manchester: Manchester University Press.

Baudrillard, J. (1983), *Simulations*, trans. Paul Foss, Paul Patton and Philip Beitchman, New York: Semiotext[e].

Baudrillard, J. (1991), 'Simulacra and Science Fiction', *Science Fiction Studies*, 18 (3), November.

Baudrillard, J. (1995), *The Gulf War Did Not Take Place*, Sydney: Power Publications.

Baudrillard, J. (2000), *The Vital Illusion*, New York: Columbia University Press.

Baym, N. (1986), 'Melodramas of Beset Manhood' in Showalter, E. (ed.), *The New Feminist Criticism*, London: Virago.

Benjamin, M. (2003), *Rocket Dreams: How the Space Age Shaped our Vision of a World Beyond*, London: Chatto & Windus.

Benjamin, W. (1972), *Illuminations*, London: Fontana.

Benthall, J. (1976), *The Body Electric: Patterns of Western Industrial Culture*, London: Thames & Hudson.

Berman, M. (1983), *All That is Solid Melts Into Air: The Experience of Modernity*, London: Verso.

Best, S. and Kellner, D. (2001), *The Postmodern Adventure: Science, Technology and Cultural Studies at the Third Millennium*, New York: Guilford Press.

Bookchin, M. (2004), *Post-Scarcity Anarchism*. Edinburgh: AK Press.

Bostrom, N. (2005), 'In Defense of Posthuman Dignity', *Bioethics*, 19(3): 202–14.

Bourdieu, P. (1984), *Distinction: A Social Critique of the Judgement of Taste*, London: Routledge.

Bowler, P.J. (1984), *Evolution: The History of an Idea*, Berkeley: University of California Press.

Boyle, C., Wheale, P. and Sturgess, B. (1984), *People, Science and Technology: A Guide to Advanced Industrial Society*, Brighton: Harvester Press.

Braidotti, R. (2002), *Metamorphoses: Towards a Materialist Theory of Becoming*, Cambridge: Polity Press.

Brendon, P. (2000), *The Dark Valley: A Panorama of the 1930s*, London: Jonathan Cape.

Bronner, S.E. and McKay, D. (eds) (1989), *Critical Theory and Society: A Reader*, New York: Routledge.

Bryld, M. and Lykke, N. (1999), *Cosmodolphins: Feminist Cultural Studies of Technology, Animals and the Sacred*, London: Zed Books.

Buchloh, B.H.D. (1989), 'The Andy Warhol Line' in Gary Garrels (ed), *The Work of Andy Warhol*, Seattle, WA: Dia Art Foundation.

Bull, M. (2005), 'No Dead Air! The iPod and the Culture of Mobile Listening', *Leisure Studies*, 24(4), October.

Burnham, J. (1962), *The Managerial Revolution*, Harmondsworth: Penguin Books.

Burroughs, W. (2001), *The Ticket That Exploded*, London: Flamingo.

Butler, J. (2002), 'Is Kinship Always Already Heterosexual', *differences: A Journal of Feminist Cultural Studies*, 13(1): 14–44.

Cadigan, P. (1991), *Synners*, London: HarperCollins.

Cantor, P.A. (1993), 'Romanticism and Technology: Satanic Verses and Satanic Mills' in Meltzer, A.M., Weinberger, J. and Zinman, M.R. (eds), *Technology in the Western Political Tradition*, Ithaca, NY: Cornell University Press.

Carpenter, F.I. (1959), 'The American Myth: Paradise (To Be) Regained' *PMLA*, 74(5): 599–606.

Carter, D. (1988), *The Final Frontier: The Rise and Fall of the American Rocket State*, London: Verso.

Castells, M. (2001), *The Internet Galaxy: Reflections on the Internet, Business and Society*, Oxford: Oxford University Press.

Castells, M. (1996), *The Rise of the Network Society* (1996). Malden, MA: Blackwell.

Cavallaro, D. (2000), *Cyberpunk and Cyberculture: Science Fiction and the Work of William Gibson*, London: Athlone Press.

Chambers, I. (1996), 'A Miniature History of the Walkman' in Du Gay, P., Hall S., Janes, L., Mackay, H. and Negus, K. (eds), *Doing Cultural Studies: The Story of the Sony Walkman*, London: Sage.

Chaplin, S. and Holding, E. (2002), 'Addressing the Post-Urban: Los Angeles, Las Vegas, New York' in Leach, N. (ed.) (2002), *The Hieroglyphics of Space: Reading and Experiencing the Modern Metropolis*, London: Routledge.

Chow, R. (1997), 'Listening Otherwise, Music Miniaturised: A Different Type of Question About Revolution' in Du Gay, P., Hall S., Janes, L., Mackay, H. and Negus, K. (eds), *Doing Cultural Studies: The Story of the Sony Walkman*, London: Sage.

Clarke, A.C. (1999), *Profiles of the Future: An Inquiry into the Limits of the Impossible*, London: Victor Gollancz.

Clarke, D.B. (1997), *The Cinematic City*, London: Routledge.

Cochran, G.M., Ewald, P.W. and Cochran, K.D. (2000) 'Infectious Causation of Disease: An Evolutionary Perspective', *Perspectives in Biology and Medicine*, 43(3): 406–448.

Cohn, C. (1987), 'Sex and Death in the Rational World of Defense Intellectuals', *Signs*, 12(4), Summer.

Cosentino, G. (2006), 'Hacking the iPod: A Look Inside Apple's Portable Music Player' in Ayers, M.D. (ed), *Cybersounds: Essays on Virtual Music Culture*, New York: Peter Lang.

Crouch, C. (1999), *Modernism in Art, Design and Architecture*, Basingstoke: Macmillan.

Csicsery-Ronay Jr, I. (1991), 'The SF of Theory: Baudrillard and Haraway', *Science Fiction Studies*, 18(3): 387–404.

Cubitt, S. (1998), *Digital Aesthetics*, London: Sage.

Darwin, C. (2004), *The Descent of Man*, Harmondsworth: Penguin.

Dear, M.J. (2000), *The Postmodern Urban Condition*, Oxford: Blackwell.

Debord, G. (1995[1967]), *The Society of the Spectacle*, trans. Nicholson-Smith, D., New York: Zone Books.

Deleuze, G. and Guattari, F. (1987), *A Thousand Plateaus*, London: Continuum.

Deleuze, G. and Guattari, F. (1983), *Anti-Oedipus*, London: Continuum.

Derrida, J. (1997[1974]), *Of Grammatology*, trans. Spivak, G.C., Baltimore, MD: The Johns Hopkins University Press.

Derrida, J. (2001[1967]), *Writing and Difference*, London: Routledge.

Easlea, B. (1981), *Science and Sexual Oppression: Patriarchy's Confrontation with Woman and Nature*. London: Weidenfeld & Nicolson.

Ellul, J. (1965), *The Technological Society*, trans. John Wilkinson and intro. Robert K Merton, London: Jonathan Cape.

Fedigan, L.M. (1992), 'The Changing Role of Women in Models of Human Evolution' in Kirkup, G. and Keller, L.S. (eds), *Inventing Women: Science Technology and Gender*, Cambridge: Polity Press.

Fiske, J. (1982), *Introduction to Communication Studies*, London: Methuen.

Ford, S. (1999), *Wreckers of Civilisation: The Story of COUM Transmissions and Throbbing Gristle*, London: Black Dog Publishing.

Foucault, M. (1978), *The History of Sexuality: An Introduction*, Harmondsworth: Penguin Books.

Foucault, M. (1980), *Power/Knowledge: Selected Interviews and Other Writings, 1972–1977*, ed. and trans. Gordon, C., New York: Harvester Wheatsheaf.

Foucault, M. (1988), *Technologies of the Self: A Seminar with Michel Foucault*, London: University of Massachusetts Press and Tavistock Publications.

Foucault, M. (1991 [1977]), *Discipline and Punish: The Birth of the Prison*, London: Penguin.

Foucault, M. (1994 [1970]), *The Order of Things: An Archaeology of the Human Sciences*, New York: Random House.

Frankel, M.S. and Chapman, A.R. (2000), *Human Inheritable Genetic Modification: Assessing Scientific, Ethical, Religious, and Policy Issues*, report prepared by the American Association for the Advancement of Science, http://www.aaas.org/spp/sfrl/projects/germline/report. pdf.

Fuller, M. and Jenkins, H. (1995), 'Nintendo® and New World Travel Writing: A Dialogue' in Jones, S.G. (ed.) *Cybersociety: Computer-mediated Communication and Community*, Thousand Oaks, CA: Sage Publications.

Fulton, V. (1994), 'An Other Frontier: Voyaging West with Mark Twain and *Star Trek's* Imperial Subject' *Postmodern Culture*, 4(3), http://www.iath.virginia.edu/pmc/text-only/ issue.594/fulton-v.594.

Gibson, W. (1986), *Neuromancer*, London: Grafton Books.

Gilroy, P. (1987), *There Ain't No Black in the Union Jack*, London: Routledge.

Gramsci, A. (1971), *Selections from Prison Notebooks*, ed. and trans. Hoare, Q. and Smith, G.N., London: Lawrence & Wishart.

Gray, C.H. (1997), *Postmodern War: The New Politics of Conflict*, New York: Guilford Press.

Gray, J. (2003), *Al Qaeda and What it Means to be Modern*, London: Faber & Faber.

Gray, J. (2004), *Heresies: Against Progress and Other Illusions*, London: Granta.

Greer, G. (2000), *The Whole Woman*, New York: Anchor.

Grimwood, J.C. (2000), *redRobe*, London: Earthlight.

Grosz, E. (1995), *Space, Time and Perversion*, London: Routledge.

Grunberger, R. (1974), *A Social History of the Third Reich*, Harmondsworth: Penguin Books.

Gunkel, D.J. (2001), *Hacking Cyberspace*, Boulder, CO: Westview Press.

Haraway, D.J. (1991), *Simians, Cyborgs and Women: The Reinvention of Nature*, London: Free Association Books.

Haraway, D.J. (1992a), *Primate Visions: Gender, Race and Nature in the World of Modern Science*, London: Verso.

Haraway, D.J. (1992b), 'The Promises of Monsters: A Regenerative Politics for Inappropriate/d Others' in Grossberg, L., Nelson, C. and Treichler, P. (eds), *Cultural Studies*, London: Routledge.

Haraway, D.J. (1997), *Modest_Witness@Second_Millennium.FemaleMan©_Meets_ OncoMouse®: Feminism and Technoscience*, London: Routledge.

Hardison, O.B. Jr. (1989), *Disappearing Through the Skylight: Culture and Technology in the Twentieth Century*, New York: Penguin.

Hardt, M. and Negri, A. (2005), *Multitude*, Harmondsworth: Penguin Books.

Haupt, A. (2006), 'The Technology of Subversion: From Digital Sampling in Hip-Hop to the MP3 Revolution' in Ayers, M.D. (ed.) (2006), *Cybersounds: Essays on Virtual Music Culture*, New York: Peter Lang.

Hayles, K.N. (1999), *How We Became Posthuman: Virtual Bodies in Cybernetics, Literature and Informatics*, Chicago: University of Chicago Press.

Heidegger, M. (1993), 'The Question Concerning Technology', in Krell, D.F. (ed.), *Heidegger: Basic Writings*, London: Routledge.

Heim, M. (1987), *Electric Language: A Philosophical Study of Word Processing*, New Haven, CT: Yale University Press.

Heim, M. (1993), *The Metaphysics of Virtual Reality*, Oxford: Oxford University Press.

Heisenberg, W. (1997), 'The Development of Philosophical Ideas since Descartes in Comparison with the New Situation in Quantum Theory' in Tauber, A.I. (ed.), *Science and the Quest for Reality*, Basingstoke: Macmillan.

Herz, J.C. (1997), *Joystick Nation: How Videogames Ate Our Quarters, Won Our Hearts and Rewired Our Minds*, Boston: Little Brown.

Hess, D.J. (1995), *Science and Technology in a Multicultural World: The Cultural Politics of Facts and Artifacts*, New York: Columbia University Press.

Hochschild, A.R. (1983), *The Managed Heart: Commercialization of Human Feeling*, Berkeley, CA, University of California Press.

Hofstadter, R. (1959), *Social Darwinism in American Thought*, New York: George Braziller.

Holmes, T (2002), *Electronic and Experimental Music*, London: Routledge.

Horkheimer, M. (1989[1938]), 'The Jews and Europe' in *Critical Theory and Society: A Reader*.

Hosokawa, S. (1984), 'The Walkman Effect', *Popular Music, Performers and Audiences*, 4: 165–80.

Hughes, J. (2001), 'The Future of Death: Cryonics and the Telos of Liberal Individualism', *Journal of Evolution and Technology*, 6 (July), available at http://www.transhumanist.com/volume6/death.htm.

Huxley, A., *Brave New World* (1977 [1932]), London: Flamingo: London.

Jameson, F. (1991), *Postmodernism or, The Cultural Logic of Late Capitalism*, London: Verso.

Kaysing, W.C. (1981 [1974]), *We Never Went to the Moon: America's Thirty Billion Dollar Swindle*. Cornville, AZ: Desert Publications.

Kember, S. (2003), *Cyberfeminism and Artificial Life*, London: Routledge.

Knabb, K. (ed.) (1981), *Situationist International Anthology*, Berkeley, CA: Bureau of Public Secrets.

Kracauer, S. (1960), *Theory of Film*, New York: Oxford University Press.

Kristeva, J. (1982), *Powers of Horror: An Essay on Abjection*, New York: Columbia University Press.

Kuhn, T.S. (1996), *The Structure of Scientific Revolutions*, 3rd edition, Chicago: University of Chicago Press.

Land, C. (2005), 'Apomorphine Silence: Cutting-up Burroughs' Theory of Language and Control', *Ephemera: Theory and Politics in Organization*, 5(3), www.ephemeraweb.org.

Latour, B. (1987), *Science in Action*, Cambridge, MA: Harvard University Press.

Latour, B. (1993), *We Have Never Been Modern* , trans. Porter, C., Cambridge, MA: Harvard University Press.

Latour, B. (2004), *Politics of Nature: How to Bring the Sciences into Democracy*, Cambridge, MA: Harvard University Press.

Le Corbusier (1964 [1933]), *The Radiant City: Elements of a Doctrine of Urbanism to be used as the basis of our Machine-Age Civilization*, London: Faber & Faber.

Le Corbusier (1988), 'Spirit of Truth' in Abel, R. (ed.), *French Film Theory and Criticism: A History/Anthology, Vol. 1, 1907–1939*, Princeton, NJ: Princeton University Press.

Leary, T. (1994), *Chaos and Cyber Culture*, Berkeley, CA: Ronin Publishing.

LeFebvre, H. (1991[1974]), *The Production of Space*, trans. Nicholson-Smith, D., Oxford: Basil Blackwell.

Levy, S. (2006), *The Perfect Thing: How the iPod Became the Defining Object of the 21st Century*, London: Ebury Press.

Lucy, N. (2004), *A Derrida Dictionary.* Malden, MA: Blackwell.

Lydenberg, R. (1987), *Word Cultures: Radical Theory and Practice in William S. Burroughs' Fiction*, Chicago: University of Illinois Press.

Lynch, L. (2003), 'Trans-Genesis: An Interview with Eduardo Kac', *New Formations: Complex Figures*, 49(Spring).

Lyon, D. (1994), *The Electronic Eye: The Rise of Surveillance Society*, Cambridge: Polity Press.

Lyotard, J.-F. (1989), *The Postmodern Condition: A Report on Knowledge*, trans. Bennington, G. and Massumi, B., Manchester: Manchester University Press.

Macey, D. (1994 [1973]), Introduction to Jacques Lacan, *The Four Fundamental Concepts of Psychoanalysis*, Harmondsworth: Penguin Books.

Maddison, S. (2004), 'From Porno-topia to Total Information Awareness, or What Really Governs Access to Porn?', *New Formations*, 52(Spring).

Magnet, S. (2006), 'Playing at Colonization: Interpreting Imaginary Landscapes in the Video Game *Tropico*', *Journal of Communication Enquiry*, 30(2).

Marcuse, H. (1991[1964]), *One-Dimensional Man*, London: Routledge.

Marcuse, P. (2003), 'On the Global Uses of September 11 and Its Urban Impact' in Aronowitz, S. and Gautney, H. (eds) (2003), *Implicating Empire: Globalization and Resistance in the Twenty-first Century World Order*, New York: Basic Books.

Marinetti, F.T. (1991), *Let's Murder the Moonshine: Selected Writings*, Los Angeles: Sun & Moon Classics.

Marx, L. (1964), *The Machine in the Garden: Technology and the Pastoral Ideal in America*, London: Oxford University Press.

Marx, K. (1990 [1867]), *Capital: A Critique of Political Economy*, Vol. 1, introduced by Mandel, E. and translated by Fowkes, B., Harmondsworth: Penguin Classics.

Marx, K. and Engels, F. (1947), *The German Ideology*, New York: International Publishers.

Marx, K. and Engels, F. (1988), *Economic and Philosophic Manuscripts of 1844 and The Communist Manifesto*, trans. Milligan, M., New York: Prometheus Books.

Massumi, B. (1993), *A User's Guide to Capitalism and Schizophrenia: Deviations from Deleuze and Guattari*, Cambridge, MA: MIT Press.

McLuhan, M. (1995), *Essential McLuhan*, ed. McLuhan, E. and Zingrove, F., London: Routledge.

McLuhan, M. (1997 [1962]), *The Gutenberg Galaxy: The Making of Typographic Man*, London: University of Toronto Press.

McLuhan, M. (1997 [1964]), *Understanding Media* , ed. and intro. Lapham, L.H., Cambridge, MA: MIT Press.

McLuhan, M. and Fiore, Q. (2001 [1967]), *The Medium is the Massage: An Inventory of Effects*, produced by Agel, J., Corte Madera, CA: Ginko Press.

Milburn, C. (2004), 'Nanotechnology in the Age of Posthuman Engineering: Science as Science Fiction' in N Katherine Hayles (ed), *Nanoculture: Implications of the New Technoscience*, Bristol: Intellect Books.

Mitchell, W.J. (2003), *ME++: The Cyborg Self and The Networked City*, Cambridge, MA: MIT Press.

Moore, D.S., Kosek, J. and Pandian, A. (eds) (2003), *Race, Nature and The Politics of Difference*, Durham, NC: Duke University Press.

More, M. (1994), 'The Terminus of the Self, Part I', *Cryonics*, 15(4): 25–35.

More, M. (1995), 'The Terminus of the Self, Part II', *Cryonics*, 16(1): 33–8.

Mudede, C. (2004), 'The Turntable' in *Life in the Wires: The CTheory Reader*, Victoria: NWP/ CTheory Books.

Murphie, A. and Potts, J. (2003), *Culture and Technology*, Basingstoke: Palgrave.

Myerson, G. (2000), *Donna Haraway and GM Foods*, Duxford: Icon Books.

Notes from Nowhere (ed.) (2003), *We are Everywhere*, London: Verso.

Neresini, F. (2000), 'And Man Descended from the Sheep: The Public Debate on Cloning in the Italian Press', *Public Understanding of Science*, 9: 359–82.

Newman, J. (2004), *Videogames*, London: Routledge.

Nye, D.E. (1994), *American Technological Sublime*, Cambridge, MA: MIT Press.

Ong, W.J. (1982), *Orality and Literacy: The Technologising of the Word*, London: Routledge.

Pawley, M. (1998), *Terminal Architecture*, London: Reaktion Books.

O'Riordan, K. (2001), 'Playing with Lara in Virtual Space' in Munt, S. (ed.), *Technospaces: Inside the New Media*, London: Continuum.

Pfeil, F. (1995), *White Guys: Studies in Postmodern Domination and Difference*, London: Verso.

Poster, M. (1990), *The Mode of Information: Poststructuralism and Social Context*, Cambridge: Polity Press.

Postman, N. (1993), *Technopoly: The Surrender of Culture to Technology*, New York: Vintage Books.

President's Council on Bioethics (2002), *Human Cloning and Human Dignity*, intro. by Kass, L., New York: Public Affairs.

Pyle, F. (2000), 'Making Cyborgs, Making Humans: of Terminators and Blade Runners', in Bell, D. and Kennedy, B.M. (eds), *The Cybercultures Reader*, London: Routledge.

Reed, E. (1978), *Sexism and Science*, New York: Pathfinder Press.

Reid, R. (1995), '"Death of the Family," or, Keeping Human Beings Human', in Halberstam, J. and Livingston, I. (eds), *Posthuman Bodies*, Bloomington: Indiana University Press.

Ritzer, G. (1996), *The McDonaldisation of Society: An Investigation into the Changing Character of Contemporary Social Life*, Thousand Oaks, CA: Pine Forge Press.

Robins, K. and Levidow, L. (1995) 'Soldier, Cyborg, Citizen' in Brook, J. and Beal, I.A. (eds), *Resisting the Virtual Life: The Culture and Politics of Information*, San Francisco: City Lights.

Rose, H. and Rose, S. (eds) (2000), *Alas, Poor Darwin: Arguments Against Evolutionary Psychology*, London: Jonathan Cape.

Rosenthal, N. (1989), 'Let us Now Praise Famous Men: Warhol as Art Director' in Garrels, G. (ed.), *The Work of Andy Warhol*, Seattle, WA: Dia Art Foundation.

Rousseau, J.-J. (1952), 'A Dissertation on the Origin and Foundation of the Inequality of Mankind' in Hutchins, R.M. (ed.), *Great Books of the Western World*, Chicago: Encyclopaedia Britannica & William Benton.

Rushkoff, D. (1994), *Cyberia: Life in the Trenches of Hyperspace*, London: Flamingo.

Russell, D. (1983), *The Religion of the Machine Age*, London: Routledge.

Russett, C.E. (1989), *Sexual Science: The Victorian Construction of Womanhood*, Cambridge, MA: Harvard University Press.

Rutsky, R.L. (1999), *High Techne: Art and Technology from the Machine Aesthetic to the Posthuman*, Minneapolis: University of Minnesota Press.

Ryle, G. (1949), *The Concept of Mind*, London: Hutchinson.

Sapir, E. (1956), *Culture, Language and Personality*, Berkeley, CA: University of California Press.

Sardar, Z. (1996), 'Alt.civilization.faq: Cyberspace as the Darker Side of the West' in Sardar, Z. and Ravetz, J.R. (eds), *Cyberfutures: Culture and Politics on the Information Superhighway*, New York: New York University Press.

Sardar, Z. (2000), *Thomas Kuhn and the Science Wars*, Duxford: Icon Books.

Sassen, S. (1998), *Globalization and its Discontents: Essays on the New Mobility of People and Money*, New York: The New Press.

Sassower, R. (1997), *Technoscientific Angst: Ethics and Responsibility*, Minneapolis: University of Minnesota Press.

Saussure, F. de (1966), *Course in General Linguistics*, ed. Bally, C. and Sechehaye, A. with Albert Riedlinger; trans. and intro. Baskin, W., New York: McGraw-Hill.

Shapin, S. and Schaffer, S. (1985) *Leviathan and The Air-pump: Hobbes, Boyle, and the Experimental Life* Princeton, NJ: Princeton University Press.

Shaw, D.B. (2000), *Women, Science and Fiction: The Frankenstein Inheritance*, Basingstoke: Palgrave.

Shaw, D.B. (2004), 'Bodies Out of This World: The Space Suit as Cultural Icon' *Science as Culture*, 13(1): 123–44.

Shelley, M. (1912 [1818]), *Frankenstein*, London: Dent.

Shields, R. (2003), *The Virtual*, London: Routledge.

Simpson, L.C. (1995), *Technology, Time and the Conversations of Modernity*, London: Routledge.

Sokal, A. and Bricmont, J. (1997), *Intellectual Impostures*, Paris: Profile Books.

Sontag, S. (2001), 'Fascinating Fascism', *Under The Sign of Saturn*, London: Vintage.

Soper, K. (1995), *What is Nature? Culture, Politics and the Non-Human*, Oxford: Blackwell.

Stallabrass, J. (1996), *Gargantua Manufactured Mass Culture*, London: Verso.

Stern, M. (2000), 'Imaging Space Through the Inhuman Gaze', in Brewer. S., Joughin, J.J., Owen, D. and Walker, R.J. (eds), *Inhuman Reflections: Thinking the Limits of the Human*, Manchester: Manchester University Press.

Stern, M. (2003a), 'Ejecting the Warp Core: *Star Trek, Voyager*, and The Reinvention of Space Travel' in Pinnell, L. (ed.), *Interceptions: Essays in the Poetics/Politics of Space*, Turkish Republic of Cyprus/North Cyprus: Eastern Mediterranean University Press.

Stern, M. (2003b), 'Shiny, Happy People: 'Body Worlds' and the Commodification of Health', *Radical Philosophy*, 118(March/April): 2–6.

Stiegler, B. (1998), *Technics and Time 1: The Fault of Epimetheus*, Stanford, CA: Stanford University Press.

Stiglitz, J. (2002), *Globalization and its Discontents*, London: Penguin Books.

Stone, A.R. (1991), 'Will the Real Body Please Stand Up? Boundary Stories About Virtual Cultures' in Michael Benedikt (ed), *Cyberspace First Steps*, Cambridge, MA: MIT Press.

Stone, A.R. (1995), *The War of Desire and Technology at the Close of the Mechanical Age*, Cambridge, MA: MIT Press.

Stuckey, C.E. (1989), 'Warhol in Context' in Garrels, G. (ed.), *The Work of Andy Warhol*, Seattle, WA: Dia Art Foundation, Bay Press.

Taylor, F.W. (1911), *The Principles of Scientific Management*, New York: Harper & Brothers.

Taylor, M.C. and Saarinen, E. (1994), *Imagologies: Media Philosophy*, London: Routledge.

Thomas, J. (1966), '*Alphaville* by Jean-Luc Godard', *Film Quarterly*, 20(1): 48–51.

Thornton, S. (1997), 'The Social Logic of Subcultural Capital' in Thornton, S. and Gelder, K. (eds) *The Subcultures Reader*, London: Routledge.

Thorpe, C. (2006), *Oppenheimer: The Tragic Intellect*, London: University of Chicago Press.

Tiptree, J. Jr. (1978), 'A Momentary Taste of Being' *Star Songs of an Old Primate*, New York: Del Rey.

Tisdall, C. and Bozzolla, A. (1977), *Futurism*, London: Thames & Hudson.

Turney, J. (1998), *Frankenstein's Footsteps: Science, Genetics and Popular Culture*, New Haven, CT: Yale University Press.

Turney, J. (2004), 'The Abstract Sublime: Life as Information Waiting to be Rewritten', *Science as Culture*, 13(1): 93–103.

Watson, J.B. (1919), *Psychology from the Standpoint of a Behaviourist*, New York: Lippincott.

Wertheim, M. (1999), *The Pearly Gates of Cyberspace: A History of Space from Dante to the Internet*, London: Virago.

Wheeler, W. (2006), *The Whole Creature: Complexity, Biosemiotics and the Evolution of Culture*, London: Lawrence & Wishart.

Whorf, B.L. (1956), *Language, Thought and Reality*, ed. Carroll, J.B. Cambridge, MA: MIT Press.

Wiener, N. (1948), *Cybernetics*, Cambridge, MA: MIT Press.

Wiener, N. (1950), *The Human Use of Human Beings: Cybernetics and Society*, New York: Da Capo Press.

Wilson, R. (1994), 'Techno-euphoria and the Discourse of the American Sublime' in Pease, D.E. (ed.), *National Identities and Post-American Narratives*, Durham, NC: Duke University Press.

Winston, M.L. (2002), *Travels in the Genetically Modified Zone*, Cambridge, MA: Harvard University Press.

Wolfe, T. (2005[1979]), *The Right Stuff*, London: Vintage.

Woolley, B. (1992), *Virtual Worlds*, Cambridge: Blackwell.

Žižek, S. (1991), *Looking Awry. An Introduction to Jacques Lacan through Popular Culture*, Cambridge, MA: MIT Press.

Žižek, S. (2004), *Organs Without Bodies: On Deleuze and Consequences*, London: Routledge.

Zukav, G. (2001), *The Dancing Wu Li Masters*, New York: HarperCollins.

INDEX

abjection, 94–5, 100
abstract space, 113–15
actor network theory (ANT), 69–71, 73, 75, 94, 173
ACTUP (AIDS Coalition to Unleash Power), 72–3
Adorno, Theodor, 18, 66, 131–3, 135–6
Africa, poverty, 32
agriculture, GM crops, 58–62, 169–70
AIDS, *see* HIV/AIDS
Akeley, Carl, 75–6
Al Qaeda, 34–5
Alcor Life Extension Foundation, 97, 98, 170–1
Aldiss, Brian, 3
Alphaville, 162–7, 172
Althusser, Louis, 157–8
Apple, iPod, 142–5
Aronowitz, Stanley, 48, 49–50
art
    aura of, 130–1
    commodification, 131–3
    ideology and, 131–3
    mechanical reproduction, 127–9, 133–4, 137–8, 172
    modernity, 125–6
    pop art, 136–8, 175
    science and, 172
astronauts, 104–10
aura, of art, 130–1, 173
autopoiesis, 91–3, 94, 173
avatar, 86, 120, 173

Bacon, Francis, 68
Balsamo, Anne, 85–7
Barthes, Roland, 128–9, 148–50
Baudrillard, Jean, 23, 61, 110–12, 117
beauty products, 53–4, 171
Benjamin, Marina, 33, 106
Benjamin, Walter, 127–9, 134–5, 172
Berman, Marshall, 10
Best, Steven, 26
bin Laden, Osama, 33–4, 77
biodiversity, threats to, 59–60
biotechnology, 56–62, 77–8
Blade Runner, 103, 105
body
    classification of, 87–9
    cyborgs, 60–1, 93–5, 101
    death of, 94–101, 151, 170
    discursive, 83–5
    dislocation, 163
    healthy, 92–3
    language and, 156–8
    machine and, 82–3, 89–92, 95
    marked, 85–7
    space and, 103
    transhuman, 96–7, 99–100
    understanding of, 81–2, 87–9
Body without Organs (BwO), 93–5, 101, 103, 120
Bostrom, Nick, 96, 100
Boyle, Robert, 46
brands, 26
Brendon, Piers, 7

Bull, Michael, 144
Burroughs, William, 158–60, 163, 165
   The Ticket That Exploded, 156–7
Bush, George, Snr., 55
Bush, George W., 33–4, 104, 107
Butler, Judith, 76

Cadigan, Pat, *Synners*, 85–7
call centres, India, 27
Canada, GM crops, 58–9
Cantor, Paul A., 66
capitalism, 11–14, 82–3
Capricorn One, 108, 117
Castells, Manuel, 27, 30, 31
Chambers, Iain, 141
Chaplin, Charlie, 6–7, 9, 11
Chaplin, Sarah, 120
Charles, Prince of Wales, 169
China, Internet policing, 36–7
Chow, Rey, 144–5, 172
cinema
   development of, 3–4
   experience of, 140
   film and aura, 129–31
   see also films by name
cities
   segregation, 119–20
   sounds of, 138–9, 140–1
civilization, nature and, 63–5
Clarke, Arthur C., 1
cloning, 72–8, 170
Code 46, 78
Cohn, Carol, 64, 152
Cold War, 19–20, 105, 108, 151–2
computers
   data processing, 162–7
   development of, 27–8
   speaking, 163–4
   surveillance by, 36–7, 40, 164–5
   video games, 117–22
consumerism, 30–1
Cosentino, Gabrielle, 142–4

COUM Transmissions, 138
cryonics, 96, 97–100, 170–1, 173
culture
   nature and, 63–5
   pre-digested, 135–6
culture industry, 131, 132–3, 173
cybernetics, 89–92, 173
cyberspace, 85–6, 115–17, 147, 172, 173
cyborgs, 60–1, 93–5, 101, 173

Darwin, Charles, 44–6
data mining, 36, 164–5, 173
data processing, 164–7, 172
Day After Tomorrow, The, 65, 67–8
death, meaning of, 94–101, 151, 170
Debord, Guy, 21–2
deconstruction, 160–3, 174
Deleuze, Gilles, 93–5, 101
Derrida, Jacques, 160–1, 167
Descartes, Rene, 46–7, 116
deviance, concept of, 50–3, 84
Diderot, Denis, 166
division of labour, gendered, 45–6, 76, 87
DNA, 88–9
Dolly, cloned sheep, 74–5
Dr Who, 138
Drexler, Eric, 170–1
Duchamp, Marcel, 3–4, 127, 137, 138
dyslexia, 155–6

Easlea, Brian, 49, 64
Echelon, 36, 165
Ellul, Jacques, 19–20, 21
email, junk emails, 157
embushelment, 55–7, 62, 174
Emerson, Ralph Waldo, 67
encyclopaedias, 166
enframing, 15–16, 174
episteme, 52, 174
eugenics, 44, 57
evolution, theory of, 44–6
expertise, scientific, 43–4, 53–4, 56, 62, 97

exploration, heroic, 104–8
extrapolation, 1–2, 23, 174

factories, mass production, 6–10
family, concepts of, 76–8
fascism, 17–18, 127–8, 134
Fedigan, Linda Marie, 45–6
film, *see* cinema
Flynn, Chris, 104
Ford, Henry, 8, 26, 150
Fordism, 8–11, 37–8, 150–1, 174
Foucault, Michel, 38–9, 52–3, 57, 76, 82, 84, 158
Frankenstein, Dr Victor, 56, 58, 64, 101
'Frankenstein Foods', 56–62
Frankfurt School, 17, 127
Freud, Sigmund, 92
Fuller, Steve, 55
Fulton, Valerie, 33
Futurism, 126–7, 130, 174

Galen, 81
Galton, Frances, 44
gender
    division of labour, 45, 76, 87
    ideology, 150
    intelligence and, 45–6
genetically modified (GM) crops, 56–62, 169–70
genomes, 57, 87–9
Gibson, William, 30, 40, 85–6
    Neuromancer, 25, 93, 103
global village, 31–5, 126, 154
globalization, 26, 30
Godard, Jean-Luc, 162–7, 172
Goldacre, Ben, 63
Gramsci, Antonio, 9–10, 127
Grand Theft Auto, 119, 120
Great Depression, 7
Green Revolution, 59, 169
Grimwood, Jon Courtenay, *RedRobe*, 140
Guattari, Felix, 93–5, 101

Gulf War, 117, 121
Gunkel, David J., 115–16

Hamer, Dean, 51
Happy Consciousness, 20–1
Haraway, Donna J., 46, 61, 70, 71–3, 75–6, 95, 101, 106, 107–8, 169, 171
Hardt, Michael, 122
Harvey, William, 81–2
Hayles, N. Katherine, 89, 90–1, 156, 165–7
Heidegger, Martin, 14–15, 17, 66
Heim, Michael, 155, 162
Heisenberg, Werner, 48
Herz, J.C., 117
hip-hop music, 139, 143
Hitler, Adolf, 17, 125–6, 128
HIV/AIDS, 72–3, 84–5
Holding, Eric, 120
homosexuality, scientific theory and, 51–2
Honda, 43
Horkheimer, Max, 17–18, 131–2, 135–6
Hosokawa, Shuhei, 140–1
Human Genome Project, 57, 87–9, 170
'human nature', 14, 63, 73, 83
Huxley, Aldous, *Brave New World*, 77, 150–1
Huxley, Julian, 96–7
hyperreality, 23–4, 30–1, 110, 113–14, 118–22, 174
hypertext, 156

ideology, aesthetics and, 131–3
immortality, 94–101
incest, taboo, 77–8
India
    call centres, 27
    Green Revolution, 59
    KRRS (Karnataka State Farmers' Association), 60, 62
inequalities, global, 32
informatics, 25, 31, 40–1, 166, 174

information technology
  cybernetics and, 90–1
  networks, 25–6, 27–31
'Informational Society', 27
intelligence
  genetics and, 57
  measuring of, 44
International Monetary Fund, 29–30
Internet, 31
  surveillance and, 36–7
iPod, 142–5
Iraq, US invasion, 121
Italy, Futurism, 126–7

Jameson, Fredric, 24–5, 54, 136

Kac, Eduardo, 89
Kass, Leon, 74
Kellner, Douglas, 26
knowledge economy, 26, 174
Kracauer, Siegfried, 140
Kristeva, Julia, 100
Kuhn, Thomas, 48–9

Lacan, Jacques, 157–8
Lang, Fritz, *Metropolis*, 6–8, 9
language
  body and, 156–8
  deconstructed, 160–3
  functionalization, 151
  literacy, 154–6
  recorded, 158–60
  scientism, 152–4
  semiotics, 147–9, 175
  word processors and, 161–3
Latour, Bruno, 69–71
Le Corbusier, 4, 111, 113
Leary, Timothy, 40
Lefebvre, Henri, 23, 111, 112–14
Levidow, Les, 121
liberal humanism, 46–7, 83, 93
linguistic turn, 23, 147, 154

literacy, technology and, 154–6
logocentrism, 160–3, 165–6, 174
Lucy, Niall, 161, 163
Lyotard, Jean-François, 43, 54

M*A*S*H*, 15–16
machines
  aesthetics, 126, 139
  body as, 82–3, 89–92, 95
  Marxism and, 11–13
  modernity and, 6–8
Maddison, Stephen, 37
Magnet, Shoshona, 121–2
maps, 110, 116, 121–2
March of the Penguins, 135
Marcuse, Herbert, 17, 20–1, 40, 84, 119,
  151–3
Marinetti, Filippo Tommaso, 126–7, 130
Marx, Karl, 10, 82–3
Marx, Leo, 66–7
Marxism, 11–14, 20, 84
mass production, 6–10
Matrix, The, 23–4
McLuhan, Marshall, 31–2, 126, 154–5
mechanical reproduction
  art, 127–9, 133–4, 137–8, 172
  film, 129–31
Mediterranean, production of space, 114
Merkle, Ralph C., 170–1
metalanguage, 149, 174
metanarrative, 5, 174
Metropolis, 6–8, 9, 103
middle landscape, 66–7
Milburn, Colin, 169–72
millennium development goals (MDGs), 32
Minority Report, 35
Mitchell, William J, 31, 35–6
Modern Times, 6–8, 9, 11
modernity, 174
  art, 125–6
  Marxism, 11–14
  mass production, 6–11

'mononaturalism', 70
Monsanto, 58, 60
monsters, nature and, 71–3
moon, landing on, 104, 105, 107, 108
More, Max, 98, 99
Mudede, Charles, 139
Murdoch, Rupert, 28–9
music
    industrial, 138–9
    machine aesthetics, 139
    personal, 140–5, 172
    popular, 132–3
    see also sound
My Own Private Idaho, 129, 130
myth, 149–50

nanotechnology, 96, 169–71, 174
nation building, 122
natural, unnatural and, 76–8, 89
nature
    culture and, 63–5
    laws of, 69
    monsters and, 71–3
    romantic concepts of, 66–8
Nazis, 17, 125–6, 132, 133–4, 172
Negri, Antonio, 122
neoliberalism, 29, 30
Neresini, Federico, 74–5
network society, 27–31, 175
normality, deviance and, 50–3
nuclear threat, 5, 56–7, 64, 151–2
Nye, David, 55

objectivity, scientific, 46–8, 52
Olympia, 134
Ong, Walter, 158, 159
ontology, technology and, 14–16
Oppenheimer, Robert, 5

panopticism, 38–9, 175
    Panopticon, 38–9
    Superpanopticon, 40, 164, 165, 176

paradigm, 48–50, 52, 175
Paris, Sorbonne occupation (1968), 22–3
Patriot missiles, 55
Pawley, Martin, 25
Pfeil, Fred, 83–4
photographs, myth of, 149–50
plastination, 101
pop art, 136–8, 175
pop music, 132–3
pornography, Internet, 37
post-normal science, 56–7, 61–2, 175
Poster, Mark, 40, 164–5
posthuman, 77–8, 100–1, 175
Postman, Neil, 44, 152–3
postmodernism, 4–5, 23, 175
printing, technology of, 155–6
psychotechnology, 133–5, 175
publishing, technology, 28–9
PWA (person with AIDS), 84–5

quantum mechanics, 47–8, 91

radio, terminology, 147, 148
Reagan, Ronald, 29
Reid, Roddey, 77
reproduction
    control of, 76–8
    as production line, 151
repurposing, 139, 175
Riefensthal, Leni, 134–5, 171
'right stuff', 104–5, 109–10, 121
Ritzer, George, 120
Robins, Kevin, 121
robots, 90, 111
Romanticism, 66–8, 175
Rousseau, Jean-Jacques, 65
Royal Society, 46
Rutsky, R.L., 125–6

Sapir-Whorf hypothesis, 148
Sardar, Ziauddin, 49, 55–6, 115
Sassen, Saskia, 30, 35

Saussure, Ferdinand de, 147–9, 160, 167
Schmeiser, Perry, 58
science
  art and, 172
  definition, 43
  observation of, 46–8
  paradigms, 48–50
  post-normal, 56–7, 61–2, 175
  power of, 50–4
science fiction, 1–2, 3, 23–4, 108–9, 162, 169
scientism, 152–3, 175
semiotics, 147–9, 175
September 11th 2001 (9/11), 33, 119
sexuality
  discourse, 84–5
  homosexuality, 51–2
  reproduction and, 76–8
Shakespeare, William, 129
Shelley, Mary, *Frankenstein*, 56, 64, 101
Shepard, Alan, 109–10, 112, 114–15
Shields, Rob, 24
simulacra, 110–12
Sinatra, Frank, 96
Singapore
  information economy, 30
  migrant labour, 32
Situationist International (SI), 22–3
social Darwinism, 44–6, 99, 105
Sontag, Susan, 134–5
sound
  play back, 158–60
  see also music
space
  abstract, 113–15
  body's place, 103
  cyberspace, 85–6, 115–17, 172
  everyday, 112–13
  exploration, 104–8
  representational, 113

representations of, 113
simulated, 108–10
virtual, 118–22
wilderness, 105–8, 172
spatial practice, 112–13
spectacle, culture of, 21–3, 175
Springsteen, Bruce, 83–4, 85
standing-reserve, 14–16, 93, 175
Star Trek, 32–3, 106–7, 116
Stelarc, 81
Stern, Megan, 100, 107
Stiegler, Bernard, 14, 81
sublime
  Romantic, 66
  technological, 24–5, 55–7, 107–8
Sumner, William Graham, 99
Superpanopticon, 40, 164, 165, 176
surveillance, 35–41, 164–5

Talk To Her, 94–6
tape recording, 158–9
taxonomy, 88
Taylor, Frederick W., 9
technocapitalism, 26–7, 176
technocracy, 19, 162, 176
technoculture, 1–6, 176
technological determinism, 6, 33, 61, 176
technological rationality, 150–2, 176
technological sublime, 24–5, 55–7, 66, 107–8, 176
technology
  development of, 2–4
  future of, 169–72
  linguistics and, 147–9
  literacy and, 154–6
  as magic, 1–2
  ontology and, 14–16
  psychotechnology, 133–5
  relationships with, 5–6
  repurposed, 139

'Technopoly', 44
Terminator, The, 60–1
Terminator Technology, 60–1
terrorism, global, 33–5
Thatcher, Margaret, 29, 74
theatre, 129–30
Thelma and Louise, 130
'Third Machine Age', 24–5, 61
Throbbing Gristle, 138–9, 141
time, regulation of, 6, 9
Tiptree, James Jr, 64
transgenics, 56–62, 89, 176
transhumanism, 96–7, 99–100, 176
transuranics, 56–7, 176
Triumph of the Will, 134–5
Turney, Jon, 56–7
2001, A Space Odyssey, 163–4

United States
    Romanticism, 66–7
    space exploration, 104–8

Van Gogh, Vincent, 136
video games, 117–22
Virgin Galactic, 114, 115

virtual reality, 117–19
viruses, 71–2

Walkman, 140–2
Wapping dispute, 28–9
war, virtual, 117–19, 121, 122
Warhol, Andy, 136–8
Watson, James, 57
Wertheim, Margaret, 110–11
Wiener, Norbert, 89–90
Wikipedia, 166–7
Wilson, Rob, 55
Wingrove, David, 3
Winston, Mark L., 58, 59, 60
wireless, terminology, 147, 148
Wolfe, Tom, 104–5, 109
women
    quest for beauty, 53–4, 171
    see also gender
Woolley, Benjamin, 112
word processors, 161–3
World Bank, 29–30

Žižek, Slavoj, 95
Zukav, Gary, 48